CARLAW® IV
THE FEDERAL GOVERNMENT'S WAR ON CAR DEALERS

CARLAW® IV
THE FEDERAL GOVERNMENT'S WAR ON CAR DEALERS

THOMAS B. HUDSON

*Counselor*Library.com, LLC

CounselorLibrary.com, LLC

CARLAW® IV The Federal Government's War on Car Dealers
© by Thomas B. Hudson, 2017.

All rights reserved. No part of this book shall be reproduced, stored in a retrieval system or transmitted by any means, electronic, mechanical, photocopying, recording, or otherwise, without written permission from the publisher. No patent liability is assumed with respect to the use of the information contained herein. Although every precaution has been taken in the preparation of this book, the publisher and author assume no responsibility for errors or omissions. Neither is any liability assumed for damages resulting from the use of information contained herein.

ISBN: 978-0-9979244-0-4

Printed in the United States of America

Project Director: Thomas B. Hudson
Production Manager: Marlene K. Locke
Production Assistant: Jean Heckhaus
Editor: Janet A. Martin
Cover and Jacket Design: Drew Robinson, Spork Design, Inc.
Book Design: Lisa A. Allen
Indexer: Sean Reagan
Printer: Sheridan Books, Inc.

CONTENTS

Acknowledgments 1

Introduction 3

Chapter 1
  2008: A Shot Across the Bow 7

Chapter 2
  2009: The Gathering Storm 13

Chapter 3
  2010: Unlimbering the Guns 25

Chapter 4
  2011: Revenge of the Consumer Advocates 53

Chapter 5
  2012: A Full Frontal Assault 113

Chapter 6
> **2013: Rolling Out the Heavy Artillery** 181

Chapter 7
> **2014: The Campaign Continues** 217

Chapter 8
> **2015: Manning the Ramparts** 259

Chapter 9
> **2016: No Truce in Sight** 297

Chapter 10
> **2017 & Beyond: The Never-Ending Struggle** 313

Appendix 1
> **Auto Finance Lexicon** 317

Appendix 2
> **Index** 323

ACKNOWLEDGMENTS

The team scores again! Drew Robinson did our jacket and cover design. Jean Heckhaus was our production assistant. Marlene Locke reprises her role on our last book as production manager. The talented and steady Janet Martin, as editor, kept me more or less on the straight and narrow. Lisa Allen did our book design. Words are poor instruments for describing the talents and abilities of this crew.

And thanks to my partners Nicole Frush Munro and Michael Benoit for letting me slip in articles that they co-authored with me.

As always, any errors are mine own.

—Tom Hudson

INTRODUCTION

The Federal Government's War on Car Dealers

Since 2010, car dealers have faced crippling assaults from Congress and federal agencies. The kickoff to trouble was the Dodd-Frank Wall Street Reform and Consumer Protection Act, signed by President Obama on July 21, 2012. That legislation created the Consumer Financial Protection Bureau (CFPB) to regulate consumer credit but supposedly exempted all, or nearly all, franchised dealers. The exemption was not entirely effective, though, since the CFPB was left with the ability to wreak havoc with the exempted dealers' operations by regulating the finance companies, banks, and credit unions that buy the dealers' financing contracts. The exemption for car dealers did not extend to dealers who hold their own retail installment contracts or to those without vehicle repair facilities.

The dealerships, and the finance companies they deal with, invited the federal government's tender attentions by misbehaving. Not all of them, by any means, but there were enough bad actors to generate a steady drumbeat of newspaper articles, TV "investigative reporter" pieces, and complaints to officials, and that steady stream, almost all anecdotes, served as the rationale for most of the subsequent legislative and regulatory attacks on dealer practices.

This book recounts the story of the dealer-bashing that has come out of Washington over the last several years, as reflected by articles that I wrote (a few with the help of my partners) as

INTRODUCTION

the events occurred. Sprinkled among these real-time observations are descriptions of the burdens that federal laws and regulations impose on dealers, and the new emphasis on enforcement by the federal agencies.

A word of warning—these articles deal with the area of law that I handle on a daily basis. That area encompasses the sales, finance, and leasing activities of dealers, with particular emphasis on what goes on in the so-called finance and insurance, or "F&I" office. Like other businesses, dealers are also subject to laws and regulations dealing with the environment, workplace safety, employment, taxes, and scads of other topics, each of which I suspect is as complicated in its way as those of concern to me. Dealers, as you see, face a very heavy regulatory burden.

As I assembled the articles for this book, I pondered about what the organization should look like. Should I present all the articles on dealer participation in one chapter, all the credit discrimination articles in another chapter, and so on, or should I gather all the Federal Trade Commission enforcement actions, then address enforcement actions by the CFPB, then turn to the Justice Department?

Finally, I decided that simply arranging the material chronologically made sense, since such an arrangement would provide a continuing narrative of the actions by the various agencies and show how the initiatives of one agency played off of the actions of the others.

Having said that, though, and by way of an introduction to this book, I'll start with a 2016 article that describes the federal approach to consumer protection over the years.

As people often say about relationships . . . it's complicated.

INTRODUCTION

The Long Arc of Consumer Protection

One advantage of having practiced law since before the invention of fire is that I have the ability to look back down the mountain I've climbed and perhaps see some things that may not be as visible to those whose time at the bar has been shorter than mine.

That happened to me a few weeks ago when I found myself thinking about an event from the early 1990s. The American Bar Association's Business Law Section does its work through committees, and one of those committees, the Consumer Financial Services Committee, was meeting in Boston. One of the highlights scheduled for the meeting was a debate between my partner Robert Cook and one of the nation's leading consumer advocates (and a good friend of ours), Kathleen Keest.

The question being debated was "Do we need more substantive consumer protection legislation and regulation, or are disclosure and consumer responsibility the answer?" I'm sure the title was catchier, but that was the gist of the debate.

Kathleen, of course, took the "more substantive laws" side, and Robert had the "disclosure is the answer" side. I believe that Robert won the debate handily, which was no mean feat against Kathleen, who, aside from being a good friend, is (1) a true believer in protecting consumers, (2) bright as a new penny, and (3) as acid-tongued as they come. I think my assessment that Robert had carried the day matched that of most of the observers, except for a few academics and die-hard consumer advocate types.

Looking back at it, though, it's pretty clear that Robert had won a battle, and not a war. For the next couple of decades, the consumer advocates kept pushing for more substantive regulation, and every time they did, a few dealers and finance companies cooperated by participating in various abuses,

INTRODUCTION

providing the fuel that stoked the legislative fires. I can draw a pretty solid line from that debate to the housing abuses, payday/title lending abuses, the economic collapse, and Lizzy Warren's success in 2011 in launching the Consumer Financial Protection Bureau (CFPB), a federal consumer financial watchdog agency with the mandate to protect consumers from abusive credit practices. The consumer advocates had pretty clearly gained the upper hand.

But then things took an interesting turn. Warren, when setting up the Bureau, decided that while more laws and regulations were nifty and all that, those laws and regulations were just temporary roadblocks that, she claimed, lawyers would just work their way around.

Nope, she had things a great deal more powerful than black and white regulations. She had the power to challenge practices that the Bureau determined were unfair, deceptive, or abusive (UDAP, or UDAAP authority) and discrimination, gray areas where the creditor's obligation varies depending on the whim and agenda of the enforcer. Why have bright lines that creditors can actually see and rules they can actually follow when you can have a "we know bad acts when we see them" standard in the hands of an aggressive federal regulator?

So we've gone from a standard developed through the 1980s and early 1990s—"disclose and let the consumer take care of himself"—to the pre-CFPB consumer advocate position that "more laws will tame the predatory marketplace" to where we are today—"we don't need no stinkin' laws—we've got UDAP, UDAAP, and superior moral judgment."

That's my take on the last 43 years of consumer protection . . . .

Chapter 1

2008: A Shot Across the Bow

CHAPTER 1

Every now and again, I get stuff wrong. That was the case when the consumer advocates started pressing Congress for a number of consumer protection reforms. At first, the proposals were "single-shot" bills that addressed some of the favorite targets of the consumer protection crowd—one bill would ban pre-dispute arbitration in consumer financial contracts, while another proposed a national finance charge rate cap of 36%.

Then, prodded by Elizabeth Warren and others, the idea surfaced of a federal agency to supervise creditors and enforce federal financial services laws.

The Obama administration had successfully pushed through Congress the health care initiative that has come to be called Obamacare, and the president evidently was feeling his oats. I figured that Obama and the Democrats had spent so much political capital on health care that they would not have anything left for financial reform.

I was wrong about that. Here's an article about the opening salvos that were to lead to an all-out assault.

December 2008
Federal Regulation: The Nanny Commission

A year or so ago, as the mortgage mess began to spin seriously out of control, one of the trade magazines asked me to do an article on the topic of how the mortgage meltdown would affect the auto finance industry. At that time, before $4-plus gasoline and a steep recession, it seemed like the answer was "not much," and that's more or less what I said.

In a later article on the same topic, I got a little closer to the mark, pointing out that because of the emerging credit crisis, it might become a lot tougher for dealers to find banks and sales finance companies willing to buy the retail installment contracts that the dealers were producing.

Still later, I wrote that some of the abuses that were evident in the defaulting consumer mortgages might stir legislators to re-regulate the auto finance industry to ban some of the more egregious practices.

Finally, I predicted that if the Democrats gained control of both the executive and the legislative branches of the federal government, we could expect to see legislation aimed at particularly business-friendly parts of the federal code, such as the Federal Arbitration Act.

But I didn't see this one coming.

Two Democratic congressmen have introduced bills that would create a federal agency to oversee the *safety* of consumer financial products, including mortgages, credit cards, car loans, and other types of credit. Car dealers will be covered by the measure because they enter into credit sales of vehicles with their customers, using retail installment contracts.

Rep. Bill Delahunt (D-Mass.) and Sen. Richard Durbin (D-Ill.) recently introduced bills in the House and Senate that would establish a Consumer Credit Safety Commission. The CCSC, as envisioned by these bills, would oversee any category of lender that extends credit to borrowers.

To this point, federal law has generally been directed at regulating the entities that offer credit, rather than credit products themselves. Content to let the states regulate actual substantive limits on credit products, the feds focused mostly on how creditors disclosed the terms and conditions of those products.

As envisioned by Delahunt and Durbin, the CCSC would focus on whether financial products offered to consumers are "safe."

CHAPTER 1

The Delahunt/Durbin bill provides for a five-member bipartisan agency that would oversee mortgages, credit cards, auto loans, savings accounts, checking accounts, and other consumer credit. The CCSC would "prevent and eliminate unfair practices that lead consumers to incur unreasonable, inappropriate, or excessive debt" and would focus on practices and product features that are abusive, fraudulent, deceptive, or predatory.

In addition, the CCSC would also collect data on the most harmful products, providing consumers with information to help them avoid "dangerous" financial products.

Specifically, the bill provides that the CCSC's objectives are to:

- Minimize unreasonable consumer risk associated with buying and using consumer credit. Who could argue with minimizing unreasonable risk? But do we want government telling us what level of risk is reasonable and what level of risk isn't reasonable? Will the feds prohibit the financing of negative equity?

- Prevent and eliminate unfair practices that lead consumers to incur unreasonable, inappropriate, or excessive debt, or make it difficult for consumers to escape existing debt, including practices or product features that are abusive, fraudulent, unfair, deceptive, predatory, anticompetitive, or otherwise inconsistent with consumer protection. The first part of this mandate sounds like federal underwriting. The second creates a redundant enforcement mechanism since the FTC and most states already prohibit unfair and deceptive acts and practices. And we will have a federal agency that will make it easier for consumers to escape existing debt. Is an obligation that reflects a 120% loan-to-value ratio "excessive" debt?

- Promote practices that assist and encourage consumers to use credit responsibly, avoid excessive debt, and avoid unnecessary or excessive charges derived from or associated with credit products. The bill doesn't say whose practices it intends to promote—those of consumers or those of creditors, but here again, we'll have a federal agency determining what is "excessive" debt and "unnecessary or excessive" charges. More federal underwriting? Is a $495 document fee to cover the preparation of paperwork an "excessive" charge?
- Ensure that credit history is maintained, reported, and used fairly and accurately. I thought that's what the Fair Credit Reporting Act did. Will pre-screening and "firm offer" mail campaigns constitute "fair" use?
- Maintain strong privacy protections for consumer credit transactions, credit history, and other personal information associated with the use of consumer credit. Don't the Gramm-Leach-Bliley Act and the FTC's privacy regulations address these concerns?
- Collect, investigate, resolve, and inform the public about consumer complaints regarding consumer credit. This would replicate duties of the FTC and state consumer protection agencies.
- Ensure a fair system of consumer dispute resolution in consumer credit. This is poorly disguised consumer advocate code for eliminating the ability of creditors to use binding arbitration agreements to reduce the risks and costs of class action lawsuits.
- Take such other steps as are reasonable to protect consumers of credit products. This catch-all provides the Commission members with plenty of discretionary room to make mischief.

CHAPTER 1

Just how the consuming public would be protected by the CCSC isn't spelled out at this early date. Would we have an FDA-type approach, where companies that want to offer financial products have to have them approved by the CCSC? Or would it be a "crash-test" rating system, with the CCSC awarding five stars to the financial products deemed safest and no stars to the ones that would eat a hole in your wallet? The intrusiveness of the CCSC could depend a great deal on the implementation details.

The bills have been referred to committees in the House and Senate and won't be going anywhere in this session. But you can look for them to be revived next year.

Just what we need. A nanny in Washington to keep all those mean old creditors in line. Time to give a call to your trade associations and crank up those lobbying machines.

Chapter 2
2009: The Gathering Storm

CHAPTER 2

The legislative effort to create a federal oversight agency described in Chapter 1 fizzled, but nothing ever dies in Washington. The same forces pushing that unsuccessful plan to reform credit regulation came charging back for more in 2009.

The reformers first tried a number of scattershot, individual bills aimed at specific issues. One bill attempted to impose a national usury rate. Another tinkered with the method of calculating the APR for credit transactions so as to include in that calculation voluntarily purchased products like GAP. Yet another sought to prohibit creditors from using mandatory pre-dispute arbitration agreements in their credit contracts.

These targeted initiatives gradually coalesced into a broad push for a new federal compliance cop. Here's what 2009 brought us.

April 2009
Here Comes Trouble!

With Congress in a full-throated pro-consumer roar and with legislators wielding pitchforks as they chase down all those business executives who got us into the mess of the 2008 financial meltdown, the old saying, "No man's life, liberty, or property are safe while the legislature is in session," comes to mind. Sometimes attributed to Mark Twain, the adage is a good description of the likely near-term legislative future of the credit industry.

For the last couple of decades, banks, finance companies, car dealers, and other players in the consumer financial services arena have had little to worry about by way of federal legislation or regulation. That is going to change soon, and in some significant ways.

The reformers' agendas are filled with plans to rectify what they perceive as either a playing field tilted toward business and away from consumers or to punish what they feel are bad acts on the industry's part. I won't attempt to list every effort we've seen so far, but here are a few of the scarier proposals.

Crash Testing Financial Products? One bill has proposed that the federal government establish a commission to measure how dangerous various financial products are. Presumably, things like variable rates and balloon payment features would increase the danger rating. It's unclear from the proposed legislation whether the commission would impose underwriting standards on creditors in an effort to make financial products safer or whether the commission would simply assign danger ratings to financial products that it believes would be dangerous to consumers' financial health. The latter system would be something like a "crash test" car rating, only applied to financial products. My read on this one is that it is a loopy idea that is unlikely to come to pass (note that I've been wrong before).

A Federal Usury Rate? Angered by what they perceive to be outrageous rates charged by payday lenders, car title lenders, and some other creditors, and emboldened by imposition of rate caps on credit extended to servicemembers, some members of Congress are proposing a federal rate cap of 36%. A cap that high wouldn't worry most car creditors (although it would kill the title loan and payday lending businesses as we now know them), except that this proposal doesn't operate like a normal finance charge cap. The new proposal defines "finance charges" by including fees and charges that the federal Truth in Lending Act excludes from the finance charge definition. While I don't think this one will pass in anything like its present form, I think it will serve as a showcase for various reform ideas we'll see in other proposals to come. And the payday and title folks will be scrambling for carve-outs for short-term credit so that they'll have a place to hide if federal usury rates ever pass.

Say Goodbye to Arbitration. Some of the Democratic Party's more influential backers are the so-called "trial lawyers." These are the lawyers who claim to bring the cases on behalf of the downtrodden against businesses (why the lawyers who represent the businesses aren't "trial lawyers" too is a mystery we'll leave for another day). At the top of the trial lawyers' wish list is a law that bans mandatory arbitration in cases involving consumers. This is one that we are likely to see in one form or another.

Increased Underwriting Burdens? As a result of the housing finance meltdown, we've heard several calls to impose a duty on creditors not to extend credit without first determining that the credit can be repaid. Some recent comments by President Obama have caused me to wonder whether he's thinking that negative equity and long-term financing are credit features he'd like to eliminate or curb significantly. Look for some of these reforms, while primarily aimed at housing, to seep over to the car side of the credit business.

TILA Amendments. When the Truth in Lending Act was passed in the late '60s, Congress decided that it didn't need to protect wealthy people who were financing personal property, so transactions in which the amount financed exceeded $25,000 were exempted. That number was never adjusted for inflation, with the result that about half the car finance transactions in the country today are not governed by TILA. That's one that should change, and it will.

There are more ideas caroming around the halls of Congress—some that are less sane than others. The credit industry needs to pray that Congress will be so busy frying bigger fish that it doesn't have the time to devote to consumer protection measures. Somehow, I think Congress will find the time to enact several headaches for creditors.

June 2009
That Thing Swinging This Way Might Be a Pendulum

I've been at this legal stuff since 1973, long enough to have seen several cycles of de-regulation, under-regulation, and over-regulation. We've enjoyed a pretty good run of de-regulation and under-regulation. That stretch is slamming to an abrupt halt.

If half of the bills presently pending in Congress pass, and if the newly energized federal agencies start cranking out regulations like I think they are going to, we're in for one of the most extensive periods of re-regulation.

Consider some of the initiatives floating around Washington at the moment.

A Federal Usury Cap? Typically, states set the maximum rates that car dealers and sales finance companies can charge for consumer credit in general and car credit in particular. Congress now wants to get into the rate regulation game.

One bill (S 500) would impose a maximum rate cap of 36% on auto credit, with a truly goofy formula for calculating interest that, unlike the APR calculation we are all familiar with, includes things like voluntarily purchased credit life insurance. It also includes amounts that are impossible to determine when credit is extended, such as late charges above a specified amount. I sense the hands of young and idealistic congressional staffers without any business or even practical experience here. They are blindly following the playbook of the more radical consumer activists, without regard for the impact of such a course.

Another bill (S 257) doesn't establish a maximum rate, as such. Instead, it provides that if a creditor charges a rate in excess of a specified amount (the lesser of 36% or 15% plus the 30-year T-bill rate, a formula that would today equal 19% or so), the creditor will essentially lose its ability to present a secured claim in a bankruptcy proceeding. That gets you to the same destination as S 500 by a different route.

Bye, Bye Arbitration? Many creditors, including many in the car sales, finance, and leasing business, have turned to the use of mandatory arbitration agreements as a first line of defense against professional plaintiffs' lawyers and their use of class claims as a way to "up the ante" and leverage a plain vanilla consumer complaint into a claim that a dealer must settle for big bucks if he doesn't want to "bet the dealership" that a court will render a huge award. So-called "trial lawyers" and consumer advocates have railed against arbitration more loudly with each passing year, and the din is now just about intolerable. My bet? You can kiss arbitration goodbye—Congress will either repeal or amend the Federal Arbitration Act. HR 1020 is a pending measure to do just that.

A Consumer Financial Products Safety Commission? I really don't know what to think about this idea. Its burden on creditors will depend on what the final arrangement looks like. Perhaps the idea is to have some sort of governmental body that looks at consumer financial services products the way that the Consumer Products Safety Commission looks at car safety. It would hand out ratings for financial products, rating, say, a 30-year, fully amortizing first mortgage with five stars and a variable-rate mortgage with a negative amortization feature and a balloon payment with no stars.

Or perhaps the model is more like the Food and Drug Administration, with creditors submitting their proposed financial products for governmental approval before they can be offered to the public after a review period of a decade or two. That one, S 566, makes my hair hurt.

A New Sheriff in Town? Another pending bill (HR 2309) would greatly expand the enforcement authority of the Federal Trade Commission, specifically directing the FTC to engage in rulemaking that would impose a cooling-off period on car financing transactions and that would regulate or eliminate spot delivery transactions, dealer finance charge markups, and the sale of F&I products, among other things. Do you recall the "Car Buyers' Bill of Rights" legislation that we've seen in the last few years at the state level? Here it is again, this time gussied up as a federal regulation.

So, boys and girls, buckle your chin straps because we're in for a rough ride. Sorta makes you long for the days of gridlock, doesn't it?

November 2009
Are You Ready for the Super Agency?

Egad!

I've just finished 595 pages of not-so-gripping prose. It's the Consumer Financial Protection Agency Act of 2009. OK, it really was about 300 pages, but the version I was working with was redlined to show the differences between the final version and the prior version, and, yes, it was 595 pages. I haven't weighed the thing, but I'll bet it weighs more than the flounder I caught a couple of hours ago.

What is this thing, you ask? I'll tell you.

This is the administration's answer to the credit and liquidity crises, as modified by Barney Frank and the Gang. Frank, a U.S. Congressman from Massachusetts, is the "Frank" of the Dodd-Frank Act. Convinced that the economy tanked because the credit police weren't tough enough, the president and Congress have decided that we need a new "Super Agency" to protect us all from those dastardly creditors. Among other powers, the Consumer Financial Protection Agency (CFPA) would enforce the Truth in Lending Act, the Equal Credit Opportunity Act, most of the Fair Credit Reporting Act, the Fair Debt Collection Practices Act, parts of the Gramm-Leach-Bliley Act, a double handful of housing credit laws, and a few other federal consumer protection laws.

If the measure is enacted, it will establish the CFPA, set forth the powers of the Agency and its Director, establish enforcement powers for the Agency, limit the powers of those creditors whose programs now depend upon the concept of federal pre-emption, establish the ground rules for balancing state and federal regulatory schemes and enforcement powers, move bodies around Washington from those agencies that currently deal with consumer credit matters to the new Agency, and make a gazillion "conforming amendments" to the various laws that now reference other agencies so that henceforth they will refer to the new Agency.

Hold on, let me catch my breath. There's more.

The new law would also regulate remittance transfers, provide the Agency with the express authority to restrict mandatory pre-dispute arbitration (that's an early Merry Christmas to the trial lawyers), require the registration and supervision of "nondepository covered persons" (entities that are not banks and credit unions), and establish the manner in which the new Agency will be funded.

Along the way, congresspersons with particular axes to grind (like bashing the community activist group ACORN, for example) managed to get in their licks, adding a little punitive measure here or a little helpful measure there, and the federal regulators who are losing staff and power to the CFPA tossed in their two cents' worth.

All in all, it reminds me of an observation that is sometimes attributed to German Chancellor Otto von Bismarck: "The less people know about how sausages and laws are made, the better they will sleep at night."

Every special interest group worthy of the name has left its fingerprints all over this one. The list of those entities that are exempted from some or all of the bill's provisions (including car dealers) would reach all the way down K Street, and it includes a number of groups that have some real clout when it comes to grassroots politicking. It appears that there was some significant horse trading going on, with an eye toward eliminating potential opposition to the measure.

Really? Horse trading? In Washington, D.C.? Ya think?

The bad news? This mess has cleared two House committees and appears to be headed for a House vote in November. The good news? There isn't much. There are some early indications that if the measure clears the House, it might face some significant opposition in the Senate.

The real game in Washington at the moment seems to be figuring out whether the health care and environmental cap and trade measures will string the CFPA bill out long enough and deplete enough of the political capital of the CFPA's advocates to result in its defeat.

December 2009
An Encore for FATHEAD?

A couple of years ago, I got so fed up with the layer upon layer of new laws and regulations coming out of Washington affecting car dealers that I invented a bogus federal agency to symbolize the problem. I named the agency the Federal Agency To Harass Enterprising Auto Dealers, or "FATHEAD."

CHAPTER 2

Little did I know that someone in the Asylum on the Hill was listening!

Now we have a new Super Agency to regulate consumer financial services being proposed in the House and in the Senate. Barney Frank is responsible for the House version, while the Senate masterpiece is from Christopher Dodd. The House bill was amended before it came out of committee to exempt car dealers who sell nearly all their retail installment contracts to third parties, but there's no such relief in the Senate bill, and the early word is that there isn't likely to be.

Both bills are hundreds of pages long (Dodd's is close to 1,000 pages), and, yup, they both would create a massive new agency with sweeping powers. Some of the powers are new, and some are borrowed from existing agencies like the Federal Reserve Board and the Federal Trade Commission. Both bills are promoted by their supporters as answers to the 2007–2009 financial and credit meltdowns. Both would impose licensing and examination requirements and other burdens on all creditors, including (unless the House exemption holds up) car dealers. Can you imagine the size of a federal agency charged with licensing and examining the tens of thousands of franchised and independent car dealerships in the country?

Talk about FATHEAD! Talk about bureaucratic bloat!

Now, I don't claim to be a scholar when it comes to the financial history of the last year plus, but I don't recall much, if anything, about the credit and financial practices of car dealers contributing to the problems experienced by consumers during that time. You would think that the chuckleheads who write our laws might have noticed that.

The mortgage industry has gotten a lot of the blame for the meltdown, and the Federal Reserve Board has come under fire for not riding herd on some arguably sharp practices by mortgage brokers and lenders. In particular, some have criticized the FRB for failing to regulate those practices.

That puzzles me. Name as many of the mortgage practices that are railed about as you can—no down payment mortgages, teaser rates, adjustable rates, pre-payment penalties, balloon payments—and I can point to a Federal Reserve Board regulation requiring that they be disclosed to the borrower. Some critics will say that the disclosure regulations could be better written, but what good would that do unless borrowers actually read the disclosures?

If these practices are bad, why not simply enact a law that prohibits them? You don't need a Super Agency for that. But Congress is reluctant to get into the business of telling lenders what features they can and cannot offer. That smacks too much of a controlled economy.

Or, you could prohibit certain products from being offered to less financially savvy consumers, drawing the line (like the Truth in Lending Act does) between savvy and unsavvy by the amount of credit extended, or maybe by credit score. But that sort of condescending Big Brother stuff doesn't go down particularly well either.

If the object is to protect consumers without having the government get into underwriting or prohibiting product features, and to do it without creating a Super Agency, why not adopt as a model the one used by those wild and crazy crash-testing folks over at the National Highway Traffic Safety Administration? You could hire a few more people to work for an existing agency like the Federal Reserve Board or the Federal Trade Commission, and these folks could assess various product features and "score" how dangerous a particular credit offering might be. A "safe" financial product, like, say, a 30-year, fixed-rate mortgage requiring a 20% down payment, escrowing taxes and insurance, with no pre-payment penalty, might get five stars, while a mortgage with a 30-year amortization schedule, a 15-year balloon payment, no down payment requirement, and a pre-payment penalty would get no stars.

Car financing is pretty simple, so there aren't too many credit features that raters could use, but a few come to mind. Financing that included negative equity or otherwise involved a high LTV might be one feature worth considering. Interest-bearing (simple interest) financing might be deemed superior to pre-computed transactions. Pre-payment penalties and balloon payments sometimes show up in car financing, where state law permits.

With such a rating scheme, there wouldn't be a need for the agency to rate every creditor's offering separately. It might be sufficient for the agency simply to invent the rating formula and let creditors rate their own products.

It would be worth a try, if we could pull the plug on FATHEAD.

Chapter 3

2010: Unlimbering the Guns

CHAPTER 3

January/February 2010
The Practical Dealer's Guide to the New Risk-Based Pricing Rule

By Thomas B. Hudson and Michael A. Benoit

In late December of 2009, the Federal Reserve Board and the Federal Trade Commission issued their joint Risk-Based Pricing Rule. The notice issued by the agencies is a mere 202 pages long.

The Rule requires a dealer that varies the cost of credit based on information in a buyer's credit report to give some buyers—essentially those who paid more for financing than some others—a risk-based pricing (RBP) notice. You, or your lawyer, will need to read the rule in detail. It is aimed squarely at dealers and is not something your finance companies can do for you.

Here's the shorthand version of the Rule, which becomes effective on January 1, 2011.

The Rule offers three ways to determine which buyers will be given the required notice. The dealer can do a case-by-case analysis of its deals, basically subjectively determining whether each individual customer is entitled to a RBP notice. Alternatively, the dealer can elect to use something called the "credit score proxy method" or the "tiered pricing method." Even the easiest of the three methods is difficult to understand, and because the agencies aren't well versed in the mechanics of indirect financing, dealers will be hard pressed to comply effectively with any of the methods.

The Rule provides a handy-dandy exception, though. If the dealer gives every customer who applies for credit (even if the customer doesn't ultimately buy the car or accept financing) a copy of the buyer's credit score and a specific notice in a form provided by the agencies, the dealer is not required to provide the RBP notice.

So you might want to simply forget about giving the RBP notice altogether and, instead, rely on the exception. There are some advantages to this approach. First, you (or your lawyer) can skip most of the 202 pages and concentrate on the parts of the release dealing with the exception. Second, unlike the "case-by-case," "tiered pricing," and "credit score proxy" methods, dealers can actually comply with the requirements that apply to the exception. And finally (you should write this down), any time the feds give you a free space in the form of a safe harbor compliance method with agency-blessed forms, you should grab it and run.

Now this article isn't entirely serious—we do have our tongue a bit in cheek—but we have provided the basics of the Rule. You and your lawyer should become familiar with the Rule and track behind us to see if you agree with our analysis. We think you likely will.

We also think that this is one of those instances in which vendors will be working up solutions that will help you comply with the new Rule. But don't wait too long for the vendors—the burden of complying with the Risk-Based Pricing Rule falls squarely on dealers, and 2011 will be here before you can blink.

March 2010
Lobbyists: Pros and Amateurs

Recently, I was speaking to a friend with a state dealer association shortly after the Federal Reserve Board and the Federal Trade Commission issued their new Risk-Based Pricing Rule. This fellow told me that one auto dealer trade association executive had stated that the RBP Rule didn't apply to car dealers, which is incorrect. When I showed the mistaken exec language from the Rule making it crystal clear that dealers were not only

CHAPTER 3

affected by the Rule, but were its intended targets, the mistaken exec responded that he was expecting a call from the FTC the following day saying the problem was fixed.

My first reaction to this statement was, "What planet is this guy from?" My second reaction was, "Where can I get some of whatever he's smoking?"

You see, the RBP Rule has been in the works for six years. That's right, S-I-X years. After six years of effort by these two federal agencies, someone representing a trade association is going to change the Rule with a phone call? The idea is absurd. Here's why:

What happens when federal agencies issue rules and regulations? First, something prods the agency into action. Some agencies simply calendar their rules for periodic review, as part of good regulatory housekeeping. In other cases, agencies will take note of a problem in the marketplace or in the courts that needs correcting.

In still other cases, an agency gets a directive from Congress to write a regulation. That's what happened with the RBP Rule. When Congress enacted the Fair and Accurate Credit Transactions Act of 2003, which amended the Fair Credit Reporting Act, it directed the Federal Reserve Board and the Federal Trade Commission to come up with risk-based pricing rules.

When the agencies gear up to create a rule or regulation, they will sometimes issue what's called an Advanced Notice of Proposed Rulemaking, in which they essentially ask the public to comment on specific issues and problems that relate to the rule. That advanced notice is followed by a period of navel-gazing during which the agency ponders the comments it has received, and then the agency works up a draft of the rule it has come up with and issues the draft with something called a "Notice of

Proposed Rulemaking." Again, the agency is looking for input from everyone, including private citizens, who wants to pipe up with comments about the draft (no lobbying registration is required to participate in this commenting process). There is a comment period within which comments must be received, and, at the close of the comment period, the agency takes all the comments it has received and reworks the rule to reflect the comments it finds persuasive.

The comment period is when the public, including trade associations, businesses, academics, consumer advocates, and plain old citizens, gets the chance to help shape the rule. Those who don't speak up during the comment period have lost the opportunity to have any influence over the content of the rule.

So, if you find yourself on the wrong end of a federal rule that has been under development for six years, that has been the subject of a comment period, and that has been issued in the form of a final rule, my advice to you is learn to live with it because—and you can write this down—you ain't gonna change it with a phone call.

And, before I drop this topic, a word about lobbying: Lobbying is different from the rulemaking process described above. Anyone can participate in a rulemaking—several of my partners regularly do so for our clients.

However, lobbying at the federal level requires several things. First, those who lobby must be registered to do so. Second, they need to know their subject matter. Third, and most importantly, they need to have mastered the process of lawmaking (Hint: That process doesn't involve calls to agency "friends" after a final rule has been issued.), and they actually must know how to persuade the folks who make laws and policy of their views.

CHAPTER 3

I'm a pretty fair car lawyer because I know the laws that deal with car sales, financing, and leasing, but I don't have the skills required to lobby. After all, knowing about the law of gravity doesn't make you a downhill skier.

If some car lawyer tells you he lobbies at the federal level, you should do some investigating before you buy the goods he's selling. First, is he/she registered as a lobbyist? What other organizations does he/she represent? Do any of the other organizations have squat to do with cars or dealers? What does his/her track record on lobbying look like?

If the only response regarding credentials is that the lobbyist "has friends at the FTC," it's time for you to run like hell.

April 2010
A Word from the Dog

Spot can't figure it out. After he finished his bowl of kibble the other morning, he trotted down to get *The Washington Post*. When he returned, he opened it, as he usually does, to the editorial page. After a few minutes, he sat up abruptly and barked, tapping his paw on the bottom left part of the page.

I picked the paper up from the floor, and, sure enough, there was yet another story claiming that a watchdog fell asleep while on duty. Spot doesn't like to see his colleagues criticized unfairly, and the editorial that offended him was, in his view, a cheap shot.

Upon reading the article, I had to agree with him. The editorial was by Steven Pearlstein, and the thrust of the editorial was that the Federal Reserve Board had not done a good job of protecting consumers and was at least partly to blame for the Great Housing Debacle and all of the other financial ills of the last couple of years.

Like so many pundits, Pearlstein states his conclusion without providing anything to back it up. Pearlstein says that until the crisis, the Fed "had a record unblemished by success." I think that his general thesis reflects a lack of understanding about the role of the Fed, and his criticism of what the Fed has done over the last several decades reflects ignorance of its many significant achievements.

Well, I earn my living by trying to keep financial institutions in compliance with federal laws and regulations, and I've accumulated a little knowledge about this topic. One of the things I've learned over the years is that federal agencies cannot make up their own mission statements. They are permitted to do only those things that Congress permits them to do.

Consider the Truth in Lending Act, for example. That law is one of Congress's primary efforts to protect consumers. The law is based on the premise that creditors should all calculate and disclose the cost of credit in the same way. TILA directed the Fed to promulgate regulations to implement TILA's disclosure requirements, and it did so, producing Regulation Z for credit transactions and Regulation M for leasing transactions.

The Fed, however, only has enforcement authority over a relatively small class of creditors. Other federal agencies—including the Federal Trade Commission, the Federal Deposit Insurance Corporation, the Comptroller of the Currency, the Office of Thrift Supervision, and the National Credit Union Administration—were given the enforcement authority for the lion's share of creditors.

Assume with me for a moment that the Fed produced a wonderful consumer protection regulation when it issued Regulation Z. If, as to most creditors, the Fed had no enforcement power regarding the Regulation, how can it be blamed for failures resulting from enforcement lapses?

CHAPTER 3

Not that there were, in my view, failures in either the drafting of the disclosure regulations or in their enforcement. I don't believe that the travails of homeowners who found themselves in difficulty over the last couple of years were the result of a failure by their creditors to disclose the terms of the credit extended to the homeowners. Those problems were, rather, caused by lax underwriting standards (can you say "no-doc loans"?), high (or no) LTV requirements or debt-to-income ratios, and the collective misjudgment of a lot of people who thought that the price of houses went only in one direction.

I might be wrong, but I don't think the Fed has any authority to require creditors as to which it has no enforcement authority to do the things that might have prevented the meltdown. It cannot require those creditors to obtain credit documents from borrowers (i.e., to stop making "no-doc" loans) or impose upon those creditors loan-to-value, debt-to-income, or other underwriting standards. I don't believe that the Fed has the authority to prohibit creditors over which it has no enforcement authority from offering those dicey loan products that President Obama would call other than "plain vanilla."

On those things that Congress actually has directed the Fed to do, such as the drafting of disclosure regulations, the Fed has done very well. I work with the Fed's regulations all the time, and I can tell you that within the mandate they have been given, they do a great job of tipping the scales toward the interests of consumers as far as they can without imposing impractical and/or costly burdens on creditors. The Fed also has a Consumer Advisory Council that includes academics and consumer advocates—just the kinds of folks you would expect to push the Fed to do all it could do, within its powers, to protect consumers.

I think Spot was right. His fellow watchdog got a bum rap. Now I think I'll see what the parakeet thinks.

2010: UNLIMBERING THE GUNS

July 2010
That'll Be the Day

Recently, my wife hauled me off to a neighborhood arts center. It was her birthday, and she wanted to go see a Buddy Holly concert. Well, not exactly Buddy himself, since he hasn't been with us since The Day the Music Died in 1959, but rather a guy in a pink sport coat, black slacks, and heavy-framed glasses, backed by a bass player, a guitarist, and a drummer.

The plain truth is that the guy playing Buddy wasn't very good. He did well enough on "Peggy Sue," "Rave On," and the other up-tempo songs, but with the slow stuff, his inability to find a note with a compass became evident. His rendition of "True Love Ways" was downright painful.

What he lacked in singing ability, though, he made up for in enthusiasm and an encyclopedic knowledge of Buddy Holly trivia. His constant patter between songs was entertaining.

One of the tidbits he dropped dealt with a song that Buddy wrote called "That'll Be the Day." It seems that Buddy went to the movies to see a 1956 John Wayne film, "The Searchers," and The Duke's character in the film punctuated a number of his scenes with that phrase.

Which got me thinking about the new federal financial reform law that Congress looks certain to enact this month to stop abuses.

That'll be the day.

I bought my first new car in 1964. Because I didn't have two dimes to rub together, I financed it. Back then, before the federal Truth in Lending Act was passed, dealers quoted finance charge rates in a bewildering variety of ways. They used "pre-computed," "add-on," and "discount" rates, among others. In the late 1960s, Senator William Proxmire took up the cause of consumer credit disclosure with the idea that everyone quoting

CHAPTER 3

credit terms ought to use the same rate calculation method and should disclose credit terms in a uniform way. The result was the federal Truth in Lending Act. Proxmire's idea was that having consumers presented with rates calculated the same way by all creditors would permit consumers to choose the best credit deal.

That'll be the day.

In the mid '70s, consumer advocates railed against the discriminatory practices of some creditors. Women and minority borrowers, in particular, were subject to credit practices that were more onerous than those visited upon men and whites. The consumer advocates thought that such discrimination was unfair. Congress heeded their arguments, and the Equal Credit Opportunity Act became law.

That'll be the day.

Also in the mid '70s, as car leasing for consumers was becoming more popular, consumer advocates argued that no federal law required lessors to provide lessees with the same sorts of disclosures that credit sellers were required to provide to credit buyers. They pressed Congress to remedy that disclosure deficiency, and the result was the Consumer Leasing Act.

That'll be the day.

There were some significant federal enactments other than these—the Fair Credit Reporting Act comes to mind—but things were generally quiet on the federal level until the consumer advocates focused on privacy. Those who received and maintained consumers' financial information weren't doing enough to keep that information from getting into the wrong hands. Perhaps, they argued, we need a federal law to remedy the problem. The Gramm-Leach-Bliley Act was the Congressional answer.

That'll be the day.

As the first decade of the new century passed the midway mark, the consumer advocates found new abuses to rail against.

The use by creditors and dealers of mandatory arbitration agreements as a first line of defense against class actions, payment packing, spot deliveries, dealer participation, and redefining the method of APR calculation to include fees and charges that aren't required to be included in the present formula have all been identified by the consumer advocates as reforms they'd like to see implemented. "Wouldn't it be great," they said," if we had a really powerful, well-funded federal regulator with sweeping rule-making authority that could implement our agenda?"

That'll be the day.

July 2010
Dealer CFPB Exemption? Maybe Not

By Thomas B. Hudson and Michael A. Benoit

Some car dealers are exempt from the regulatory reach of the Consumer Financial Protection Bureau created by the Dodd-Frank Act, which is the moniker they've hung on the federal financial reform legislation. But some aren't. Determining which ones are in and which ones are out requires a review of the language in the bill dealing with the exemption.

Congressional bills can be hard to read. This one's no different. Following, we've set forth the auto dealer exclusion provision in the bill and what we hope is a mostly English language translation of it.

SEC. 1029. EXCLUSION FOR AUTO DEALERS.

(a) SALE, SERVICING, AND LEASING OF MOTOR VEHICLES EXCLUDED.—Except as permitted in subsection (b), the Bureau may not exercise any

CHAPTER 3

rulemaking, supervisory, enforcement or any other authority, including any authority to order assessments, over a motor vehicle dealer that is predominantly engaged in the sale and servicing of motor vehicles, the leasing and servicing of motor vehicles, or both.

Translation: Dealers primarily engaged in the sale and servicing of motor vehicles, the leasing and servicing of motor vehicles, or both, are excluded from the regulatory reach of the CFPB. Note that the dealer must have a servicing function and a sales and/or leasing function. If an independent dealer maintains a servicing department, and some do, that dealer qualifies for the exemption.

(b) CERTAIN FUNCTIONS EXCEPTED.—Subsection (a) shall not apply to any person, to the extent that such person—
(1) provides consumers with any services related to residential or commercial mortgages or self financing transactions involving real property;

Translation: The exclusion won't apply to any motor vehicle dealer engaged in consumer real estate financing, regardless of whether he would be excluded in subsection (a).

(2) operates a line of business—
(A) that involves the extension of retail credit or retail leases involving motor vehicles; and
(B) in which—
(i) the extension of retail credit or retail leases are provided directly to consumers; and
(ii) the contract governing such extension of retail credit

or retail leases is not routinely assigned to an unaffiliated third party finance or leasing source; or

Translation: No exclusion for dealers who engage in consumer lease and installment sale financing and who keep those obligations or sell them to their affiliated finance companies. These dealers will be subject to the jurisdiction of the CFPB.

(3) offers or provides a consumer financial product or service not involving or related to the sale, financing, leasing, rental, repair, refurbishment, maintenance, or other servicing of motor vehicles, motor vehicle parts, or any related or ancillary product or service.

Translation: The exclusion won't apply to a dealer who offers or provides consumer financial services not related to the vehicle sale or lease, e.g., it would not apply to a dealer who offers home improvement credit in addition to selling or leasing vehicles.

(c) PRESERVATION OF AUTHORITIES OF OTHER AGENCIES.—Except as provided in subsections (b) and (d), nothing in this title, including subtitle F, shall be construed as modifying, limiting, or superseding the operation of any provision of Federal law, or otherwise affecting the authority of the Board of Governors, the Federal Trade Commission, or any other Federal agency, with respect to a person described in subsection (a).

Translation: This section keeps the authority of other agencies with respect to motor vehicle dealers intact. So, even if

CHAPTER 3

a motor vehicle dealer qualifies for the exclusion, it will still be regulated in the same manner it has been to date.

> (d) FEDERAL TRADE COMMISSION AUTHORITY. — Notwithstanding section 18 of the Federal Trade Commission Act, the Federal Trade Commission is authorized to prescribe rules under sections 5 and 18(a)(1)(B) of the Federal Trade Commission Act, in accordance with section 553 of title 5, United States Code, with respect to a person described in subsection (a).

Translation: This section expands the FTC's authority with respect to motor vehicle dealers. The FTC will now have express authority to write rules regulating dealers with respect to unfair and deceptive practices. The FTC also gets new authority to makes rules defining unfair and deceptive practices in accordance with the federal Administrative Procedures Act, which will allow the FTC to draft and implement a rule in as little as six months. So dealers exempt from the CFPB's authority shouldn't be overly happy—Congress giveth with one hand and taketh away with the other.

> (e) COORDINATION WITH OFFICE OF SERVICE-MEMBER AFFAIRS.—The Board of Governors and the Federal Trade Commission shall coordinate with the Office of Servicemember Affairs, to ensure that—
> (1) servicemembers and their families are educated and empowered to make better informed decisions regarding consumer financial products and services offered by motor vehicle dealers, with a focus on motor vehicle dealers in the proximity of military installations; and
> (2) complaints by servicemembers and their families

concerning such motor vehicle dealers are effectively monitored and responded to, and where appropriate, enforcement action is pursued by the authorized agencies.

Translation: The Federal Reserve Board and the FTC will now be required to work with the Office of Servicemember Affairs to provide education regarding automobile finance. It also appears that the legislation mandates these agencies to focus on specific dealers in close geographical proximity to military bases. The agencies are also required to monitor complaints about dealers from servicemembers, and respond to such complaints. Where warranted, the agencies are to see that the appropriate regulators undertake enforcement actions.

> (f) DEFINITIONS.—For purposes of this section, the following definitions shall apply:
> (1) MOTOR VEHICLE.—The term "motor vehicle" means—
> (A) any self-propelled vehicle designed for transporting persons or property on a street, highway, or other road;
> (B) recreational boats and marine equipment;
> (C) motorcycles;
> (D) motor homes, recreational vehicle trailers, and slide-in campers, as those terms are defined in sections 571.3 and 575.103 (d) of title 49, Code of Federal Regulations, or any successor thereto; and
> (E) other vehicles that are titled and sold through dealers.

Translation: The definitions are fairly straightforward but raise some interesting questions regarding certain goods in certain states (e.g., an all-terrain vehicle not required by law to be titled).

CHAPTER 3

> (2) MOTOR VEHICLE DEALER.—The term "motor vehicle dealer" means any person or resident in the United States, or any territory of the United States, who—
> (A) is licensed by a State, a territory of the United States, or the District of Columbia to engage in the sale of motor vehicles; and
> (B) takes title to, holds an ownership in, or takes physical custody of motor vehicles.

Translation: Again, mostly straightforward, but where do companies fit that only lease cars and are not licensed to sell them? What about rent-to-own? What about consignments, in states where they are permitted?

So, there's the auto dealer exclusion language from the bill, in all its majesty, and there's our initial attempt to translate it into something like English. The bill itself is over 2,000 pages long, and we haven't digested the entire thing yet. It may be that dealers foreclosed from the Section 1029 exclusion could qualify for other exclusions contained in the bill, but that remains to be seen.

We suspect that as the dust settles, more questions will arise. When they do, check back with us—assuming the bill passes (and that's likely but not guaranteed as we write this), we'll probably still be trying to figure out what it all means.

August 2010
The Consumer Financial Protection Bureau and Car Dealers: More Questions than Answers

My partners Michael Benoit and Anne Fortney did a webinar on the new Consumer Financial Protection Bureau that has been established by the Dodd-Frank federal financial regulation overhaul bill that President Obama has signed into law.

Michael and Anne did a crackerjack job, but, no sooner had the webinar ended and the computers started cooling off, we began getting emails and phone calls asking for details on how the CFPB was going to affect dealers in general, and specifically what its effect would be on franchised dealers, independent dealers, and BHPH dealers.

Apart from being able to say that nearly all franchised dealers and some independent dealers (those with service capabilities who don't hold their own retail installment contracts) have an exclusion from the CFPB's jurisdiction, I can't provide much of an answer to these questions beyond, "It's gonna get rough."

I can't give specifics because there aren't many yet. I can, however, hazard a few educated guesses about where we think the CFPB and the newly energized Federal Trade Commission (the entity that will regulate all dealers, including those excluded from CFPB jurisdiction) will want to move first.

I expect the CFPB and the FTC will begin to issue proposed regulations as soon as they get their computers plugged in, although it may take a little while for the CFPB to accomplish that. In any event, it will be those proposed regulations that will tell us what these cops are interested in addressing first.

Can I read the tea leaves and forecast those topics that will be the subject of the proposed regulations? I've tried, and my list appears below. Some of the topics are more likely than others to end up being addressed, and some are more far-fetched. In each

CHAPTER 3

case, I've mentioned the topic and why I think it's likely that it will be the subject of a proposed regulation.

Race discrimination: A decade or so ago, Nissan Motors Acceptance Corporation and General Motors Acceptance Corporation were sued in Tennessee in private class actions alleging racial discrimination in connection with credit extended to car buyers. The Justice Department filed amicus briefs in the actions, and lawyers from our firm have met with a group of Justice Department lawyers regarding auto finance issues. I think we'll see an initiative here, and it will probably be an enforcement action rather than rulemaking.

Payment packing: This is a practice that state AGs have targeted as unfair and deceptive. I'd not be surprised to see the Bureau and FTC agreeing.

Arbitration: Banning the use by dealers of pre-dispute arbitration clauses in their sales and credit agreements with consumers is probably #1 on the consumer advocates' hit list. The Bureau is required to conduct a study of this practice and is authorized to ban or restrict it consistent with the study.

Dealer participation and spot delivery: Capitol Hill testimony by consumer advocates attacked these common dealer business practices. It's possible they'll both show up on the Bureau's and the FTC's radar screens.

Three-day cooling-off period: This topic keeps popping up in proposed "car buyer bill of rights" proposals and was also mentioned in the Congressional testimony of consumer advocates.

Pricing or markup (of the vehicle and ancillary products): I don't have much to support this one other than a few AG inquiries and a queasy feeling in my stomach. The new CFPB prohibition of "abusive" practices might be used to attack pricing, and the FTC may decide to define certain products as per se unfair and deceptive. At a recent independent dealer association meeting, one survey reported that used car markups exceeding 100% weren't unusual. It's not unusual in the restaurant business either, but I'm not sure anyone makes the same connection. While I'm suspecting that the new federal sheriff might think current industry markup practices need regulating, I'm hoping rational agency economists will provide a buffer.

APR calculation methods: I think it's possible that the CFPB will be pushing the so-called "FAIR" formula, requiring fees and charges for optional products and services as well as fees like late charges and NSF charges to be included in the APR and finance charge calculations. The FAIR formula concept appeared in two federal rate cap bills introduced last fall. While the bills did not go anywhere, beware the power of a catchy acronym. A change in the APR and finance charge calculation formulas would probably require an act of Congress, so look for the CFPB to urge an amendment to the Truth in Lending Act for this purpose.

Advertising: State AGs are currently very active in this area and will likely continue to be.

Rent-to-own/lease-to-own/title pawn: These areas are the closest thing on the car finance side to payday lending. Consumer advocates really hate these businesses.

A ban (or limitations) on self-help repossession: This is based on the 2010 Public Citizen Repo Madness publication. I think that this one's a low-percentage possibility since self-help repo is permitted in some form in all states and is economically more efficient for all parties involved.

If this list looks like a recipe for regulatory disaster to you, perhaps it's time for you to get active in your state and national dealer associations. The Bureau will start rolling out proposed regulations in a few months. The only way to curb the influence of the consumer advocates who will be pushing initiatives like these will be to participate often and loudly in the comment process, educating the Bureau and FTC on the economic value of all segments of this industry and letting them know the economic impact their proposals will have on consumers. Buckle up. It's going to be a bumpy ride.

November 2010
No More Advertising "Business as Usual"

Have you ever walked out the door and instantly said, "A storm's on the way," and later wondered how you knew the weather was about to change? Maybe the ancestral part of your brain picked up the change of pressure or humidity, or maybe somewhere in our prehistoric past we were able to pick up wind gusts that moved in a certain way. However you did it, your initial instincts were correct, and you made it to your car just before the bottom fell out.

My instincts these days tell me a storm's on the way. This one is coming out of Washington, D.C., and it's tracking toward dealers and their advertising.

How do I know? Well, I guarantee you that I didn't pick it up from things my ancestors learned on the Serengeti plains.

I have, though, picked up some signs. Here they are.

Sign: Congress passes the Dodd-Frank Wall Street Reform and Consumer Protection Act, creating the Bureau of Consumer Financial Protection.

Sign: Dealers who are exempt from the Bureau's authority fall squarely into the sights of the Federal Trade Commission.

Sign: Dodd-Frank beefs up the FTC's rulemaking authority. No longer will the FTC be hobbled by its creaky old rulemaking authority—now it will be lean, mean, and fast.

2010: UNLIMBERING THE GUNS

Sign: The FTC has created a task force to address the practices of car dealers.

Sign: State attorneys general have been on a rampage on the subject of dealer advertising violations for the last few years. AGs who have been successful attacking dealer advertising have attended meetings where the state AGs gather and talk about their enforcement initiatives. That has led to other enforcement activities.

Sign: The FTC's new dealer task force is very familiar with the AGs' initiatives.

Sign: The FTC's new dealer task force will be looking for some low-hanging fruit to give it some early successes.

All these signs are what folks in the detective business refer to as "clues." And it doesn't take a Perry Mason, a Columbo, or a Monk to piece these clues together and conclude that a storm's on the way.

Now, maybe you already run all your ads past your dealership's lawyer. If you do, you can probably quit reading this now.

If not, and if whoever is in charge of your dealership's advertising isn't very well trained on the legal aspects of advertising, now would be a good time to put your lawyer and your advertising person together for a crash course. The lawyer will no doubt point out the advertising rules contained in Federal Reserve Board Regulations Z and M, governing credit sales and leases generally. Your mouthpiece will also probably walk you through the state laws that you'll need to pay attention to. These can be found in your state's credit sale and lease laws, in the state's general advertising laws and regulations, in laws prohibiting unfair and deceptive practices, and in state motor vehicle dealer laws and regulations. Some states hide provisions relating to advertising—especially those provisions dealing with

CHAPTER 3

lotteries and games of chance—in odd places like the state's criminal code.

Your lawyer likely also knows that there are some worthwhile resources available for your advertising person from the Federal Trade Commission's website, from the National Automobile Dealers Association, and from your state dealer association.

Using all these resources, your advertising person, with your lawyer's help, should create advertising guidelines and a checklist to apply to every ad that he or she approves and keep a record of each ad, with the checklist attached.

When folks from the FTC's task force land on your doorstep and ask you for your advertising manual, wouldn't it be helpful if you actually have one?

November 2010
Time to Put a Lock on the Fax Machine?

Every day, we check a bunch of Internet sites to see what the various federal agencies are up to that might affect car dealers. When we find items of interest, they go out as an "Alert" to the subscribers of our several online compliance services. Usually we'll pick up some action by the Federal Reserve Board or the Federal Trade Commission, but occasionally an item from another agency turns up.

Recently an item from the Federal Communications Commission caught my eye. Actually, I should say several items, and they were identical, except for company names and numbers. One such entry read:

- Forfeiture Order—(September 16, 2010) Monetary forfeiture issued in the amount of $806,500 against SMC, LLC for delivering at least 145 unsolicited advertisements to the telephone facsimile machines of at least 84 consumers.

Eight more nearly identical items followed. The dollar amount of each forfeiture and the number of unsolicited faxes for each one were as follows:

$1,533,000	145
$139,000	31
$125,000	23
$4,500	10
$144,000	32
$27,000	6
$50,000	63
$257,000	56

According to my handy Radio Shack calculator, that's a $3,000,000-plus day for the FCC from unsolicited faxes (makes you wonder why, with all that penalty income, we pay taxes, but I digress).

"Hmmmm," says I, "I wonder if this would be a practical problem for car dealers?"

That led me to fire off an email to a friend who runs a dealership. I asked, "Is there actually any possibility that a dealership employee might send unsolicited faxes in an attempt to drum up business?"

Here's the dealer's reply:

I don't think there is much real risk that an employee would personally send unsolicited faxes to drum up business. After all, I don't think most dealerships will have lists of fax numbers lying around. I just checked our credit app (provided by one of the captives), and it doesn't ask for a fax number. I also just looked in our CRM, and fax numbers aren't listed with the customer information. Frankly, if you told me to fax an ad to all the customers in my database today, I don't know how I'd do it. But, I

CHAPTER 3

think the bigger risk is that some marketing company would offer to do a bunch of faxes on the dealership's behalf. Such a company would likely claim to have its own customer lists, and would use these lists to advertise things for the dealers. The dealer would provide the content, and the fax company would get it out there. I get calls from every type of marketing outfit you could imagine—it wouldn't surprise me to get a call from a fax marketing company. That being said, I still don't think that there is a huge risk that a dealer would send out a bunch of faxes. My guess is that most dealers know that the faxes just sit on the fax machine in the admin office anyway, and aren't as effective as, say, a 20-foot inflatable gorilla in front of the dealership.

I don't like raising an alarm when a potential threat is only theoretical, so I decided to ask my friend Denny Long, Vice President of DBD Communications in Powell, Ohio, whether he thought an article on faxing would be worthwhile. Denny has been involved with dealer advertising since before the invention of the wheel, and if anyone had ever heard of dealers using faxes to advertise, it would be Denny. Here's his response:

Although I don't believe a lot of dealers will do this, there is always that one employee that might think it's a good idea. I could definitely see where a dealership that wants to go after commercial or fleet sales might be tempted to try a fax blast.

I did find one 2002 article where a dealer was fined $6.5 million (OUCH!) for sending 33,000 faxes. My bet is that most people don't know about the law and I believe it is a good idea to inform them especially since based on your information it sounds like the FCC is getting very aggressive with their fines. I also found that there are quite a few companies that still offer "blast fax" services.

I would hate to hear that a dealer tried this a few months from now and received a big fine when it could have been avoided if he had read your article. My vote is to publish the article.

2010: UNLIMBERING THE GUNS

Denny's response persuaded me. Maybe there's not a huge risk here, but a risk nonetheless. The risk, and the ultimate exposure, would be even less if the dealership has a written "Do-Not-Fax" policy. You do have one of those, right?

With penalty numbers like those in the FCC's release at stake, maybe when that ad guy with the blast fax program comes calling, you'll want to ask him about his selection of inflatable gorillas.

December 2010
When the FTC Letter Arrives ...

When my car dealer client called, he was in a blind panic. It seems that when he arrived at his dealership that morning, lurking in the mail was a letter from the Federal Trade Commission, or, more specifically, from the FTC's Division of Financial Practices, Bureau of Consumer Protection.

The letter announced that the FTC was conducting a "nonpublic investigation" to determine whether the practices of my client's dealership (and naming the dealership) complied with the FTC's Trade Regulation Rule Concerning Preservation of Consumers' Claims and Defenses. The letter requested that the dealer voluntarily provide, "in lieu of compulsory process," (hint, hint) a boatload of information, and requested copies of a number of documents, including copies of all consumer credit contracts executed by the dealership on or after October 1, 2009.

A little background is in order at this point. The Rule referenced in the FTC's letter is commonly called "The Holder Rule," and it has been on the FTC's books since the Pilgrims landed at Plymouth Rock. The Holder Rule was the FTC's response to a particular abuse it had identified in the credit sale

CHAPTER 3

of consumer goods. Way back when, a merchant who sold a shoddy refrigerator on credit could assign the consumer's installment contract to a finance company, and, when the consumer quit making payments to the finance company, claiming the refrigerator was a piece of junk, the finance company could claim that it was a "holder in due course" of the customer's obligation and, by virtue of that status, was immune from the consumer's claims.

The FTC's Holder Rule brought those practices to a grinding halt. The Rule required credit sellers to include a provision in their contracts stating that the holder of the contract was subject to the claims and defenses of the consumer. Problem solved.

I was a new lawyer when the Holder Rule became effective, and I still recall the anguished screams of banks and finance companies that bought retail installment contracts from car dealers and that thought they would become targets for all of the car buyers who had claims or defenses against the dealers who sold them their cars.

It never happened. Dealers and finance companies stuck the required language in their credit contracts, and banks and finance companies amended their dealer agreements to provide that dealers were on the hook for any consumer claims and defenses asserted using the Holder Rule, and business went on as usual. Sure, there were a few problems here and there, but the world didn't end, and the Holder Rule seemed to operate pretty much as intended. For decades and decades.

So why, you ask, did the FTC suddenly get its shorts in a twist about dealers' compliance with the Holder Rule? The short answer is that I have no idea.

About the only thing that I can come up with is that the members of the FTC's newly formed Auto Dealer Task Force were sitting around a table trying to figure out a good first move in showing they are serious about curbing abuses in the credit sale marketplace, and decided to gather some facts about one of their early consumer protection initiatives to see how it was working. To my knowledge, the FTC has never taken any steps, formal or otherwise, to assess the Holder Rule's effectiveness.

If that is what is going on, I predict that the FTC will be mightily pleased with what it finds. I haven't seen a retail installment contract printed since the Holder Rule went into effect that didn't contain the language mandated by the Rule. The industry should end up with nothing but gold stars on this one.

So, back to my dealer client. After he recovered from passing out, I told him that unless he had encountered a particular problem lately, it was not likely that the FTC had a particular interest in his dealership, and that it was more likely than not that such a letter had been sent to a random sampling of dealers in an attempt by the FTC to test industry compliance with the Holder Rule.

This particular story has a happy ending. The dealer forwarded the FTC's letter, and we worked with the FTC's staff to scale down the scope of what our client would produce. That way, our client does a little leg work for the Commission, and he can rest easy that he isn't in the FTC's gunsights.

The next story might take a nastier turn, though. Industry compliance with many FTC rules and regulations isn't what it should be, and the next letter might be directed at practices where dealers are much more vulnerable. If you haven't had lunch lately with your friendly dealership lawyer, now might be a good time.

CHAPTER 3

Chapter 4

2011: Revenge of the Consumer Advocates

CHAPTER 4

The year 2011 got downright interesting. As it became more and more evident that the CFPB was on a regulatory and enforcement tear like nothing else that the car industry has ever seen, some push-backs emerged. One of those consisted of unsuccessful attempts to hobble the Bureau by pushing legislation to restructure it. Another pushback, of sorts, involved the Federal Trade Commission. The FTC, seeming to smart from criticism that it had been a weak credit law enforcer and from defections of a number of its experienced staffers to the fledgling but higher-paying CFPB, decided to stake a claim on part of the auto dealer compliance turf. The FTC held three "Roundtable" discussions on auto sales, finance, and leasing over the course of the year.

All the usual suspects showed up at these Roundtables. With the consumer advocates ignoring the FTC's plea for data and pushing the usual consumer sob stories instead, and proffering advocacy disguised as "research," these events were predictably, well, predictable.

Articles describing all three FTC Roundtables appear below, and it's fair to say that in 2011, the FTC made it clear that it intended to be a player in the auto business enforcement arena. The FTC's ramped-up enforcement in connection with dealer advertising and other practices in 2012 are traceable to the Roundtable fact finding of 2011, but I'm getting ahead of myself.

Here's how the year unfolded.

January/February 2011
Are You a Bottom Feeder?

When you are a lawyer, your friends insist on telling you every lawyer joke they hear. One of my favorite recent ones: "What's the difference between a lawyer and a carp?" The answer, after my obligatory "I give up," was, "One's a scum-sucking bottom feeder, and the other one's just a fish."

I immediately thought of that joke when I read that Federal Trade Commission Chairman Jon Leibowitz, in a speech to the U.S. Chamber of Commerce, used the term "bottom feeder" in describing the FTC's agenda for the coming year in light of the creation of the Bureau of Consumer Financial Protection, with which the FTC will share enforcement authority over financial services companies.

Leibowitz, in an effort to calm criticism by the business community of any increase in regulation, said that the agencies would not impede the business community and that, in the exercise of their overlapping jurisdiction, they did not want to "double-team" legitimate business. He said that the CFPB will not be "devising new hoops for already stressed businesses to jump through" because it "will be too busy going after the multitude of truly bad actors, the bottom feeders, on the consumer financial protection stage."

He's selling, but I'm not sure I'm buying. I recently attended an American Bar Association meeting that featured a panel discussion about the FTC's and the Bureau's likely agendas over the course of the new year. The panelists included two FTC lawyers, an industry lawyer, and a consumer advocate. While I wasn't particularly alarmed by the FTC lawyers or the industry lawyer (my partner Michael Benoit, by the way), the consumer advocate lawyer made it clear that the business practices the Bureau should focus on include some very

CHAPTER 4

mainstream dealership and finance company practices such as dealer participation in the finance charge, spot deliveries, and the use of arbitration agreements. You can bet she'll be bending ears at the Bureau as it begins to write new rules.

Perhaps industry will be pleasantly surprised, however, and the Bureau and the FTC will actually focus on "bottom feeders."

Maybe the FTC and the Bureau will focus on parts of the credit industry that have seen a lot of recent criticism—like payday loans, tax refund anticipation loans, and title loans—and leave dealers alone for a while. But I'm thinking that won't be the case and that at least "bottom feeding" dealers will get some attention.

If that's the case, what sorts of dealers and dealer practices will we see under attack? I have a few candidates.

- High on my list would be the high-pressure shops that hide the ball from the customer, packing payments and quoting payment amounts that include a "leg."
- And how about those F&I departments that dummy up credit applications and supporting documents to make credit applicants look more creditworthy than they actually are in order to "get the deal bought"?
- Have you heard of "power booking"? Some F&I shops add phantom equipment to the car that will serve as collateral for the finance company to which they intend to assign a buyer's retail installment sales contract, hoping by doing so to increase the assignee's advance amount.
- Some dealers have never had their advertisements reviewed by a lawyer and pay no attention to the federal and state legal requirements that govern their ad practices. The fruit here hangs so low it touches the ground.
- And finally, some dealers essentially ignore compliance requirements and "fly under the radar" when it comes to

complying with things like the rules relating to privacy notices and Safeguarding Policies, OFAC checks, the Red Flags Rule, and the new Risk-Based Pricing Rule. I expect that we will see some early efforts by the FTC and the Bureau to see who's naughty and who's nice.

Those are some of my early candidates for "bottom feeder" attention. If any of these descriptions fit your shop, it might be time to work your way out of the muck and head toward the surface.

January/February 2011
Do I Hear a Squeaky Wheel?

I write article after article, and give presentations at dealer conferences every other day, or so it seems, and I seldom get any feedback about whether I'm doing any good when it comes to helping dealers with the thorny details of compliance. So it's gratifying to get a letter indicating that at least some dealers are drinking the Kool-Aid I'm selling. It's even more fun when the writer has a sense of humor. Here's a recent letter from a dealer who had recently bought our latest book, ***CARLAW*** III *Reloaded*. Evidently, the mailman was able to deliver the letter despite our dog Spot's best efforts to dismember him:

Tom,
I hope you and yours are having a wonderful holiday season. I'm currently plugging my way through your book Reloaded. *It's an easy read, but when I got to the section about advertising, I felt like I was reading a Stephen King novel.*

You see, I'd recently been dragged kicking and screaming into "the Internet Age." By my staff. Who assured me we're Doing Everything Right. So, when I got to the section of your book that

CHAPTER 4

made me feel like "Something Wicked Had Already Arrived" I did the following, and I'm only on Chapter 6 in the book . . .

- *Shut down the website, and I'll email you particulars why when I get a few more minutes.*
- *Told them that they can only put cash cars on Craigslist, must disclose that we are dealers, and don't put any pricing at all.*
- *Prayed for divine intervention in hoping no one printed off any of the junk that the website host put on as "extras" that the staff thought was great.*
- *Told my husband, who's been running this place for almost 40 years, that he can no longer just throw the customer's drivers license on the counter til they get back from a test drive.*

I can write an entire chapter or two for your next book, but suffice it to say that as much money as we spend on everything else, I'm demanding that ALL of the new regulations (and some that aren't new, just being enforced more often) are going to be taken quite seriously.

Now, I know this writer. I'd spoken to her several times over the years at various conferences, and my impression of her and her husband is that they are bright, thoughtful people and good business people. So I was a little surprised to hear her say that she thought her compliance efforts weren't up to snuff. I'd have bet that she had her store turning pretty square corners when it came to the rules and regulations that apply to her business.

I suspect that she is like most dealers I know, and probably like I would be if I were a dealer. Compliance efforts aren't exactly a profit center, and the dealers that we work with seem to operate frequently using the concept of the squeaky wheel—they address compliance when there's a problem.

Well, some pretty big wheels are about to squeak. The new federal Bureau of Consumer Financial Protection (editor's note: this was what the CFPB was called early in its history) is in the process of organizing. When it begins its work, auto dealers will be on the short list of businesses the Bureau will target. And for those dealers who are fortunate enough to enjoy an exemption from the Bureau's jurisdiction, the Federal Trade Commission has just assembled an auto dealer task force (the "auto dealer" reference in the task force title is what detectives call a "clue").

If my letter writer follows through and addresses the compliance problems she has identified so far, then goes a step further and does a review of the rest of her store, she just might be ready when those wheels begin to squeak.

January/February 2011
For Compliance Advice, Who Are You Gonna Trust?

By Thomas B. Hudson and Nicole Frush Munro

If you have marked off January 1 on your compliance calendar, then you have also gotten your dealership into compliance with the Risk-Based Pricing Rule, you've had your privacy forms redone, and you're ready for the Federal Trade Commission to knock on your door to ask about your level of compliance with the Red Flags Rule. If that describes your dealership's level of compliance preparedness, you can quit reading this and get back to cleaning up after your Super Bowl party.

When our law firm does dealership compliance reviews, we frequently find that even large dealers have made no efforts to comply with privacy and other rules that are now several years old. That leaves us with the suspicion that a large majority of smaller dealers also haven't done anything to meet the new January 1 compliance requirements.

CHAPTER 4

In our experience, smaller dealers generally don't spend money on compliance. They look for ways to meet their compliance needs that don't involve hard cash.

They often turn first to the Internet. However, they usually find that an Internet search produces a huge number of hits, but precious little in the way of analysis or practical advice. And when they actually find such analysis or advice, they are unable to determine whether it is accurate.

State and national dealership associations' efforts to find and distill state and federal requirements range from horrible to pretty good. I recently visited the website of a major national auto dealer trade association to see how the association was helping its members with the Risk-Based Pricing Rule requirements. What I found was that the association had posted a copy of the Rule—from the *Federal Register*—with no explanations and no analysis. That's about as helpful to a dealer searching for compliance help as a cornbread recipe.

State and federal agencies (the Federal Trade Commission is a good example) offer some helpful assistance on their websites, but the dealers we know tell us that you often need to be a computer whiz to determine how to search these sites and a lawyer to figure out how to analyze information when you're lucky enough to find it.

Some dealers turn to their vendors for free compliance help. Again, the quality of information we see coming from vendors ranges from awful to excellent. Vendors with good lawyers on staff or with good outside firms often offer very valuable compliance solutions. Others, however, not so much. We've received phone calls from dealers who have gotten legal advice from vendors and lived to regret it. How can you know whether your vendor is giving you the straight skinny or a bunch of drivel? And what happens if you rely on the vendor's advice and get into mischief? Will the vendor step up to any losses, penalties, and fines you incur? Very few will.

The business of selling cars, selling cars on credit, and leasing cars is one of the most highly regulated areas of commerce. The 2010 Dodd-Frank Act, the Bureau of Consumer Financial Protection it created, and a beefed up enforcement effort against dealers that is being implemented by the Federal Trade Commission are about to make things that were already complicated a lot more so. It is no exaggeration to say that any dealer who attempts to handle the legal aspects of his or her dealership on a "do-it-yourself" basis needs not just a law degree, but a number of years' experience dealing with the legal problems that dealers face. Those nonlegal "do-it-yourself" folks must look good in a single-colored jumpsuit or really enjoy becoming friendly with their regulators.

If your dealership doesn't have a lawyer on staff or on call, you need one. And not just any lawyer. Your wife's cousin may be a wonderful general business lawyer or may be able to draft a spiffy will, but he or she probably will not know the laws and regulations that apply to your business. If you cannot get a recommendation for a good, experienced dealership lawyer, go to the website of the National Association of Dealer Counsel. This organization is composed of 500+ lawyers who know a great deal about the legal problems of dealers. Not all are compliance lawyers—some deal with franchise issues, employment issues, and other areas—but I'm pretty confident that if the lawyer you call isn't in the compliance area, you'll get a referral to someone who is.

You've seen those TV commercials that say, "Don't try this at home," and you've heard the old saying, "You get what you pay for." Sometimes, there's just no substitute for professional advice.

CHAPTER 4

March 2011
On Safari

Sometimes when I'm huffing and puffing away on the treadmill, I'll run out of crime dramas, Clint Eastwood movies, or other assorted mindless drivel and will end up watching one of the nature shows. You know the sorts of shows I mean—the lions stir themselves from their resting spot beneath the only tree for 10 miles in any direction, stretch slowly, and then mosey on down toward a passing herd of wildebeests. Or, that is, the females do. Since the females are the hunters, the males won't wake up 'til food appears.

The shows never vary. The females crouch in the grass and edge closer and closer to the herd, until one of the hunters breaks cover and charges. The wildebeests, suddenly alarmed, put it into gear, and the chase is on.

The lions, by mental telepathy, zero in on one of the big hooved critters and try to cut it from the safety of the herd. Then, nipping and slashing from all sides, they try to bring it down.

I couldn't help thinking of that scenario as I saw headlines about the attempts by Congress to curb the power and influence of the Consumer Financial Protection Bureau. With Republicans in control of the lower chamber, evidently some members of Congress think there might be a chance of limiting the Bureau's power and influence.

The attacks on the Bureau so far are aimed at two areas where critics think the Bureau might be vulnerable—oversight and funding.

The Dodd-Frank Act made an effort to provide the Bureau with as much independence as possible. Although the Bureau is to be housed at the Federal Reserve Board, it will have only the most limited sort of oversight by an oversight council. Most observers believe the council will not provide much of a brake on the Bureau's activities. A bill has been introduced that will change this cozy arrangement by moving the Bureau to the Justice Department, where it will enjoy less freedom to maneuver.

The most recent attack is on the funding of the agency. Knowing that the power and effectiveness of the Bureau would be directly affected by the number of dollars in its budget, the drafters of the Dodd-Frank Act intentionally put the funding of the Bureau as far away as it could from the political process. They did this by providing that the lion's share (sorry) of the funding would be calculated as a percentage of a certain line item in the budget of the Federal Reserve. In addition, Congress was to provide additional early funding for the Bureau's startup period. I've seen estimates of the amount of the Bureau's first-year budget that range from $500 million up, which isn't exactly chump change, even in Washington, D.C.

House Republicans are pressing to limit the CFPB's funding by adding a provision to the continuing resolution (an interim funding bill) that would limit Federal Reserve transfers to the Bureau to $80 million (President Obama's 2011 budget allocated $134 million to the CFPB, increased to $329 million in 2012).

House Financial Services Chairman Spencer Bachus (R-Ala.) said, "Since this new government bureau has virtually unlimited powers over a huge part of our economy, accountability demands that Congress exercise appropriate oversight. So until we know more about the bureau and its needs, it is entirely sensible to limit its funding to $80 million."

Elizabeth Warren tried to fend off the budget slashers by accusing them of trying to chip away at the Bureau's independence "by subjecting it entirely to Congressional

CHAPTER 4

appropriations without any dedicated funding from the Federal Reserve."

It's too early to tell whether the lions will dine or the wildebeest will escape, but you can count on seeing variations of this drama frequently as the Bureau's critics gear up for the fight to limit its powers.

March 2011
Pitch the Bath Water. Keep the Baby.

Dealers think that the ability to spot deliver a car provides customers with a valuable benefit. The ability to leave the dealership with a vehicle pending the assignment of a customer's retail installment contract to a finance source makes the dealer happy and makes the customer happy. The spot delivery process gives the dealer and the finance company an opportunity to confirm that information provided by the customer is complete and accurate and lets the customer enjoy his or her new ride while this process is underway. Done correctly and ethically, a spot delivery transaction is one of those win-win situations.

Done incorrectly and/or unethically, though, the spot delivery transaction can be seen by consumer advocates, state regulators, and courts as an unfair, deceptive, or abusive dealer practice. Consumer advocates have for several years railed against spot delivery transactions, calling them "yo-yo" deals. In the eyes of the consumer advocates, dealers intentionally spot deliver cars to customers when the dealers know that they will be unable to assign the customers' retail installment contracts without requiring the customers to return to the dealership and re-contract with new terms detrimental to the consumers. The consumer advocates point to anecdotal evidence that such

2011: REVENGE OF THE CONSUMER ADVOCATES

abuses occur but, when pressed, can offer little or no evidence of the frequency of such practices.

Undeterred by the lack of such evidence, the consumer advocates want the practice of spot delivery outlawed. They have pressed the issue before Congressional committees in hearings on bills that eventually led to the Dodd-Frank Act, and you can bet the keys to your pickup that they will be pressing the issue with the Consumer Financial Protection Bureau.

When they do, they will point to stories like these:

- A customer buys a car, which is spot delivered, only to be called back to the dealership two months later and told that her deal is being rescinded.
- A customer trades in his car on a car that is spot delivered and three days later is told the dealer cannot assign his retail installment contract. He returns to the dealership only to find that the car he traded in has been sold. He receives the wholesale value for the trade-in and, if he owed money on the trade-in, must repay the lienholder. Meanwhile, he's walking, not driving.
- A customer buys a car, which is then spot delivered, and signs a retail installment sales agreement. She does not sign any sort of rescission or "unwind" agreement, however, and no rescission or unwind language is contained in the retail installment sales agreement. Notwithstanding the absence of any contractual right to require the customer to return the car, the dealer, unable to assign the retail installment contract, demands that the customer return the car and re-contract. When the customer refuses, the dealer repossesses the car, even though the buyer is not in default.

I have no doubt that these sorts of things happen occasionally. Sometimes they happen because the dealer has

CHAPTER 4

never had the spot delivery process vetted by the dealer's lawyer. Sometimes they happen because of mistakes. And, no doubt, sometimes they happen because the dealer is abusing the spot delivery process.

When the new Consumer Financial Protection Bureau addresses spot deliveries, as I'm afraid it will, I hope that it doesn't throw the baby out with the bath water. If President Obama appoints me as the Director of the Bureau (I'll let you know right away if that happens), I would first tell my staff to do some research and determine how frequently abusive spot deliveries occur, rather than rely on the sorts of anecdotal "evidence" we have seen so far. Only if the staff determined that abusive spot delivery practices were occurring in significant numbers would I have them consider regulating spot deliveries.

If, based on real evidence, the staff determined that dealers were behaving badly when they engaged in spot deliveries, I'd have them address the practices they believed to be harmful to consumers, rather than ban spot deliveries altogether.

The staff might well then come up with a regulation based on the "best practices" of dealers who do spot delivery transactions day in and day out without problems. They might, for instance:

- allow for mutual rescission until the contract is assigned;
- require a dealer to keep the customer's trade-in until the customer's retail installment contract is assigned;
- provide a reasonable period (say, 10 business days) for the assignment of the retail installment contract, beyond which the deal could not be unwound;
- prohibit a dealer from imposing any fees on the consumer other than charges for excess wear and use or damage to the car;

- prohibit a dealer from requiring a customer to re-contract if the retail installment contract could not be assigned;
- prohibit any unwinding of a deal unless the customer has agreed in writing to the unwind (this last one, in my view, isn't necessary, since a dealer generally has no unwind rights absent the customer's written agreement, but the prohibition might still serve a useful educational purpose for dealers and consumers alike).

No doubt there are other consumer protections and dealer prohibitions that the staff might come up with. As long as they are based on real evidence, and on the best practices of those dealers who currently are doing spot deliveries correctly and ethically, they might well be acceptable to the industry.

At the end of the day, spot deliveries have their uses and, done correctly, can benefit dealers and customers alike.

Pitch the bath water. Keep the baby.

April 2011
Paving the University's Walkways

The new federal Consumer Financial Protection Bureau has been tasked by Congress with (1) writing some new consumer protection regulations, like those on debt collection, and (2) rewriting some old standbys, like Regulations Z, M, and B. It will be very interesting to see what sort of philosophy the Bureau brings to its drafting chores.

Perhaps it will take a lesson from a wise old university dean. Assigned to a brand new campus, the dean not only was in charge of academic matters but also had to oversee the basic construction of the campus facilities. Attending a planning meeting one day, she listened attentively while her staff discussed construction details. At some point, the staff began to argue about where paved walkways should be laid. After listening to various views, the wise old dean interrupted and said, "We won't establish where walkways will be until we've occupied this campus for a year. Initially, we'll just plant grass. Then, a year later, we'll simply pour the concrete where the students have worn paths in the grass."

I'll admit that this approach doesn't always exactly translate into wise regulation writing. But if your business is writing credit regulations, there is something to be said for carefully observing what the best companies are doing, and understanding why they are doing it, before you take pen to paper (does anyone ever do that now?) to write regulations.

My experience is that most dealers and sales finance companies are honest and ethical and make a serious attempt to comply with the laws and regulations that apply to their activities. Sure, there are cowboys in every industry—those who flaunt the rules in search of quick profits, regardless of who gets hurt in the process. The technical term for these people is "crooks," and there are some of these folks in the car business doing bad things to their customers. I could point out that nearly every one of these bad things—unfair, deceptive, or abusive practices—that consumer advocates and the Bureau can identify will already violate some law, so we don't need new regulations to further outlaw them, but that's an argument for another day.

If the Bureau makes an effort to identify "best practices" in the auto sales, lease, and financing world and fashions its regulations to reflect those best practices, it will be much more likely to end up with regulations with which those who are regulated can actually comply. Such regulations will also be much more likely to gain the support of those ethical and honest dealers who lose business to those dealers who engage in "worst practices."

Even "best practices" regulations will end up stifling or at least slowing innovation. The Bureau will not be able to predict where the next bright new idea will come from or what it will look like, and regulations generally are not flexible enough to accommodate products and services that did not exist when the regulations were written. Any regulations the Bureau crafts will by necessity force program development into channels dictated by the terms of the regulations. New ideas will suffer.

The Bureau is in luck. The grass was planted years ago. Honest and ethical dealers and finance companies have worn readily identifiable paths in the grass. These paths show where those walkways should go.

April 2011
The FTC Is Making Its List and Checking it Twice

The Federal Trade Commission has just released the list of top consumer complaints received by the agency in 2010. The list showed that for the 11th year in a row, identity theft was the number one consumer complaint category.

Since the FTC has recently formed an Auto Dealer Task Force, I was sure that the agency had piles of complaints from consumers about their car buying, financing, servicing, and repair experiences. Otherwise, who would need a task force? So I knew I would see dealers listed in the Top 10 categories, and maybe in first place.

Nope.

The FTC says that it received 1,339,265 complaints in 2010. Of those, a whopping 250,854—or 19%—dealt with identity theft.

OK, I suppose I can see that. Lots of folks are out there pretending to be somebody else, trying to make a fast buck.

CHAPTER 4

But auto dealers, in order to get their very own task force, had to be in at least second place, right?

Wrong again. Debt collection complaints were in second place, with 144,159 complaints. I suppose that's to be expected toward what we all hope is the end of a very bad economic period. But where were the car dealers?

I resigned myself to read the list to find how badly those car dealers had performed. Guess what? They weren't on the list at all!

Here's the FTC's final complaint tally:

RANK	CATEGORY	NUMBER OF COMPLAINTS	PERCENTAGE
1	Identity Theft	250,854	19%
2	Debt Collection	144,159	11%
3	Internet Services	65,565	5%
4	Prizes, Sweepstakes, and Lotteries	64,085	5%
5	Shop-at-Home and Catalog Sales	60,205	4%
6	Imposter Scams	60,158	4%
7	Internet Auctions	56,107	4%
8	Foreign Money/ Counterfeit Check Scams	43,866	3%
9	Telephone and Mobile Services	37,388	3%
10	Credit Cards	33,258	2%
??	**AUTO DEALERS**	??	??

OK. Let me get this straight.

Auto dealers don't even appear in the FTC's Top 10 list. That means that the FTC had fewer than 33,258 complaints involving them. When you consider how many transactions the nation's new and used car dealers engage in each year—sales, leases, servicing, repairs, and the like—their absence from the FTC's Top 10 list of consumer complaints is all the more remarkable.

I made a similar observation about the absence of car dealers from the FTC's rankings in an article several years ago and was taken to task by a critic for suggesting—gasp—that car dealers were not mugging, looting, and pillaging among the consumer population. My critic had a point. The FTC isn't the only organization that consumers complain to when they have problems. A number of state attorneys general release similar lists each year, and it's true that dealers show up on many such lists. I still find it remarkable that they don't make the FTC's Top 10 list, however.

The new federal Consumer Financial Protection Bureau, created by the 2010 Dodd-Frank Act, has been given the job of being "Complaint Central." The Bureau has been tasked by Congress with the job of collecting consumer complaints, resolving them, and reporting to Congress about the resolutions.

With a new, central place for consumer complaints to be filed, and with the Bureau and other consumer protection groups urging consumers to avail themselves of the new complaint process (see the Bureau's website at www.consumerfinance.gov to see how the Bureau is urging that consumers file complaints), it will be very interesting to see if the volume of complaints increases dramatically (I predict it will) and if car dealers will show up on the Bureau's Top 10 list (again, I predict they will, but I don't think that they will rank very far up the list).

CHAPTER 4

I promise that I'll write this article again right after the Bureau issues its report on 2011 complaints. Do you suppose that car dealers will be mentioned in enough complaints to justify that task force? Stay tuned!

May 2011
Impressions from the FTC's Detroit Roundtable

The FTC's first "Roundtable" was held on April 12 at Wayne State University Law School in Detroit. The FTC billed it as a "listening tour."

The event was well attended, as these things go. I'd guess that the crowd numbered perhaps 100, and it included dealers, finance company representatives, class action lawyers, consumer advocates, academics, state and federal regulators, and lawyers, like me, who represent the industry.

In order to "listen," the FTC divided the day into discussions by six panels, each addressing a different subject. The panels, and those who participated on them, were billed as follows:

Panel 1
Understanding the Motor Vehicle Sale and Credit Transaction, From Both Prime and Subprime Perspectives
Moderator: **Joel Winston**, Associate Director, Division of Financial Practices, FTC
Panelists
JJ Hornblass, Executive Editor and Publisher, *Auto Finance News*
Thomas B. Hudson, Partner, Hudson Cook, LLP
Chris Kukla, Senior Counsel for Government Affairs, Center for Responsible Lending

Thomas A. Moore, Jr., President, National Automotive Finance Association and President/CEO of First Investors Financial Services
John Van Alst, Attorney, National Consumer Law Center
David W. Westcott, President, Westcott Buick GMC Suzuki

Panel 2
Interest Rates, Dealer Reserves, and Markups
Moderator: **Reilly Dolan**, Assistant Director, Division of Financial Practices, FTC
Panelists
Delvin Davis, Research Analyst, Center for Responsible Lending
Randy Henrick, Associate General Counsel, DealerTrack, Inc.
Andrew D. Koblenz, Vice President and General Counsel, National Automobile Dealers Association
Peter J. Sheptak, Vice President and General Counsel, World Omni Financial Corp.
John Van Alst, Attorney, National Consumer Law Center

Panel 3
Payment and Locator Devices and Consumer Policy
Moderator: **Kate White**, Attorney, Division of Privacy and Identity Protection, FTC
Panelists
Michael Benoit, Partner, Hudson Cook, LLP
Bill Brauch, Special Assistant Attorney General, Consumer Protection Division, Iowa Office of Attorney General
Will Lund, Superintendent, Maine Bureau of Consumer Credit Protection
Charles Pearce, Chief Legal Officer, Credit Acceptance Corp.
Joseph S. Taylor, Vice President, Recovery Industry Services Company

CHAPTER 4

Panel 4
Spot Delivery
Moderator: **Carole Reynolds**, Attorney, Division of Financial Practices, FTC
Panelists
Bill Brauch, Special Assistant Attorney General, Consumer Protection Division, Iowa Office of Attorney General
Michael G. Charapp, Partner, Charapp & Weiss, LLP
Ian Lyngklip, Senior Member, Lyngklip & Associates
S. Allen Monello, CEO, Automotive Industry Center for Excellence
Keith Whann, General Counsel, National Independent Automobile Dealers Association

Panel 5
Contract Add-Ons
Moderator: **Katie Worthman**, Attorney, Division of Financial Practices, FTC
Panelists
Rob Cohen, President, Auto Advisory Services, Inc.
Greg Grzeskiewicz, Assistant Attorney General, Illinois Office of Attorney General
Christopher M. Leedom, President & CEO, The Leedom Group, Inc.
Community Auto Finance Association, **Dani Liblang**, Senior Partner, Liblang & Associates, P.C.

Panel 6
Vehicle Title Problems and Dealer Bankruptcies
Moderator: **Robin Thurston**, Attorney, Division of Financial Practices, FTC
Panelists
Greg Grzeskiewicz, Assistant Attorney General, Illinois Office of Attorney General
Keith Kiser, Director, American Association of Motor Vehicle Administrators
J. Peter Kitzmiller, President, Maryland Automobile Dealers Association
Rosemary Shahan, President, Consumers for Auto Reliability and Safety
Keith Whann, General Counsel, National Independent Automobile Dealers Association

I stayed throughout the day and tried to follow the discussions carefully. Here are my "30,000-foot" impressions.

Overall, I'd say that the FTC representatives who served as moderators seemed to be neutral on the issues that the panels discussed. That was a welcome development since the questions that the FTC had published in the *Federal Register* in advance of the event had seemed, at least in some instances, to be hostile toward industry. The state regulators were also neutral, for the most part. Easily the most effective presenter of the day was NADA's Andy Koblenz, who made a very cogent argument in support of the current system of dealer participation.

The FTC's Joel Winston set the tone for the day by stating that the FTC wasn't very interested in anecdotes, but was instead looking for data—real live facts. That statement set a high bar for the consumer advocates, who seem to have no end

CHAPTER 4

of stories about dealers and finance companies abusing widows and orphans and drowning kittens, but, when asked about how frequently such abuses occur in the marketplace, always seem to come up empty-handed.

The consumer advocates didn't show particularly well. Notwithstanding Joel Winston's admonition that he was looking for facts, they kept trotting out their anecdotes, many of them years and sometimes even decades old. The industry participants kept pointing out that anecdotes weren't favored.

One National Consumer Law Center representative tried to point to a recently issued "survey" by the NCLC (the release of the survey was conveniently timed just before the first FTC Roundtable) that purported to show that dealer abuses were rampant in all states. Since the "survey" was nothing but a compilation of the answers to a short questionnaire by 48 lawyers who handle auto cases for consumers, no one seemed to pay it much mind. It certainly wasn't exactly anything that would be seen as either impartial research or scholarship, if you catch my drift.

The consumer advocates staked out the most radical consumer protection positions, arguing for an end to, or serious limits on, common dealer practices such as dealer participation and spot delivery. In support of their positions, the consumer advocates kept coming back to their stories about dealer misdeeds, only to be countered in nearly every instance by the industry representatives who stated that the dealer's actions were already illegal under either state or federal law, and there was no need for further regulation. At one point, I turned to the person next to me in the audience and whispered that if discussions about practices already banned by federal and state laws had been prohibited, the entire Roundtable would have taken about 15 minutes.

The conflicting agendas of the consumer advocates and the industry representatives produced sparks on the topics of dealer participation, spot deliveries, the sale of ancillary products, and credit discrimination. Other panels were much more sedate, with the surprise of the day being the panel that discussed GPS and starter interrupt devices. The panel participants seemed to be in general agreement that the use of the devices was OK but that perhaps there were some privacy issues regarding the safekeeping of location data.

Industry did better than the consumer advocates. In fairness, the industry participants were not very long on data themselves, but the tone of the day seemed to be that the burden of proof was on those asserting bad acts, and not on the industry to show that it behaved well.

If you missed watching the Roundtable (it was streaming live), the video and a transcript are available on the FTC's website, as noted in the box on page 4. OK, "Law & Order" it's not, but if you are in the car sales, finance, or leasing business, you need to see it.

May 2011
The Garbage Factory

A reputation is a valuable thing to lose. The Boston-based National Consumer Law Center (NCLC) has for years enjoyed a reputation among compliance lawyers as a producer of really first-rate legal publications on compliance topics such as automobile fraud, the cost of credit, credit discrimination, and the like. The publications have a pro-consumer flavor, and I warn our young lawyers to beware the occasional editorial slant, but the books are so good that I know few industry compliance lawyers who don't have all of the NCLC volumes in their libraries.

CHAPTER 4

Then came the 2010 "Repo Madness" report. That piece of claptrap disguised as research made the case in loud press releases that self-help repossession of vehicles by creditors was more dangerous than defusing improvised roadside bombs. The uncritical press echoed NCLC's claims, as did many who didn't bother to, you know, actually READ the so-called "report." Those who did read it recognized it for what it was: typical anecdotal stuff posing as research that resulted in shrill headline claims that bore no relation to the content of the report.

Well, regrettably, the NCLC has done it again.

This time the headline screamed, "New National Consumer Law Center Survey Finds Consumer Abuses in Auto Sales and Financing Are Common Throughout the United States." Timed for release just as the Federal Trade Commission held its first auto sales and lease "Roundtable," its prominent bullet points claimed:

- 87% of attorneys said they receive between 21 and 200 or more requests for assistance each year from consumers experiencing problems buying and/or financing a vehicle.
- 91% of attorneys turn people away who said they suffered abuses in auto dealer sales/finance transactions due to too many requests for help.
- 83% of attorneys said that the consumers they interviewed "always" or "often" received a product (car or financing) from an auto dealer that was different from what was described to them during the car purchasing transaction.
- 96% of attorneys said that the abuses their clients suffered were part of a general industry practice.

Do these bullet points support the screaming headline? You be the judge.

When you actually READ the survey, a few things jump out at you.

2011: REVENGE OF THE CONSUMER ADVOCATES

First, who were these lawyers who were surveyed? NCLC says that they were "participating legal aid and private attorneys working on consumer auto issues."

Oh. Lawyers who hold themselves out as consumer lawyers get a lot of consumer complaints. Wait a minute while I stop the presses.

OK, next question. How broad was this survey? In a paragraph buried on the last page of the survey results, we learn that the NCLC sent a questionnaire to 400 lawyers who identified themselves as working on auto issues as part of their practices. A less-than-overwhelming 48 lawyers responded.

So, 352 of the 400 lawyers declined to respond to the NCLC's questionnaire. Although the NCLC crowed that "[t]he results [of the survey] represent [the experiences of] practicing attorneys in all regions of the United States," those who bothered to dig deeper than the headline and the bullet points learned that exactly three lawyers from the Southwest bothered to respond, while the response from other regions was sparse— seven from the Northeast, eight from the West, 10 each from the Mid-Atlantic and the Midwest, and 12 from the South.

And oh yeah—well over half of the lawyers (32 of 48) indicated that they handled 100 or fewer requests for assistance from consumers each year. That is, at the very most, 3,200 requests. And the NCLC's completely unsupported assumption is that all those complaints are valid.

I sometimes wonder whether the NCLC has any appreciation of the size of the new and used car marketplace in the United States. With 13 million new cars and maybe twice that many used cars (I'm guessing) sold each year, any unbiased reader of the survey would say, "OK, there are some crooked dealers in the United States, and these responding lawyers are trying hard to clean them up."

79

CHAPTER 4

What an unbiased reader certainly would not say is, "New National Consumer Law Center Survey Finds Consumer Abuses in Auto Sales and Financing Are Common Throughout the United States."

I have a loud and clear message to the NCLC: Taking a survey of 48 lawyers whose practices involve consumer auto claims and asking if they see abuses is like taking a survey of the choir members to see if they believe in God. You can pretty well predict the answers before you ask the questions. If you value your reputation for excellence, stop producing garbage.

I don't often say so in public, but I have a master's degree in social science research and actually know how to do research on issues like this. Think I ought to apply for a job at the NCLC?

Naaah. They evidently have no need for someone who knows how to do this stuff. Besides, who wants to work for a garbage factory?

July 2011
FTC Roundtable II

The Federal Trade Commission has announced its second auto dealer roundtable, to be held August 2–3 at the St. Mary's University School of Law in San Antonio, Texas. The FTC says it wants Roundtable II to focus on financing for servicemembers, credit discrimination, and financial literacy.

What can we expect from Roundtable II? My crystal ball's a bit murky these days, but we can probably get some ideas from Roundtable I, held in Detroit in April. Based on what happened at the April event, here are a few predictions.

1. Where's the data? The FTC will once again be in "referee" mode, attempting not to show favor to any particular points of view. An FTC moderator will begin, as in Roundtable I, by stating that the FTC is looking for data, not anecdotes. Anecdotes are what the consumer advocates usually proffer when they are asked for proof of abusive practices by dealers and finance companies. For the remainder of the day, the consumer advocates who participate in Roundtable II will cheerfully ignore the FTC's admonition and will offer anecdote after anecdote. Industry representatives will use every opportunity to point out that these anecdotes are not the "data" the FTC is looking for.

2. Here's some. Or not. In an effort to appear to offer the data that the FTC says it is looking for, some consumer advocacy group will come out with a purported "study" in advance of Roundtable II. Just before Roundtable I, the National Consumer Law Center released a "study" concluding that consumer fraud was a national plague. It made for a great press release, but if you actually bothered to, you know, read the thing, you'd find that the "study" was based on an NCLC survey of 400 lawyers specializing in consumer law, 48 of whom bothered to respond. Not surprisingly, these consumer lawyers reported that they saw lots of problems in auto sales, finance, and leasing transactions since that's what they did for a living. It wouldn't surprise me to see the release of something similar before Roundtable II.

3. Wait—isn't that already illegal? The consumer advocates' anecdotes will nearly all involve egregious actions on the part of some dealer and finance company—actions that already violate one or more state or federal laws. If the ground rules for Roundtable I had precluded discussion of acts and practices that are already illegal, it would have lasted about 15 minutes rather than all day. Look for more of the same from Roundtable II.

4. How about things that have happened in this century? In Detroit, one reaction of many industry observers was that many of the consumer advocates' horror stories and recitations of bad

CHAPTER 4

acts and practices on the part of industry reflected things that went on in the industry 10 or 15 years ago, but which were not descriptive of current business practices. Expect more of the same in San Antonio.

5. Mum's the word. The consumer advocates will not utter a word about the government's already-powerful arsenal of laws that, if enforced, would address the evils that they will bemoan. Consider, as an example, the Pentagon's assertion that predatory lending practices undermine the combat readiness of our armed forces, then consider that every base commander in the United States has the authority to stop servicemembers from frequenting a business that the commander believes is treating servicemembers unfairly (you'd think that if commanders actually believed that their combat readiness was imperiled, they'd use that power). You aren't likely to hear about that from consumer advocates.

You have to commend the FTC for its "listening tour," and for what has thus far been an even-handed approach to understanding the business of auto sales, finance, and leasing. I'll be encouraged if Roundtable II continues the FTC's approach.

You can actually join me and attend Roundtable II—for Roundtable II details, go to the FTC's web page at www.ftc.gov/bcp/workshops/motorvehicles/. Transcripts of the panel discussions are available on the FTC's website.

July 2011
Cobweb Compliance

I've become acquainted with a very persistent spider. Every morning, I put on the coffee, then wander a couple of hundred feet down to the street to fetch the paper. The path meanders down a hillside, through lots of azaleas, and I have the morning sun at my back. Nearly every morning, there's a huge, complex spider web that's maybe eight feet across that catches the sun's rays, revealing the spider's latest art. I usually wreck it, to make sure he has something to do for the remainder of the day, only to repeat the process the next day.

Those cobwebs are a thing of beauty, but whenever I see them, I think of cobwebs that aren't so pretty—compliance cobwebs.

Compliance cobwebs appear in dealerships that are savvy enough to make a serious stab at compliance but that aren't savvy enough to follow through on all of their compliance responsibilities. Let me give you an example.

The Federal Trade Commission's Safeguarding Rule requires that a dealership create a safeguarding policy to make sure that nonpublic financial information of its customers doesn't end up in the wrong hands. The policy can range from fairly simple to complex, depending on the dealership's operations, and it has to be written down. The policy must name a dealership person to be chief in charge of safeguarding, and the policy must be updated from time to time.

The guys over at Cobweb Motors attended an industry conference and heard a compliance presentation about this new safeguarding requirement. They hadn't been in business long, so they decided that they'd try to save some money by crafting their safeguarding policy themselves.

They spent a lot of time on the FTC's website and did a pretty good job of coming up with a policy that complied with the rule. Because their operation was confined to one lot, and because they had very little in the way of technology, their policy was on the fairly simple side. Their policy stated that it would be subject to review from time to time, and it named Joe Doaks, their General Manager, as the person in charge of their safeguarding policy.

CHAPTER 4

More than a little pleased with themselves, they put a copy of the policy on their bookshelf and promptly forgot it.

A few short years go by. Cobweb Motors has become very successful, with a dozen stores in three states, new computer equipment, websites, social networking programs, and deals with lead providers and a number of other vendors. Joe Doaks didn't work out all that well and has moved on.

The dealership's safeguarding policy, however, still sits, undisturbed, on the bookshelf. Cobweb compliance.

Then one day, the FTC shows up and asks to see the safeguarding policy. When the policy as written has little or no resemblance to the policy needed for Cobweb Motors's expanded operations, and when the FTC determines that there hasn't been anyone in charge of things since Doaks left, the FTC decides a little enforcement action is in order.

Meanwhile, the folks over at Careful Motors had a similar experience. They developed their safeguarding policy, named Sandy Smith to be in charge, and put it on the bookshelf. Their policy, however, called for a review of the policy every six months, with a notice of the required review calendared for several members of the dealership's management team (an easy thing to do with Outlook) so that in case Sandy moved on to another job, the review would still occur.

Every six months, Sandy would pull the policy off the shelf and read through it to determine whether it was still appropriate and accurate for the dealership. She would then document that she had done so and add the documentation to the policy. Most of her reviews would take no more than a half hour or so.

When the FTC comes calling on Careful Motors, will we be likely to see an enforcement action? Probably not.

The Safeguarding Rule isn't the only federal regulation that requires dealerships to review and reassess their earlier attempts at compliance. The Red Flags Rule, for example, contains such a requirement as well.

And even when there is no express regulatory requirement for a periodic review of forms and operations, dealers need to periodically check to make sure that the cobwebs haven't crept in. Laws and regulations change, forms companies revise and replace forms, and lawsuits require forms and procedural changes as well. When you're scheduling those required safeguarding and red flags reviews, why not include as many of your dealership's other forms and procedures as you can?

Get rid of those cobwebs!

July 2011
CFPB Watch

No News on Elizabeth Warren. Again.
"It's simply great, mate, waiting on the levy, waiting for the Robert E. Lee," or so sang Al Jolson (or Mickey Rooney and Judy Garland, in "Babes on Broadway"). It's not so great, mate, waitin' on President Obama to name a director for the CFPB. By the time this issue of *Spot* is published, we'll be two or three weeks away from the July 21 designated transfer date—a date important to many of the Bureau's activities—and still no director. As we said last month, something's got to give on this front, and shortly.

Looking for a Job?
It seems like the Bureau is looking for "a few good men" (or women). We went to lunch with two of the CFPB's recently hired staffers a couple of weeks back. They wanted to pick our brains about who they might hire who would be knowledgeable regarding the car business they are about to start regulating.

CHAPTER 4

Although they weren't ruling out lawyers, they emphasized that they were looking for folks who weren't lawyers. So, if you like stifling heat coupled with oppressive humidity in the summer, and an occasional 56-inch snowstorm in the winter, and can stand the constant sharpshooting between the Democrats and the Republicans (or, as we refer to them down at the beach, "Democrabs" and "Repelicans"), shoot us an email with your resume attached, and we'll forward it along to D.C.

Drafting Disclosures

Last month, we reported that the CFPB had issued prototype mortgage "shopping sheets" on which it sought public input. This month, the CFPB has issued new versions of those forms. The new disclosures—called by those lighthearted bureaucrats at the CFPB "Redbud" and "Dogwood"—appear at www.consumerfinance.gov/knowbeforeyouowe/ and present standard information regarding typical mortgage loan terms in different ways. According to the CFPB, these forms intend to be more effective at "communicating closing costs." The Dodd-Frank Act directed the CFPB to propose model disclosures combining disclosures required under the Truth in Lending Act and two sections of the Real Estate Settlement Procedures Act into a single, integrated disclosure. Dodd-Frank gave the CFPB one year from the designated transfer date of July 21, 2011, to develop the combined disclosure, which aims to improve consumer understanding of mortgage costs. Car industry folks may find the CFPB's approach to this rulemaking instructive when the time comes for the CFPB to address auto finance and lease forms.

August 2011
Wanna Buy Your Lawyer a Yacht? (Part II)

Skipping over Raj Date, about whom there was some buzz from those speculating about who might get the nod, Obama selected Richard Cordray, formerly attorney general for the state of Ohio, as the first director of the CFPB.

In June 2000, I wrote an article titled "Wanna Buy Your Lawyer a Yacht?" The article bemoaned the fact that people in the car business were aiding and abetting the plaintiffs' lawyers and consumer advocates who are so intent on bringing lawsuits against dealers and finance companies. I went on to urge a vocabulary change. In the decade-plus since then, I'm sorry to report that things haven't changed much. Here's that article.

At a recent conference of subprime finance companies and dealers, every agenda item and every speaker seemed to deal with "loans" or "lenders." Finally, I could stand it no longer. When the time came for me to speak, I ranted instead. Why? Because no one at the conference was making loans, and no one there was a lender. And what you call things can sometimes matter—a lot.

In a typical motor vehicle retail installment sales transaction, a dealer extends credit to a consumer. How? The dealer exchanges a perfectly good (we hope) vehicle for a piece of paper containing the consumer's promise to pay for the car over a time period of, say, 36 months. The dealer and the consumer have not engaged in a "loan" transaction, they have engaged in a "credit sale."

The dealer then sells the credit contract to a finance company. (Note that the finance company isn't lending money to anyone—it is buying a contract from a dealer in what is, in reality, a secondary market commercial transaction. OK—if you are an Ohio dealer, you may actually be acting as agent for a bank that is really making a loan to your buyer, and some Colorado dealers use

CHAPTER 4

a very peculiar credit sale form that is titled as a note—I'm talking here about normal dealers.)

Does anyone (besides blood-sucking lawyers) really care what you call this transaction? Well, you need to care, unless you feel like paying a lot of money to those blood-sucking lawyers.

Here's the problem. The documents a dealer uses to complete a credit sale have been designed to comply with state retail installment sales laws and with federal laws regulating credit sales. These laws are different from the laws that govern loans. A plaintiff's class action lawyer looking for a way to sue you may allege that the transaction is not really a credit sale but rather is a disguised loan.

The lawyer's next step is to argue that the dealer, or the dealer and the finance company, should have complied with the loan laws rather than the credit sale laws. Lawyers call this a "recharacterization" attack—the plaintiff's lawyer is trying to "recharacterize" the credit sale as a "loan." If the judge takes the bait and agrees with this argument, the defendants are in trouble because the judge's next step will be to declare that all the transaction documents violate the loan laws—laws that the dealer and the finance company never intended to abide by.

Imagine for a moment that your dealership or finance company is the defendant in one of these suits. What will the plaintiff's lawyer find when he or she reviews your company's internal books and records during the discovery process? Will your internal documents be filled with incorrect references to "loans" and "lenders"? If so, you are manufacturing ammunition for the enemy. These faulty references, by themselves, probably won't be decisive, but you can bet that the plaintiff's lawyer will beat the judge or jury over the head with your own references to "loans" and "lenders."

So, how do you defend against one of these attacks? The plaintiff will argue that the dealer never carries his own paper, and that the dealer would never enter into a credit transaction with a consumer if the dealer had to carry its own paper, and doesn't enter into such a transaction with a consumer until some bank or finance company has reviewed the consumer's credit history. The argument that naturally follows is that the dealer is the agent of the finance company or bank and that the finance company is actually a "lender."

Here's the defense. The dealer is the creditor. Sure, the dealer assures that he can sell the consumer's contract before he completes the credit sale. But think about a typical dealer agreement between a dealer and a finance company. After the dealer gets an approval from the finance company of the consumer's credit and enters into the contract with the consumer, what happens if the dealer decides not to assign the contract to that finance company? Can the finance company force the dealer to assign the contract? Nope. At least not under any dealer agreement I've ever written or reviewed. Under most dealer agreements, the finance company has to buy the contract from the dealer if the finance company has approved the consumer's credit and everything else is as the dealer has represented, but the dealer has no obligation to assign any contracts. In stock market terms, the dealer has a "put," but the finance company does not have a "call."

Let's say that the dealer enters into a contract with every intention of selling that contract to a finance company, then decides that rather than selling the contract to the finance company, he'll keep it and collect payments directly from the consumer—the finance charge that results from an 18% APR looks like a pretty good return for his retirement program. Is there anything the finance company can do about the dealer's change of heart?

Nope. Nothing. Nada. The finance company has no right to force the dealer to assign the contract. If that's so, how can the

CHAPTER 4

dealer be the finance company's agent? Once a judge or jury understands this, the dealer should win the case.

The plaintiff's lawyer will scream and jump up and down (the plaintiff's lawyer's refrain—when there's danger, when there's doubt, run in circles, scream and shout), arguing that this scenario is purely theoretical—that the dealer has never held onto a contract and never will. But the dealer's theoretical right to hold the contract is, or should be, controlling.

But let's make it even tougher for the plaintiff's lawyer. Let's quit talking about "loans" and "lenders." Let's get those references out of our company's records. Let's train everyone in the company (and for that matter, everyone in the industry) to call these things by their correct names. Let's deprive the plaintiff's lawyer of the easy evidence. Maybe he'll think twice and not bring the suit.

Doesn't that make a lot more sense than buying a yacht for him, or for your defense lawyer?

The message of this article is, if anything, more relevant today than it was in 2000. With the Federal Trade Commission and the new Consumer Financial Protection Bureau breathing down the necks of dealers and sales finance companies, it's becoming more and more important for us industry types to accurately describe the way that indirect auto finance works. I'm betting, though, that I'll be writing this article, or one like it, in 2020.

August 2011
Flying Under the Radar

My client was a buy-here, pay-here dealer. I was reviewing the dealership's compliance—at his request—and just finished telling him why the way he financed repairs violated state and federal law. I also told him what he'd have to change in order to continue the practice without breaking the law.

2011: REVENGE OF THE CONSUMER ADVOCATES

He was quiet for a long moment, then scrunched up his face in something between a frown and a scowl. He clearly wasn't happy.

Finally, he spoke, "I think we'll just keep on flying under the radar on that one. After all, we aren't charging our customers any interest on the cost of the repairs. We're really doing them a favor, when you think of it. I can't imagine anyone coming after us for that. And anyway, we've never been sued."

That got me thinking about the phrase "flying under the radar." In this over-regulated world, a dealer who seriously tries to comply completely with every law and regulation that applies to the business of selling and financing vehicles needs to go to law school before attending his first dealer auction.

Most dealers don't do that; nor do most dealers have a compliance lawyer on staff or on retainer. Most dealers make some effort to comply, then, by being "mostly compliant," hope they "fly under the radar," avoiding big lawsuits and heavy-handed regulator action through luck and good customer service.

I can't tell a client to fly under the radar or condone it when he does. All I can do is tell the client what the law is and advise him about whether his practices are legal. It's up to the client to heed or ignore my advice.

The scope and complexity of the regulations applicable to the sale and financing of cars leads to a sort of risk triage, a process in which the dealer does some mental calculus (price of compliance minus risk and cost of legal action vs. ability to serve customers plus ability to make money) and determines that, given the likelihood of liability, it makes more sense to ignore some laws than to comply with them. Viewed like this, "flying under the radar" can make a lot of business sense. If I were a car dealer, I might be tempted to push the stick forward and lose a little altitude myself.

CHAPTER 4

But (and you knew there was a "but" coming) flying under the radar requires some knowledge of the terrain, lest you wind up crashing nose first into the side of a regulatory mountain. Putting it another way, taking risks when you know the potential for disaster is one thing, but taking risks when you don't know the odds is stupid.

Here are a few questions you might want to ask yourself when you are tempted to fly under the radar.

Are there criminal penalties for your proposed conduct? It's one thing to do something that constitutes a breach of contract for which your customer could sue you. It's something else again to commit a crime that could expose you to the loss of your dealership, large fines, and perhaps even prison time. And those criminal penalties can be found in some unexpected places. I've never heard of anyone going to jail for violating the Truth in Lending Act, but TILA has criminal penalties for some violations.

How frequently will you engage in the low-flying activity? If you finance repairs a couple of times a year, that's one thing, but if you are illegally charging some fee on every deal you do, that's another thing entirely. The radar is a lot more likely to pick you up if it has a lot of opportunity to do so.

Will the "I'm being nice to my customers" defense save you? You may think that a particular practice is so beneficial to your customers that they will be so abjectly grateful for the help that they couldn't possibly file a lawsuit against you. Alas, that's not how the legal world works. You might have helped your customer, but when she later defaults, and you repossess her car, she won't remember the help, but she will remember the repossession. And when she visits her lawyer, he will be combing through all your documents looking for any violations, no matter how benign, that will support his demand for a big settlement check. And if instead of facing your customer, you are the target of an investigation by a state or federal agency, you can bet that the "Look how nice I was" defense won't fly if the investigation turns up violations. "Nice" doesn't keep a regulator from ordering restitution, compelling fines, or, worse, pulling your license.

Can you really avoid being detected by the radar? For the last few decades, we haven't seen a lot of enforcement activity against dealers by their principal federal cop, the Federal Trade Commission. The Dodd-Frank Act split the regulation of dealers, with some still answering to a beefed-up FTC and others answering to the new Consumer Financial Protection Bureau, which calls itself the "new cop on the beat." Odds are that enforcement activity will pick up dramatically. In other words, the radar's getting stronger, and, right now, we have no radar detector, so we don't know where the CFPB or the FTC will strike first.

The next time you are tempted to push the nose over and head for lower altitude in an effort to avoid doing what the law requires, pull this article out and give some thought to these questions. As they say, "Don't do the crime . . . ."

September 2011
Impressions from the FTC's Second Roundtable

The Federal Trade Commission's second "Roundtable" was held August 2–3, 2011, in San Antonio. As in Detroit, a good crowd showed up. The audience included finance company representatives, class action lawyers, consumer advocates, academics, state and federal regulators, and lawyers, like us, who represent the industry.

In its press release issued before the event, the FTC announced that the event, intended to gather information on

CHAPTER 4

consumers' experiences in the sale and financing of motor vehicles at dealerships, would cover topics related to military consumers' experiences in buying and financing motor vehicles, the role of financial literacy in consumers' understanding of that process, and fair lending issues. The FTC, as it did before the Detroit Roundtable, characterized the event as part of a "listening tour."

In order to "listen," the FTC divided the day into discussions by nine panels, each addressing a different subject. Below, I'll summarize what I consider to be the most noteworthy points made by each panel.

Panel 1, titled "Military Consumers and the Auto Sales and Financing Process," started by addressing the military's authority to declare businesses that take advantage of servicemembers "off limits." That power, wielded by the Armed Forces Disciplinary Control Board, is one, said the military panelists, that is cumbersome to invoke and not used frequently.

The panel next discussed education of servicemembers, with the panelists noting that, in some ways, servicemembers were in better shape than others to learn how the buying and financing process works because the military branches provide some level of financial education and servicemembers have access to those who can advise them.

The military panelists next identified a problem that servicemembers face—lienholders won't let cars go overseas, leading to voluntary repossessions. They noted a related problem—warranties and service contracts provided by some dealers sometimes cannot be enforced or honored overseas or out of state.

The next topic dealt with differences between civilian and military transactions. Specific questions dealt with the percentage of servicemember buyers who arranged their own financing, the degree to which servicemembers negotiate financing with the dealer, and whether menu presentations were done differently with servicemembers. The conclusion seemed to be that there were few such differences.

The CFPB's Holly Petraeus then raised the issue of dealer markups of finance charge rates. An industry panelist responded that there is expense associated with the F&I process.

Panel 2, titled "The Online Auto Process for Military and Other Consumers," addressed the online vehicle sales process.

After describing his dealership's online process, Texas dealer Steve Hall began by noting that all consumers are seeking more control over the buying process and that the Internet provided an important tool to increase that control.

Consumer advocate Thomas Domonoske drew a distinction between information and advertising, and noted that real-time price comparisons are not possible on the Internet unless every dealer sells his vehicles at the advertised price. He asserted that while consumers could get a lot of information online, they can't do comparison shopping online. He complained that some "finance" sites are really dealer lead sites and that some dealers advertise cars they don't have. Finally, he observed that jurisdictional issues arise frequently in connection with transactions involving servicemembers when, for instance, a servicemember based in State A buys a car in State B and then moves to State C.

Jeremy Anwyl pointed out that consumers can negotiate online. He asserted that the tools are available but that not many consumers avail themselves of them, in part because the buying public is stratified in terms of Internet savvy, Internet use varies by the consumer's level of Internet sophistication, and the demographics of those using the Internet have worked their way toward the mainstream.

CHAPTER 4

Military panelist Dwain Alexander voiced the opinion that education of servicemembers is important but noted that he didn't want the seller as the educator. He noted that servicemembers are young, and while they use Internet for social networking, they tend not to use Internet tools.

Hall observed that consumers tend to overpay with their wallets or overpay with their time. Consumers can research the dealer, the dealer's website, vehicle photos, history reports, and financing availability over the Internet. The more information the consumer can get online, the more transparent the dealership is likely to be. Consumers arrive at the dealership knowing what competitive rates are and about extended warranties, GAP, and other products. Today's online consumers, he said, are "everyday" consumers.

Panel 3, titled "Military Consumers, Sales Representations, and Financing Process Issues," started with a discussion of how military transience affects a servicemember's ability to buy and finance a vehicle. Michael Archer pointed out that younger servicemembers move more frequently early in their careers.

Alexander noted that the most vulnerable time for servicemembers was during the first tour. Car dealers, he said, say junior people don't "push back."

Industry lawyer Shawn Mercer observed that servicemembers decide when they will buy cars and are aware that they are subject to transfer. He referred to the "20-week Rule," evidently a prohibition against buying vehicles during the first 20 weeks of enlistment.

The discussion then turned to bird dog, or referral, fees. The consumer advocates offered anecdotes about outrageous bird dog fee activity and outrageously high bird dog fees but, as usual, were unable to provide data showing that bird dog fee abuses were commonplace. Terry O'Loughlin pointed out that bird dog fees are illegal in many states, that during his tenure with the Florida AG's office, bird dog fee issues were rare, and that when they occurred, bird dog fees usually involved amounts of $50 to $150.

Mercer noted that bird dog fees are common in a lot of industries and that paying such fees is a widespread practice. The practice in the auto retailing business, though, can create licensing issues.

Alexander then described the military's "internal" bird dog fee problem that arises when servicemembers are steered to dealers by other servicemembers (who are sometimes retired servicemembers) and sometimes by their superiors, who are paid to do the steering. The "victims," he said, are often reluctant to "squeal" on those who have received bird dog fees. Finally, he noted, placing a dealer off limits is sometimes not effective.

When Mercer asked why the military doesn't simply stop its internal bird dog problem, Archer complained that he does not have investigators, but has to wait for complaints. He identified procedural problems, as well, saying that he first had to send a warning letter, then had to wait for more complaints. In addition, the Control Board meets quarterly, so it can't act quickly, and once a dealer agrees to stop doing bad things, the Board has to let the dealer off the blacklist.

The next topic was the practice of spot delivery (the industry term) or "yo-yo financing" (the consumer advocates' term). This is one where the opposing sides regularly talk past one another, with the consumer advocates pointing out abuses by dealers in the spot delivery process and refusing to acknowledge that spot deliveries can be and are done fairly and ethically.

Mercer described a spot delivery as the dealer allowing a buyer to leave the dealership with a car without financing in

CHAPTER 4

place. He asserted that all deals are conditional and that problems that result in financing difficulties are often created by the consumer (e.g., information provided by the consumer is wrong). Sometimes the incorrect information is identified by follow-up interviews by the finance company considering buying the consumer's credit contract. Mercer noted that spot deliveries vary by the way they are documented and said that he doesn't see spot deliveries as being a pervasive problem. When a deal falls through, the customer is within his or her rights to walk away, and we usually see that the price of the car goes down as a means of permitting the dealer to save the deal.

Domonoske then ranted for a few minutes, but, in the process, made some valid points. He focused on the state of mind of the buyer as he or she leaves the dealership, claiming that the dealer seeks to mislead the buyer as to the possibility that the transaction might not be final. His remarks underscored the precautions that ethical dealers take to carefully disclose to the customer the fact that financing is not yet in place. He took the position that there is no reason for a spot delivery when the buyer is in the military.

Alexander asserted that some dealers make a customer sign a promissory note when a car is spot delivered, while others may charge fees when the deal goes south. He did not admit that these practices were already illegal in many states, nor did he offer anything to suggest such practices were prevalent.

Terry O'Loughlin, with Reynolds & Reynolds, opined that he did not see dealers doing abusive spot deliveries frequently and that nearly all deals go through as written. Most buyers, he said, know when a deal is contingent, and most dealers don't want to see the customer have to return to the dealership when a deal falls through.

2011: REVENGE OF THE CONSUMER ADVOCATES

Alexander then described a successful Norfolk-area program put together by the Better Business Bureau and the Virginia Independent Auto Dealers Association to combat dealer abuses, including price gouging and yo-yo sales.

The panel then turned to negative equity and add-on services and products, rehashing the same ground covered in the Detroit Roundtable. Again, the consumer advocates railed about abuses using anecdotes, and the industry participants responded that such abuses already violated existing laws.

Panel 4, titled "Military Consumers, Vehicle Title Problems, and Repossessions," was dullsville. We heard more anecdotes about consumers with title problems, often in circumstances in which the dealer had gone bankrupt. Consumer advocate John Van Alst trotted out his laughingly ridiculous National Consumer Law Center "study," "Repo Madness," arguing that the violence that occurs in connection with repossessions justifies doing away with self-help repossession by vehicle creditors. He seemed impervious to the observation that his own "study" illustrated that such episodes of violence are rarer than hen's teeth. Keith Whann, General Counsel for the National Independent Automobile Dealer Association, observed that current law made it illegal to breach the peace in the process of repossession.

Van Alst then criticized starter interrupt devices, claiming that a car could be made inoperable under dangerous circumstances. He then noted that self-help repo is used as a threat by creditors. (Well, yeah!)

Duller than even Panel 4, Panel 5 was titled "Financial Literacy and Capability for Military Consumers." Pam McClelland started the discussion by bemoaning the fact that there isn't enough time to teach young servicemembers everything that needs to be taught. She stated that the military

CHAPTER 4

does have some teaching tools to help servicemembers learn about financing and gave, as examples, gaming and a cell phone app that provides five questions that a servicemember should ask at a dealership when buying and financing a car.

Panel 6, titled "Special Programs to Enhance Consumers' Financial Literacy," consisted of Susie Irvine promoting the American Financial Services Association's (AFSA) MoneySkill program and its excellent consumer education booklet "Understanding Vehicle Finance." Ever the constructive one, Van Alst opined that there is very little empirical evidence that such educational materials change consumers' behavior and that what we need is—you guessed it—more regulation. Greg Zak pointed out that credit problems start at home and that the most effective training is one-on-one.

I couldn't quite figure out how Panel 7, titled "Financial Literacy and New Approaches for Auto Sales and Financing," was going to cover anything other than what Panel 6 had covered, so I was surprised when it started with the concept of simplifying credit scores, making them like school grades, so that it would be easier for consumers to understand them.

Alan Mosher challenged the concept of education, saying that you could not create an educational program that would get consumers to care. Consumers, he said, care only about monthly payments, down payment, and "Can I get a car?"

Anwyl opined that people are deluded that they know more about buying a car than they really do. He pointed out that describing a car online is the same for all customers, but dealing with credit ability and scores varies from person to person. Edmunds, he said, tries to "tease" consumers into looking at important credit information, but that creates frustration. He ended by stressing that consumers shouldn't get fixated on any single aspect of the credit transaction.

2011: REVENGE OF THE CONSUMER ADVOCATES

Irvine said that AFSA urges consumers to get their credit scores before they go to the dealership. AFSA also has middle school materials that teach about secured borrowing. When asked about whether consumers should be taught to focus on one specific factor in the credit transaction, she responded that she thought the proper analysis would be a holistic one.

The panelists then batted around a nonstarter of an idea—creating an "invoice" for used cars. Mosher pointed out that there is nothing in the used car market that compares with a new car invoice because there are too many variables. There are some guides, but they contain ranges of prices.

We finally hit some fireworks with Panel 8, titled "Fair Lending—Interest Rates, Markups, and Payments." First, Chris Choate, with some help from Andy Koblenz, explained the various components of the "buy rate."

Koblenz, General Connsel to the National Automobile Dealers Association, in answer to a question from the moderator, observed that the ECOA applies to auto finance transactions and that he had not seen any broad-based fair lending problems.

Kukla responded that we can't verify that there is no fair lending problem because we don't have a database comparable to the HMDA information available in housing finance. The available data is private.

The discussion then turned to the topic of dealer markup. Koblenz noted that retail installment contracts contain a disclosure that the APR may be negotiable with the dealer, and that competition constrains dealers' ability to mark up rates. Kukla responded that by the time the consumer sees the disclosure, it's too late to negotiate.

Consumer advocate Delvin David proposed that dealers should be required to disclose the amount of the markup, a proposal that the Federal Reserve Board has twice considered

CHAPTER 4

and rejected. That led to a blistering response from Koblenz, who argued that direct lenders don't have to disclose the components of the rates that they impose.

From there, the discussion parroted the discussion on this topic that we heard in Detroit, with the consumer advocates pushing the same arguments and the industry representatives defending with their now-familiar themes.

That is, with one teeny-weeny little exception. When David trotted out his "Under the Hood" Center for Responsible Lending "study," economist Thomas Durkin shredded the work's methodology, pointing out flaw after flaw and calling it an "advocacy study" that started with a conclusion and ignored evidence that did not support the conclusion. Many of those listening, me included, had been critical of the so-called study, but no one had skewered it quite so well.

One continuing theme from the consumer advocates was that any discretion on the dealer's part to increase the buy rate increased the risk of discrimination. If Kukla said that once, he said it a half-dozen times.

Panel 9, titled "Fair Lending—Compliance, Risk, and Liability," featured Kukla again, with several more admonitions that dealer discretion increased discrimination risk.

It also featured a pretty interesting monologue by Stephen Harvey, who held forth on the topic of "who should be liable for fair lending violations." Harvey described intentional discrimination and disparate impact discrimination, which is difficult to prove, and concluded by saying that the question could not be answered in the abstract.

Jon Seward agreed with much of what Harvey said and, with respect to disparate impact cases, pointed to the limited data available for such cases. He said that Justice has current investigations under way. Seward mentioned the argument that dealers don't discriminate because dealers "only see green." But where you have discretion, discrimination risk goes up. Dealer turnover is high, and former employees will "rat out" a dealer. Sometimes discrimination patterns can break down to a particular finance officer, with, for example, an individual officer regularly charging more to women. Justice has a current investigation of a buy-here, pay-here operation using reverse redlining.

The rest of Panel 9 was largely nonproductive, with two exceptions. The first involved a suggestion that dealers have a written mark-up policy and that they record deviations from that policy and the reasons for the deviations. Harvey retorted that it would be more effective to teach dealership employees the requirements of the ECOA.

Harvey also got in the last word about discretionary pricing, stating that doing away with it would be a giant policy change and that there's no data to support such a change.

I haven't tried in this limited space to report every comment by every panelist and have ignored many panel contributions that I thought failed to lead to anything worth reporting. If you want the blow-by-blow, the transcript and the video of the San Antonio proceedings are available on the FTC's website. If that's the way you decide to go, block out a day and a half for the experience.

November 2011
A Regulatory Mouse Click Away

When Jerry Voegler, Executive Director of the South Dakota Independent Auto Dealers Association, asked me to come to Deadwood, South Dakota, to do a legal session for his dealers, I jumped at the chance. My wife and I had never been to that part of the world, so we treated it as a mini-vacation. We saw Mount

CHAPTER 4

Rushmore, the Crazy Horse Memorial, Spearfish Canyon, Roughlock Falls, and Horsethief Lake, and took in the spectacular scenery from Needles Highway.

From the road, as we traveled, we saw one unusual thing after another. Where else would you see a sign for "Croft's Saddlery" or billboards for "Red Ass Rhubarb Wine"? We passed on the Red Ass but dropped in on the Stone Faces (Mt. Rushmore—get it?) Winery. We saw motorcycles everywhere (mostly Harleys), along with old cars. A large herd of people driving Jeeps stayed overnight at our hotel.

The hotel was a little on the rustic side but it was on par with a lot of the better hotels we've stayed in, and the restaurant was remarkably good. I'd just come from Vegas and was worn out from steak houses, so on the first night I tried the walleye. It was so good and fresh that I had it twice more before we left.

Jerry's conference seemed to be a smashing success—well attended with a lot of vendors. My legal session was lively with dealer participation.

Jerry, if you decide to do it again, sign me up.

Before you lunge for your computers and phones to remind me that this is supposed to be a legal column, let me turn to a thought I had on this trip that might be worth passing along.

At Jerry's conference, one of the speakers preceding me was Chip Perry of AutoTrader. Chip did his usual excellent job of walking the dealers through effective and ineffective ways of selling cars on the Internet. About halfway through his presentation, a little light bulb in my head switched on.

Chip hadn't said anything that was incorrect, but, just that morning, I had been perusing the dealer ads in the Rapid City paper, looking for federal advertising violations (I know, I need to get a life). As usual, I found several, but, as I did, I thought to myself, "Right, the Federal Trade Commission is going to subscribe to the Rapid City paper, and papers from all over the U.S., so that it can go after dealers for advertising violations." Pigs will fly first.

But as Chip talked about dealer websites, I had a flash! Guess what? The FTC has Internet access!

Yep, all those Internet websites, set up to draw customers to the dealerships, also serve as regulatory windows the FTC, the Consumer Financial Protection Bureau, and other regulators can use to take a look at some of the practices of dealers. Of course, ad violations come to mind first, but I've seen things on websites that would form the basis for claims under the federal Truth in Lending Act and the Equal Credit Opportunity Act, as well as claims under state unfair and deceptive acts and practices laws.

And keep in mind that it isn't just the FTC and the CFPB that dealers need to worry about—I have it on good authority that more than a few plaintiffs' class action lawyers have Internet access, too.

Twenty years ago, the distant reaches of South Dakota might have been far from the ebb and flow of consumer credit enforcement actions. Now, dealers in that area, and all over the country, are just a regulatory mouse click away. Is it time for a legal review of your website and your Internet sales practices?

December 2011
Venus and Mars

On November 17, the Federal Trade Commission held its third, and likely final, so-called "Roundtable" dealing with automobile sales, finance, and leasing issues in Washington, D.C. The idea was to have a morning session on leasing, followed by several panels to rehash what was discussed at the two earlier Roundtables.

CHAPTER 4

I had been a panelist at the first Roundtable in Detroit on April 12 and had watched the streaming video of the second Roundtable in San Antonio. The FTC invited me back as a panelist for this final wrap-up.

I listened as the morning sessions went on. The leasing panel addressed issues not covered before, but the rest of the day offered nothing new. The consumer advocates jumped on their favorite horses and rode them hard. They railed against spot delivery practices, dealer participation, the sale of ancillary products and services, and the use by dealers and sales finance companies of mandatory arbitration clauses.

My panel led off the afternoon session, discussing "Which Practices, If Any, Cause Significant Harm to Consumers, and What Are Potential Solutions?" My panel, along with the one before and the one after, was given a specific topic to handle under the general heading of "Motor Vehicle Selling, Financing and Leasing: What Have We Learned from the Roundtables and Where Do We Go from Here?" I decided to spend a minute addressing the "what have we learned?" topic. I'll repeat my comments here.

One thing we have certainly learned is that the consumer advocates, on the one hand, and the dealers, dealer trade associations, and lawyers who represent dealers, on the other hand, live in different worlds.

The consumer advocates were unable to offer data about the frequency of dealer transgressions, but began and interspersed their presentations time and again with something like, "I see this _____ [fill in the blank with whatever bad thing a crooked dealer did to an elderly person or a student or a member of the military], and this type of behavior happens all the time." They then went on to describe some egregious practice that violates 417 federal and state laws and regulations that already apply to dealers and already prohibit the described conduct.

These consumer advocates are, for the most part, good, honest folks who are not misrepresenting their day-to-day experiences. I'm certain that they do see abusive dealer practices. As one of our panelists pointed out, dentists see a lot of people with tooth problems. It isn't exactly a "stop the presses" revelation to hear that a lawyer whose specialty is representing consumers who are suing car dealers hears a lot of stories about dealers violating the law.

The industry representatives were quick to acknowledge that there are dealers who violate the law. I can't speak for the rest of the industry panelists, but my view is that there are some, but very few, dealers who intentionally violate the law, and many of the unintentional legal violations that occur are due to the complexity and incredible scope of the laws and regulations that govern auto sales, finance, and leasing activities.

I'll admit that I experience some of the same kind of "universe-narrowing" effect that the consumer advocates experience. When my phone rings, the dealer on the other end of the line is one who is interested in complying with that rat's maze of laws and regulations, not one who is looking for ways to lie, cheat, steal, or defraud his or her customers. Folks who intend to defraud consumers don't tend to ask us compliance lawyers for assistance.

In short, the consumer advocates are from Venus, while the industry folks are from Mars. We don't recognize the world that they live in, and they don't recognize ours. The language barrier keeps us from communicating effectively, even though on some things we agree.

The result of this situation is that we've spent a lot of energy at three Roundtables talking past each other. Now, the FTC

CHAPTER 4

needs to decide whether the auto sales, finance, and leasing world is filled with bad actors determined to flim-flam customers at every turn to make a buck or if that world overwhelmingly consists of honest businesspeople who struggle to get things right, treat customers well, and create customers for life.

I recognize one of these worlds. The other one is in a galaxy far, far away.

December 2011
They'll Never Catch Me!

Yeah, that's what Butch and Sundance said, too.

It's a rare conference I attend that I don't end up talking with dealers about some of the more dangerous things that some of them do, like financing repairs without doing their legal homework, pricing cars higher for poor-credit buyers, or jacking up their car prices and then purporting to offer "no interest" car credit.

Sometimes the dealers I discuss these topics with will appear to listen closely, as if they're seriously considering taking the advice I'm giving, but I can hear the wheels turning. While they are listening with their right ears to me, a little devil is sitting on their left shoulders saying, in a firm voice, "They'll never catch me." And, despite my efforts to educate, the dealers walk away thinking, "They'll never catch me."

Well, Butch and Sundance had a long run without being caught, but even they eventually went down in a hail of bullets. Many dealers who believe that they will never get caught will have a similarly unhappy end—at least that's what my crystal ball tells me.

Here's how.

2011: REVENGE OF THE CONSUMER ADVOCATES

First, the long arm of the law just got longer. Dealers have always had to worry about the state authorities who regulate dealers, state consumer credit regulators, and state attorneys general. But now the posse includes the federal Consumer Financial Protection Bureau, a powerful new federal regulatory and enforcement agency that has car dealers squarely in its sights, and a newly invigorated Federal Trade Commission also drawing a bead on the dealers it regulates (some dealers are subject to the FTC's jurisdiction, while others will be regulated by the CFPB, but explaining all that is a whole 'nother column).

The posse also beefed up its firepower. The new Dodd-Frank Act gave state AGs some powerful new weapons, and the FTC now has expedited rulemaking authority.

The posse has gotten smarter, too. In addition to the increased firepower, the FTC has been "going to school" on the topic of dealer practices, having just concluded the last of three "Roundtable" meetings around the country that were billed as a "listening tour" to which dealers, finance companies, trade associations, state regulators, and consumer advocates were invited. It's safe to say that the FTC got an earful at the Roundtable events, although most of the information was in the form of anecdotal nonevidence preferred by consumer advocates.

Some dealers, especially those in less populous states and in rural areas, have told me that they don't worry too much about the law's heavy hand. They believe it's unlikely that they will see federal or state enforcement actions way out in the hinterlands. Since one way that the authorities find out about bad dealer practices is investigative journalism, and since small markets likely have less of that than large markets, they probably feel that exposure from that source is unlikely.

CHAPTER 4

I might agree with that risk assessment if it weren't for a couple of problems. Granted, enforcement budgets are stretched, and an enforcement agency, federal or state, might feel constrained to stick close to its home base, especially if it concluded that there was plenty of low-hanging fruit within easy reach. And maybe regulators will look toward bigger players, so hitting smaller dealerships might not be first on the agenda.

But, what if someone was blowing the whistle on misbehaving dealers?

Who would do such a thing, you ask? I can think of a couple of possibilities.

First, dealers will rat out other dealers in a heartbeat when they see them doing illegal stuff. A dealer friend of mine recently gave a call to the attorney general's office to complain about a competing dealer's advertising violations. Most dealers are OK with good old competition but don't like it when the other fellow's advantage arises because he's breaking the law.

Second, employee turnover at dealerships is high, I'm told. With all of those employees coming and going, there are bound to be some who leave a dealer's employment under less-than-pleasant circumstances and who feel that they have an ax to grind. These folks are a telephone call away from telling your regulators everything that they have learned about your dealership. If you've taught them to do things that aren't legal, you can bet that they will pass that information on to the dealership cops.

And don't forget the Internet. Not all dealer misdeeds can be uncovered by a visit to the dealer's website, but certainly advertising, pricing, and sometimes documentation problems can be found with nothing but a bit of web crawling. And it doesn't cost a lot for a regulator sitting in her cubicle in Washington, D.C., to do that sort of investigation.

"They'll never catch me?"

Dream on, my friend. It's only a matter of time. Just ask Butch and Sundance.

CHAPTER 4

Chapter 5

2012: A Full Frontal Assault

CHAPTER 5

The year 2012 caught the CFPB in what was primarily a reconnaissance mode. While some of the Bureau's staff members had been poached from other agencies, like the Federal Reserve Board and the FTC, and were experienced, very competent and business-savvy, the more typical CFPB staffer was inexperienced, did not know the auto sales and finance business and came equipped with a pro-consumer agenda that reflected a high degree of suspicion and hostility toward the auto industry.

The CFPB staffers took to the road, attending industry conferences and, for the most part, observing. Occasionally, they would accept an invitation to speak, but the Bureau kept its folks under such tight control that they seldom said anything that their audiences had not previously seen on the CFPB website or in its press releases. But they watched, and they learned, and returned to their Washington fortress to share what they had learned with the rest of the troops.

Industry had welcomed the CFPB's "watch and learn" initiative, but they would soon discover that the Bureau's learning had been quite selective, with the staffers absorbing bits of knowledge supporting their agenda but often refusing to believe things that refuted their world view.

While the Bureau was in "soak up the knowledge" mode, the Federal Trade Commission began to assert itself in the auto sales and finance world. Going for some of the lowest-hanging fruit, the FTC hammered dealer advertising in several enforcement actions that asserted violations of some basic and long-standing advertising regulations. Dealers, it seemed, had gotten very lax about worrying over advertisement compliance. The FTC set out to fix that, and to establish its own "street cred" as an enforcer of consumer protection laws. The FTC seemed to want to show that it was just as tough as "the new sheriff in town"—the CFPB.

The following articles reflect the way the year unfolded.

January/February 2012
Wash Out Your Mouth with Soap!

That's what my mother would tell me when I'd slip up and use a four-letter word in her presence. She'd scold me, telling me that those four-letter words were the sign of a weak vocabulary.

I was thinking of that admonition the other day when I was contemplating some of the words and phrases that dealers and finance companies use in their ads and websites—words they ought to strike from their vocabularies. Let's start with some of the four-letter variety.

First on my list are "loan" and "note." If you are a dealer selling cars to consumers on credit by having your buyers sign retail installment contracts, then your business has nothing to do with loans and notes. Those words are common, sloppy industry shorthand for the instruments that dealers create when they sell cars on credit, but they are not accurate, and the misuse of them can have dire consequences for your business.

The same goes for the somewhat longer word "lender." The bank that makes your dealership a working capital loan is a "lender." A bank or other company that provides your dealership with inventory financing, or floor planning, is a "lender." A bank, credit union, or sales finance company that buys your retail installment contracts is not a "lender." If you need a generic phrase that accurately describes these folks, maybe you could use "financing source," but don't use "lender."

"Free" is another very dangerous four-letter word that dealers would do well to forget. Pick up a weekend paper, and turn to the car section, or take a look at that mailer you just got from the dealer down the street, and you're likely to see that if you buy a car from the dealer, you'll get something (a gas card, tires for life, a date with Lady Gaga) free. The Federal Trade Commission and a lot of state attorneys general

CHAPTER 5

will land on you like a ton of bricks if they see the word "free" employed improperly.

OK, it isn't a word, and it's only three letters, not four, but my next candidate is "WAC." That term, which stands for "with approved credit," appears in dealer ads all the time. Presumably the dealer placing the ad understands what it means, and industry lawyers like me know what it means, but [NEWS FLASH—HOLD THE PRESSES] ordinary people don't have a glimmer of a clue what "WAC" stands for. And you see it used in ads that have plenty of white space, where spelling out "with approved credit" would not be a problem. It wouldn't surprise me to see a state regulator challenge a dealer's use of the term.

"Warranty" makes my list as well, at least when used incorrectly, as it frequently is. Under federal law, a warranty can be offered only by a manufacturer or a seller and does not involve a separate charge. You hear dealers talking about "extended warranties" all the time. The problem is that the products they describe are not warranties at all but are service contracts or mechanical breakdown protection contracts. State laws work this way as well. Warranties are part of the "basis of the bargain" for the goods purchased. Translation: There is no separate charge.

And one of the worst offenders is the phrase "all applications considered." That's a dealer's cute attempt to imply that all credit applications are "approved," when that is not the case. That attempt is one that AGs don't like and have frequently challenged.

Do any of these words or phrases pop up in your advertising or on your website? If so, it's time to reach for that bar of soap.

January/February 2012
Trying to Read the Tea Leaves

For centuries, people have tried to divine what the future holds. Reading tea leaves, gazing into crystal balls, and searching the heavens for divine messages all have had their adherents.

When the subject is the future agenda of a federal agency, however, none of those methods seems to work very well. If you're interested in where an agency like, say, the Consumer Financial Protection Bureau is headed, you look for pronouncements, announcements, planned events, and the agency's website to try to figure out what its next move, and particularly its next move relating to auto finance and leasing, will be.

Until recently, the Bureau has been pretty quiet about auto stuff. We saw a flurry of housekeeping announcements, some significant mortgage disclosure movement, some credit card activity, and some student loan noise, but not much about cars.

Then a couple of CFPB staffers showed up at the National Alliance of Buy Here, Pay Here Dealers event in Atlanta in early November. Shortly thereafter, we get an announcement detailing the approach the Bureau will use in examining "nonbanks," a term that will include many auto finance companies.

Next comes an announcement by Richard Cordray, the Bureau's new director, that the Bureau is interested in buy-here, pay-here (BHPH) dealers. That announcement followed an article in the *L.A. Times* that appeared to make no distinction between the industry's bad apples and the large majority of reputable BHPH dealers. The article claimed that BHPH dealers made direct loans, which is generally incorrect (they enter into retail installment sales transactions with their customers), and that they charged rates as high as 30%. Those rates are legal for most car finance transactions in California, yet there was no

117

CHAPTER 5

indication that rates that high are common, but nothing gets in the way of a good story, don't you know. Cordray claimed that his interest in this topic came, in part, from Holly Petraeus, who evidently gave him an earful about sharp practices of BHPH dealers around military bases.

January 17 brought yet another Cordray announcement. In this one, he set forth the Bureau's top three priorities. Cordray identified them as the Bureau's "Know Before You Owe" project dealing with real estate finance disclosures, the policing of nonbanks, and (drum roll, please) "cracking down on law breakers."

From these sources we can begin to get some idea of where the Bureau is likely to flex its muscles first. The initiative involving nonbanks might pick up some of the larger auto sales finance companies. Cordray's comments about BHPH dealers and his emphasis on enforcement actions as one of the Bureau's top three priorities point to a storm brewing for BHPH dealers, and especially for BHPH dealers who do business near military bases.

If you're a BHPH dealer, it might be time to put on your helmet and flak jacket.

March 2012
Wars and Rumors of Wars

The Bible says that near the end of days, there will be "wars and rumors of wars." I'm not Mayan (the Mayan calendar ends in 2012, if you haven't heard), and I don't think we are nearing the end of the world, but I can tell you that the rumors are flying.

I got a call a few days back from a New England dealer who was in a real dither because he had heard that the new federal Consumer Financial Protection Bureau was going to impose caps on the rate of finance charges that dealers can impose in connection with selling cars on credit.

"Tell me it ain't so," you say.

OK, "it ain't so." The Dodd-Frank Act, which created the Bureau, expressly states that the Bureau has no authority to establish maximum finance charge rates. However, that doesn't mean that the Bureau can't create problems regarding rates. It could, for example, revise Reg. Z to redefine what is and what is not a finance charge for federal disclosure purposes. For example, the Bureau might change the Reg. Z definition of the term "finance charge" to include fees and charges that are now excludable from the finance charge. That wouldn't necessarily create a problem since Reg. Z deals with disclosures, not caps. It would still be up to the states, as it is now, to establish maximum finance charge rates. The damage might come, however, if state legislatures adopt the new federal definition without also raising their maximum rates to accommodate the expanded definition.

It's hard to tell where this rumor came from, but I'm betting that someone heard of a pending California bill that would cap finance charges for buy-here, pay-here dealers and didn't quite get the facts right. In any event, there's nothing to it.

The second rumor was that the Bureau was requiring BHPH dealers to post the prices of their cars on the cars. That one's not true either, at least not yet. The Bureau might get around to taking such action as a way of trying to force dealers into pricing their cars in a way that does not violate Reg. Z. There are dealers who will price a car at one price to a cash buyer and at a higher price to a buyer on credit. That can create Reg. Z violations, and the Bureau might eventually get around to making such a rule. If it does, it will have to do it through a lengthy rulemaking proceeding, unless it determines that the practice is "unfair, deceptive, or abusive," in which case it could

CHAPTER 5

proceed by initiating an enforcement action. In any event, there's no such rule yet.

My guess is that this one originated with another pending California bill that would require BHPH dealers to post the value of their vehicles on the cars themselves. There's no telling whether or not the California measure will go anywhere—the proposal presents a host of problems—but, after all, it is California.

And there's the biggest rumor of all: that the Republicans will retain their House majority, win the Senate, take the presidency, and repeal all the Dodd-Frank reforms, including the one that created the Bureau. As nearly as I can tell, the source of this one is talk radio stations, and if you believe this stuff, I have some Florida swampland that you really need to see.

March 2012
Musings from Las Vegas

If hanging around Las Vegas for nearly a week is your cup of tea, you need to take in the American Financial Services Association's (AFSA) Automotive Finance Conference for three or four days, then top it off by staying around for the National Automobile Dealers Association (NADA) annual meeting. Those events started on February 1 and continued into the following week, and I was around for most of the time.

The AFSA conference was noteworthy for a couple of reasons. First, there were sightings of Consumer Financial Protection Bureau staffers during the course of the AFSA meetings. Rick Hackett, who is the head person in charge of the Bureau's unit that will oversee installment credit (that's us, folks), and Eric Reusch, an analyst-type at the Bureau, showed up for some valuable face time with the AFSA folks and, more specifically, with the lawyers for the AFSA member organizations.

Hackett reiterated the message we've heard from the Bureau, as well as from the Federal Trade Commission—that he, and the Bureau, are in "information gathering mode" and that no one should expect any new regulations from the Bureau until the information gathering phase has been completed.

That statement complemented the interest that the FTC's Roundtables stirred up regarding several industry practices, including dealers' spot delivery procedures. We've been waiting since the last Roundtable for the FTC's interest to result in some sort of action. Based on the comments by the FTC staff at the Roundtable events, most observers expect that the FTC will soon be doing its own prospecting for information regarding dealer practices.

And both of those pieces of information echo the message that the FTC and the Bureau have been sending since the beginning of the FTC's Roundtable sessions in February 2011—the feds are looking for facts, not anecdotes, before they start making rules.

Before that gives you a case of the warm and fuzzies, remember that new rules and regulations are only part of the federal arsenal. The Bureau and the FTC both have formidable enforcement powers, and those enforcement powers can be exercised in response to consumer complaints. In other words, don't assume that the FTC and the Bureau will be idle until they are finished gathering facts and information.

Although they are not law related, I have a few additional observations about the AFSA and NADA events. First, both were very well attended compared to previous years. There were significantly more attendees and exhibitors for both. The atmosphere was markedly more upbeat, as well—a lot less gloom and doom than a couple of years ago.

CHAPTER 5

The NADA Exhibit Hall was bustling. Each year, there seems to be a new emphasis on some part of the car business. This year, I was puzzled by the number of exhibitors offering marketing help to dealers. I don't recall that there were nearly so many in past years.

I was also disappointed that the manufacturers didn't bring more concept cars to the exhibit hall. Eye candy is good.

So, that's my take on Vegas in February. If you weren't there, plan to attend next year. There are few better places to take the pulse of our industry.

April 2012
FTC's Complaint Report—Another Big Yawn for Car Dealers

Some articles I could write in my sleep. This is one of them.

Why? Because I've written essentially the same article for several years in a row.

On February 28, the Federal Trade Commission released a list of the top consumer complaints it received in 2011. For the 12th year in a row, identity theft complaints topped the list. Of the more than 1.8 million complaints filed last year, 279,156 were identity theft complaints. That's 15 percent.

OK, but the FTC is the federal agency that scheduled three "Roundtables" around the country last year in order to learn about all the bad stuff car dealers were up to that consumer advocates complained about, right? So, complaints about car dealers and their abusive practices had to be in second place, right?

2012: A FULL FRONTAL ASSAULT

Nope. The next nine complaint categories were as follows:

Category	Number of Complaints	Percentage
Debt Collection	180,928	10%
Prizes, Sweepstakes, and Lotteries	100,208	6%
Shop-at-Home and Catalog Sales	98,306	5%
Banks and Lenders	89,341	5%
Internet Services	81,805	5%
Auto-Related Complaints	77,435	4%
Imposter Scams	73,281	4%
Telephone and Mobile Servicess	70,024	4%
Advance-Fee Loans and Credit Protection/Repair	47,414	3%

So, out of 1.8 million complaints, 77,435 involved "auto-related" complaints. If, like me, you are math challenged, that is less than one-half of one percent. Even that amount isn't a reflection of problems that consumers encounter when dealing with car dealers, though. Why not? Because the FTC calls a complaint an "auto-related" complaint if it involves "misleading or deceptive claims regarding auto warranties; repair/maintenance issues with newly purchased used or new cars, including dissatisfaction with service provided by auto mechanics; price fixing and price gouging concerns against gas stations and oil companies; etc."

Let's be charitable and assume that about half of the 77,435 complaints actually involved problems with car dealers. That leaves about 38,750 complaints. Then consider that there were,

123

CHAPTER 5

what, about 13 million new car sales in 2011. I don't know the used car sales number, but assume that it was double the new car number. If that's roughly accurate, that's 38,750 complaints arising from 39 million transactions. If I did the math right, that equals a complaint in less than one-tenth of one percent of the transactions.

If complaints about car dealers and their practices are so numerous that they deserved FTC attention in the form of three Roundtables during 2011, wouldn't you think that the FTC would have a complaint category that isolated dealer misdeeds from complaints about mechanics and the price of gasoline? And wouldn't you think that there would be a big enough number of such complaints to move the needle just a little bit?

April 2012
FTC Hammers Dealers on "Upside Down" Ads

Five car dealers have agreed to Federal Trade Commission settlement orders that require them to stop running ads in which they promise to pay off a consumer's trade-in no matter what the consumer owes on the vehicle. In this action, the FTC evidently used a large-bore cannon, hitting dealers in Connecticut, North Carolina, South Dakota, and West Virginia.

The FTC charged that the ads, which ran on the dealers' websites and on sites such as YouTube, deceived consumers into thinking they would no longer be responsible for paying off the balances on their trade-ins, even if the balances exceeded the trade-ins' values (i.e., the trade-ins had "negative equity"). Instead, said the FTC, the dealers rolled the negative equity into the consumers' new vehicle finance contracts (the FTC erroneously called these "loans") or, in the case of one dealer, required consumers to pay it out of pocket.

2012: A FULL FRONTAL ASSAULT

The proposed settlements bar the dealers from making similar deceptive representations in the future. I could not recall a previous advertising complaint by the FTC against a dealer, and the FTC itself said that the cases were the first of their kind brought by the FTC. It wasn't clear whether "their kind" referred to advertising cases or cases dealing with negative equity.

The Commission also issued a new consumer education publication titled "Negative Equity and Auto Trade-ins" to help consumers understand these types of ads.

"Buying a new car or truck is a major financial commitment, and the last thing consumers need is to be tricked into thinking that a dealer will 'pay off' what they owe on their current vehicle, when they really won't," said David Vladeck, Director of the FTC's Bureau of Consumer Protection. "The Federal Trade Commission is constantly on the lookout for potentially deceptive ads, and brings actions to stop them when appropriate."

The FTC alleged that despite the dealers' claims, consumers still end up being responsible for paying the difference between what they owe and what their vehicles are worth. The complaints charged that the dealers' representations that they will "pay off" what the consumers owe are false and misleading, and violate the FTC Act. Examples of the allegedly deceptive advertisements include:

- "Credit upside down? Need a new car? Go to Billionpayoff.com. We want to pay off your car."
- "Uncle Frank wants to pay [your trade] off in full, no matter how much you owe."
- "I want your trade no matter how much you owe or what you're driving. In fact, I'll pay off your trade when you upgrade to a nicer, newer vehicle."
- "[Dealer] will pay off your trade no matter what you

125

CHAPTER 5

owe . . . even if you're upside down, [Dealer] will pay off your trade."

If those ads sound familiar, it's because it would be hard to open a newspaper, listen to the radio, or watch TV without encountering very similar wording in dealer ads.

What's going on here, you ask? After all, didn't these dealers actually pay off the balance due on the customer's trade-in vehicle?

It appears that the dealers did, in fact, pay off those balances (at least nothing in the FTC's release indicated to the contrary). What the FTC appears to have its shorts in a twist about is that the dealers were paying off the trade-in balances by using the consumers' own money, in the form of financed negative equity, to do so. When a dealer does that, the FTC says that the dealer is misrepresenting the identity of the party paying off the trade-in.

The proposed orders also require the dealers to keep copies of relevant advertisements and materials that substantiate claims made in their advertisements and to provide copies of the orders to certain employees. Finally, the dealers must file compliance reports with the FTC to show they are meeting the terms of the orders, which will expire in a mere 20 years.

That 20-year reporting requirement is just ugly.

How can your dealership avoid ending up in the FTC's crosshairs like these dealers did?

If I were you, I'd be scheduling an advertising review with your lawyer for early tomorrow morning—before breakfast. And the advertising review shouldn't be limited to the issue of negative equity—you ought to vet every ad against every law and regulation that applies to it. The review shouldn't be limited to print, radio, and TV ads either. Your website, any Internet sales site you are using, and all that fancy new social media stuff can also be subject to the advertising laws. One outcome of the review should be advertising guidelines you can follow in the future and a plan to update those guidelines periodically.

Or you can skip the review and fill out reports to submit to the FTC for the next 20 years.

April 2012
The FTC's Next Shot

"A good hockey player plays where the puck is. A great hockey player plays where the puck is going to be."—Wayne Gretzky

My wife is particularly fond of that Gretzky quote. How a quintessential Southern lady from Atlanta became a semi-rabid hockey fan who quotes Gretzky is a story for another day, but I thought of that quote, and Gretzky's concept, when I saw all of the Internet chatter following the Federal Trade Commission's enforcement action against five dealers over ads that described the dealers' negative equity policies.

Evidently, the FTC believes that the phrase "We'll pay off your trade" is verboten in ads when the dealer and the finance company buying the dealer's retail installment contracts are financing the negative equity as part of the new deal.

Dealers everywhere are scrambling to check their ads to see whether they are vulnerable to a similar enforcement action. Gretzky would call those dealers "good."

Great dealers, however, are looking past this FTC initiative and trying to figure out what the FTC's next advertising enforcement move will be.

You won't be surprised to hear that I have a few candidates. Here are three.

If you review dealer ads frequently, as I do, often you will see, as the last item in the mouse type where example credit disclosures appear, the letters "WAC." Those letters mean, I am

127

CHAPTER 5

told, "with approved credit." Dealer ads use "WAC" even though there is plenty of white space where "with approved credit" could be spelled out. Guess what, dealers? Probably fewer than one consumer in 10,000 has a clue what "WAC" means. That makes it a meaningless disclosure. I'm betting the FTC doesn't like meaningless disclosures.

Some dealers run ads that show prices that assume that the buyer can and will qualify for every dealer and finance company discount and special offer that exists, even when very few (or no) buyers will qualify for all of them. So, if your ads show a price that has been computed by subtracting the senior citizen discount, the first buyer's discount, the loyal customer discount, the college student discount, the returning war fighter discount, and the Girl Scout discount (all right, I made that one up), you might want to begin to assemble your sales records so that you can show the FTC that you occasionally have a customer who qualifies for all those discounts at the same time. Good luck with that.

My final entry is the one I often see in the literature that those weekend marketing companies use. You know the folks I'm talking about—they take over your dealership for a weekend, promising scads of sales. They send out a lot of direct mail, much of it with questionable content and, as far as I can tell, none of it reviewed by a lawyer. I can't tell you how many times I've reviewed these mailers and have come across the phrase "all applications accepted" or something similar. The writer of the ad is, of course, trying to convey the thought that everyone's credit application will be "approved." Since that doesn't happen, the ad writer substitutes "accepted" for "approved," thinking that most readers will equate the two terms. I'll bet that's another FTC no-no.

Those are my three candidates for where I think the puck is likely to be when the FTC takes its next shot at misleading ads.

There are many more possibilities out there—you may have some ideas of your own.

So, when you've gotten those negative equity ads in order, I suggest that you do a thorough legal scrubbing of all your ads (don't forget your website, Internet sales sites, and social media activities), and try to identify where the puck will end up next.

May 2012
State AGs Urge Spot Delivery Regulations that Mirror Industry Best Practices

After the conclusion of the Federal Trade Commission's Roundtables, the FTC asked interested parties to submit any additional comments dealing with the topics covered at the Roundtables. The attorneys general of Alaska, Arizona, California, Colorado, Connecticut, Delaware, District of Columbia, Georgia, Hawaii, Idaho, Illinois, Iowa, Maine, Maryland, Massachusetts, Minnesota, Mississippi, Missouri, Nevada, New Hampshire, New Jersey, New Mexico, New York, Ohio, Oregon, Pennsylvania, Rhode Island, Tennessee, Utah, Vermont, Washington, and West Virginia got together and submitted comments for the FTC's further consideration.

One of the topics most frequently discussed during the Roundtables was the practice of spot delivering vehicles. The practice was roundly denounced by the consumer advocates, who call spot deliveries "yo-yo sales" and contend that the practice is always unfair or deceptive. "Nonsense," said the industry Roundtable participants (including me), who agreed that some spot delivery practices could be abusive but contended that a spot delivery can be done in a nonabusive manner.

Neither industry nor the consumer advocates were able to proffer any data to show how often dealers spot delivered cars or

CHAPTER 5

how often the spot deliveries were the type that both industry and the consumer advocates would characterize as abusive. At the conclusion of the Roundtables, I felt that the industry had pretty much won the argument that spot deliveries, when done properly, served a useful purpose and were not abusive.

The AGs' comments seem to indicate that the AGs mostly agree with the industry. In their comments, they urge the FTC to regulate spot deliveries to prohibit abusive practices. The AGs' recommendations read very much like "best practices" that dealership lawyers have been urging dealers to institute in connection with these transactions. Here are the specific practices that the AGs want to have addressed by rule:

- Require dealers to retain consumers' trade-in vehicles until financing is approved.
- Preclude dealers from threatening to repossess or repossessing vehicles in a manner that does not comply with state law, and from threatening to file or filing a theft or other police report due to the consumer's refusal to return the vehicle to the dealership if financing is not approved.
- Bar dealers from charging consumers for mileage, for wear and tear, or for any other reason, pending approval of financing.
- Require dealers to offer consumers either a complete unwinding of the deal or credit under other terms, with the consumer having the choice to decide which of the two alternatives to accept, and bar dealers from making any representations to the contrary concerning the consumers' obligations or rights.
- Bar dealers from retaining portions of down payments or deposits when a deal falls through.
- Require dealers to disclose to consumers that if the first finance agreement is rejected, the consumer has the right to

2012: A FULL FRONTAL ASSAULT

walk away from the deal and has no obligation to the dealer.
- Prior to completing a spot delivery, require dealers to clearly disclose to consumers that financing has not been finalized and the responsibilities and potential consequences for consumers.

With a couple of exceptions, these recommendations echo those that I and other lawyers have been making to dealers for several years. Compare the AGs' list above with the following list from an article I wrote more than a year ago (arguing that spot deliveries, done correctly, are not abusive), titled "Pitch the Bathwater, Save the Baby":

- Allow for mutual rescission until the contract is assigned.
- Require a dealer to keep the customer's trade-in until the customer's retail installment contract is assigned.
- Provide a reasonable period (say, 10 business days) for the assignment of the retail installment contract, beyond which the deal could not be unwound.
- Prohibit a dealer from imposing any fees on the consumer other than charges for excess wear and use or damage to the car.
- Prohibit a dealer from requiring a customer to re-contract if the retail installment contract could not be assigned.
- Prohibit any unwinding of a deal unless the customer has agreed in writing to the unwind (this last one, in my view, isn't necessary, since a dealer generally has no unwind rights absent the customer's written agreement, but the prohibition might still serve a useful educational purpose for dealers and consumers alike).

The proposal by the AGs mostly tracks these industry "best practices," and I hope the FTC follows through with either rulemaking or enforcement actions to address abusive practices in connection with spot delivery transactions.

CHAPTER 5

May 2012
You Shouldn't Be in the BHPH Business If . . .

After listening to Jeff Foxworthy's "You might be a redneck" routine, it occurred to me that if Ole Jeff wrote an article to convey a cautionary message to anyone thinking about going into the BHPH business about the ways state and federal law apply to selling cars on credit, it might sound a bit like this one.

You shouldn't be in the BHPH business if . . . you've done your pro forma and you have not included anything for legal compliance costs, both for startup and as an ongoing expense item.

You shouldn't be in the BHPH business if . . . you don't know the difference between promissory notes and retail installment contracts. I am floored by the number of times I review BHPH deal jackets and find dealers using nothing but a promissory note to reflect the buyer's obligation. A dealer using nothing but a promissory note doesn't have a security interest in the vehicle, cannot legally repossess the vehicle upon default, and has almost certainly violated state and federal law.

You shouldn't be in the BHPH business if . . . your idea of obtaining documents that comply with state and federal law is to photocopy the deal jacket documents from the last place you worked. We've seen franchised dealers and substantial BHPH dealers using documents that are outdated, designed for use in other states, copyrighted, crafted by lawyers who don't know what they are doing, or otherwise screwed up.

You shouldn't be in the BHPH business if . . . you don't know the difference between pre-computed retail installment contracts and interest-bearing (so-called "simple interest") retail installment contracts. We've seen dealers using pre-computed contracts and servicing them as interest-bearing contracts, and vice versa. That's a no-no.

2012: A FULL FRONTAL ASSAULT

You shouldn't be in the BHPH business if . . . all of your prior experience in the car business is with dealerships that sell their retail installment contracts to unrelated financing sources, and you haven't learned how the activities of servicing, collection, repossession, and sale of repossessed vehicles are regulated (and they are heavily regulated). Without knowing those areas, you'll be flying blind with regard to half of your business.

You shouldn't be in the BHPH business if . . . your accountant and your lawyer are not well versed in the BHPH business. Missing critical tax advice because your accountant is inexperienced in BHPH is a shortcut to the poorhouse. Getting your BHPH legal advice from your lawyer brother-in-law whose practice is general corporate work, estates and trusts, or criminal work is, well, criminal.

You shouldn't be in the BHPH business if . . . you don't intend to spend the money necessary to learn what you are doing and to stay abreast of changes in the legal landscape that affect you. First, you have to learn the laws that regulates BHPH, then, because those laws aren't static, you have to stay on top of every change to those laws. That means getting trained in the first place; subscribing to publications and attending conferences; joining dealer associations and 20 groups; and creating, implementing, updating, and funding a credible compliance program for your dealership. If you aren't going to do the compliance stuff right, open a bait shop instead. Worms are simple.

You shouldn't be in the BHPH business if . . . you have never heard of the new Consumer Financial Protection Bureau. That's the new very powerful federal cop that has enforcement and rule-writing jurisdiction over BHPH dealers. The creation of the Bureau is a game changer—this business will not be the same in a few short years. You need to get to know the Bureau as well as it is getting to know your business.

CHAPTER 5

And before you email me to complain about my making fun of rednecks, you need to know that, as a card-carrying Georgia redneck, I get a pass.

May 2012
Earthquakes

Here on the Right Coast, earthquakes are rare. This isn't California, after all. So when one hits, as it did last August, we really notice it.

In our area of law—consumer financial services—earthquakes are rare, too. As a matter of fact, we've had only two in my memory.

The first occurred in the late 1960s, a few short years before I started practicing law. A fight had been brewing in Washington, D.C., and the topic was consumer protection by the federal government. Everyone was "for" protecting consumers (they were for apple pie and motherhood, too). The fight was about the best way to go about providing that protection.

On the one hand were those who believed that the answer to consumer protection was disclosure. Creditors would not be subject to substantive federal regulations, like, for example, maximum loan terms or required grace periods for late payments. Instead, creditors would be required to disclose, in a uniform way, the principal terms and conditions of the credit that they offered. Consumers, armed with the knowledge provided by the disclosures, would then be in a better position to protect themselves.

On the other hand were those who believed that disclosures were ineffective and that the only way to deter creditor misbehavior was to have rules that addressed the substance of credit transactions.

2012: A FULL FRONTAL ASSAULT

Wisconsin Senator William Proxmire, a Democrat, led the disclosure proponents. Proxmire and his allies prevailed, and the result was the federal Truth in Lending Act, with its implementing Federal Reserve Board Regulation Z. TILA and Reg. Z have some substantive provisions, but, for the most part, they deal with disclosure. Creditors, it's fair to say, breathed a sigh of relief.

Fast forward about 20 years. At an American Bar Association Business Law Section Consumer Financial Services Committee meeting in Boston, my partner, Robert Cook, squared off in a panel discussion about "Disclosure vs. Substantive Regulation." His opponent was Kathleen Keest, a consumer advocate and one of the brightest credit lawyers in the country.

The argument was a close one, but no one threw any knockout punches. On balance, I thought Robert emerged as the winner on points. Maybe that's just my bias talking.

The presentation by Robert and Kathleen was evidence that the fight had not been settled, though, and did nothing to resolve the continuing dispute. Fast forward another 15 years.

The U.S. experiences a near collapse in its financial markets. Sharp lending and underwriting practices by mortgage lenders and brokers are widely believed to have played a central role in the process. The credit disaster is hailed by the substantive regulation crowd as proof that disclosure doesn't work.

Those favoring substantive regulation were now in the ascendancy, and they got the ears of Messrs. Dodd and Frank. The resulting Dodd-Frank Act created the Consumer Financial Protection Bureau, and the CFPB will be more than a little bit interested in the substantive regulation of credit. The ground begins to shake again—this is the second earthquake to hit the consumer financial services markets.

CHAPTER 5

Will the new emphasis on substantive oversight work? We'll see.

I actually think that most of the bad stuff creditors have done to consumers for the last 50 years could have been prevented or limited if the federal enforcement agencies had enforced the laws already on the books. If the disclosure laws are replaced by or supplemented with substantive regulation, we won't see any changes unless the new rules are enforced. Time will tell whether or not the feds will effectively enforce the new laws.

Maybe we'll check back in another 50 years, when the next quake will probably hit.

May 2012
Things You See Out of the Corner of Your Eye

My friends who are hunters tell me that when they are out in the early morning, and it's still dark, they can make out objects better if they don't look directly at them. Evidently, in such situations, peripheral vision is better than whatever you call direct vision.

I thought about that when I saw the recent proposed rule issued by the Consumer Financial Protection Bureau that would permit credit card issuers to offer so-called "fee-harvester" credit cards to people with poor credit histories (the "fee-harvester" moniker was thunk up by the consumer advocates, who are geniuses at coming up with pejorative names for financial products).

The Federal Reserve Board, when it had the rule-writing authority under the federal Truth in Lending Act applicable to these cards, issued a rule dealing with these cards. The rule prohibited the issuers of these cards from excluding charges incurred before the cards were issued from congressionally

2012: A FULL FRONTAL ASSAULT

imposed limits on fees the issuers could assess. Last fall, the FRB's rule was overturned by a federal court, which concluded that the rule went beyond the law and that the agency had exceeded its authority. The Bureau's proposed rule would permit those pre-issue charges, angering the consumer advocates.

How does this relate to peripheral vision? Well, those of us in the auto finance and leasing business have been watching the CFPB carefully for signs of its enforcement and regulatory intentions. So far, at least, there haven't been too many developments directly related to our area. But if you watch out of the corner of your eye, you can pick up developments like this one that might offer some hints as to where the Bureau might go when it decides to address the auto world.

The significance of this "fee-harvester" rule, I think, is that it is an indication that the Bureau might pay less attention than we supposed to the pressure brought to bear by the consumer advocates, who roundly denounced the Bureau's proposed rule, and more attention to, you know, the law. Evidently the Bureau staff looked at the court's decision overturning the FRB's rule, looked at the law, and determined that the court's analysis was correct. Go figure.

The Bureau's rule should cheer creditors in the often-maligned subprime and buy-here, pay-here parts of the auto finance and lease marketplace, businesses that are very unpopular with the consumer advocates. The proposed rule evidences an even-handedness that many observers were predicting we would not see from the Bureau.

Many auto dealer and finance company practices were discussed at the FTC's 2011 Roundtables, including dealer participation, spot deliveries, the sale of ancillary products, the use of GPS and starter interrupt devices, payment packing, and the like. Most of the bad practices that were discussed are illegal,

137

CHAPTER 5

but many of them are legal. The legality of the practices doesn't stop those consumer advocates from tearing their hair out and jumping up and down screaming about how abusive those practices are (despite, in many instances, absolutely no facts to support their positions).

Perhaps the Bureau's show of backbone in connection with its proposed regulation on the fee-harvesting cards will carry over to its enforcement and regulatory actions dealing with auto finance and leasing. Or, perhaps the baying crowd will push them to ban otherwise legal practices. I'll keep an eye out for the answer.

June 2012
Facts, Anyone?

Facts about the prevalence of dealer practices that harm consumers seem to be hard to come by.

The Federal Trade Commission's Roundtables proved that no one has much hard data about the prevalence of bad practices by car dealers. Consumer advocates came to the events armed, as they always are, with sad stories about individuals who had been victimized by dealers. The consumer advocates claimed, with little or no proof, that the practices they described were pervasive and representative of the way that dealers treat consumers. Industry representatives responded that, while there were certainly dealers who did not comply with laws regulating their transactions with consumers, there wasn't a shred of evidence regarding the prevalence of such practices. The industry representatives were correct.

To come up with the prevalence of a practice requires a fraction. The numerator of the fraction would be the number of bad acts. The denominator would be the total number of transactions in which the bad acts might take place.

Surprisingly, the information necessary to determine that fraction doesn't seem to exist.

For years, the Federal Trade Commission has collected consumer complaints, each year publishing a "Top 10" list. One of the categories on the list deals with auto-related complaints, but the category is so broad that it includes complaints that have nothing to do with F&I practices, such as complaints about repairs and servicing. It even includes complaints to manufacturers about car problems. The list is, I suppose, better than no information at all, but not by much.

The Consumer Financial Protection Bureau has also begun to collect consumer complaints. The Bureau focused on credit cards and student loans first, but you can bet that it won't be long before it begins to receive and compile complaints from car buyers (I hope that they do a better job of categorizing the complaints than the FTC has done).

Neither the FTC nor the Bureau seems to try to determine the validity of the complaints they receive. It's likely the case that some complainants later resolve their complaints without telling the Bureau. It's also possible that some consumers are misinformed about their transactions and file complaints that are baseless. For instance, a consumer might believe that she has a three-day right to rescind a car purchase made at a dealership and complain when the dealer refuses to rescind. It's also possible (dare we say so) that there are some consumers who will never be happy about any transaction and whose complaints are baseless. And we haven't even gotten to complaints filed by outright crackpots and by the dealer down the street seeking to smear an honest dealer.

But I digress. I was musing about the collection of complaints by the FTC, the Bureau, and other consumer protection organizations that have a complaint collection process. When you

CHAPTER 5

add up all these complaints (which might be duplicative if consumers complain to more than one organization), you end up with only a very rough numerator of the fraction you need to determine if any complained-of practice is pervasive enough to address with regulations or enforcement actions.

The other part of a fraction is the denominator. In order for the fraction to be a meaningful measure of prevalence, the numerator and the denominator must be counting the same things. If the FTC's complaint file is the numerator, and if it includes sales, finance, lease, warranty, repair, and service complaints, then the number that is used as the denominator needs to be the total of all of the transactions out of which those complaints arise. I don't think anyone knows what that number might be.

But let's speculate. If there are 50,000 complaints registered in a marketplace where there were 100,000 transactions, most of us would agree that there's likely a problem there someplace. If there are 50,000 complaints in a marketplace of 250 million auto-related transactions (which might be a really low guess when you throw in everything but the kitchen sink, the way the FTC does), you might tend to think that the FTC and the Bureau could do more for consumer protection by focusing on, say, identity theft.

The FTC and the Bureau have both made public statements that they are interested in facts regarding the prevalence, or not, of various dealer practices decried by the consumer advocates. If they are serious, they will need to determine a denominator that is appropriate for whatever number of consumer complaints they identify. The failure to do so would render their conclusions meaningless.

Facts, anyone?

July 2012
FTC Charges Car Dealer and Debt Collector with Exposing Sensitive Personal Information on File Sharing Networks

A recent Federal Trade Commission announcement caught my eye because it illustrates so well a compliance lesson that I try to teach to dealers. On June 7, 2012, the FTC announced that it had charged EPN, Inc., a Utah debt collector, and Franklin's Budget Car Sales, Inc., a Georgia car dealership, with illegally exposing sensitive personal information of consumers by allowing peer-to-peer (P2P) file sharing software to be installed on the companies' computer systems. Files shared to a P2P network are available for viewing or downloading by any computer user with access to the network. In general, a shared file cannot be removed permanently from the P2P network. In addition, files can be shared among computers long after they have been deleted from the original source computer.

EPN collects debts for a variety of clients, such as health care providers, commercial credit organizations, and retailers. According to the FTC's complaint, EPN's installation of P2P file sharing software on its computer network caused consumers' sensitive information, including Social Security numbers, employer names, health insurance information, and medical diagnosis codes of approximately 3,800 hospital patients, to be made available to any computer connected to the P2P network. The FTC alleged that EPN did not have an appropriate information security plan, failed to assess risks to the consumer information it collected and stored, did not adequately train employees, did not use reasonable measures to enforce compliance with its security policies and procedures, and did not use reasonable methods to prevent, detect, and investigate unauthorized access to personal information

CHAPTER 5

on its networks. Because of EPN's failure to implement reasonable and appropriate data security measures, the FTC charged EPN with committing unfair or deceptive acts or practices in violation of Section 5(a) of the Federal Trade Commission Act.

Franklin's Budget Car Sales allegedly compromised consumers' sensitive personal information by allowing P2P software to be installed on its computer network as well, in violation of the FTC Act, the Safeguards Rule, which implements Section 501(b) of the Gramm-Leach-Bliley (GLB) Act, and the Privacy Rule, which implements Section 503 of the GLB Act. The dealership sells and leases new and used vehicles and also provides financing for its customers. Because of its alleged failure to implement reasonable security measures to protect its customers' personal information, the FTC charged that, among other personal information, the names, addresses, Social Security numbers, dates of birth, and drivers' license numbers of approximately 95,000 consumers were made available to the P2P network. Franklin's also allegedly failed to provide annual privacy notices and failed to provide a mechanism by which consumers could opt out of information sharing with third parties, in violation of the GLB Privacy Rule.

Settlements with the debt collection business and car dealership will bar misrepresentations about the privacy, security, confidentiality, and integrity of any personal information and will require the companies to establish and maintain comprehensive information security programs as well as to undergo data security audits.

Here's the lesson that I took from the FTC's announcement.

Many dealers who have made an attempt to comply with the federal privacy laws and regulations, with the federal "Red Flags"

142

requirements, and with the federal "Risk-Based Pricing" rules have bought "one-size-fits-all" manuals for these programs. Other dealers have made more of an effort, some of them even enlisting their lawyers to assist with preparing the required manuals. But, regardless of which compliance road the dealers have followed, most of them have one thing in common. Once the dealers adopt the policy, they put it on the bookshelf and ignore it.

With technology developing at warp speed, those manuals need to be revisited, and revisited frequently, by people who understand the technology developments need to be involved. These reviews need to be scheduled on a periodic basis, with the frequency determined after consultation with the lawyers and the techies. And when the reviews are done, they should be documented so that the dealership can show its regulator that it does periodic reviews.

Would these steps have made any difference if they had been implemented by the debt collector and the dealer? Perhaps not, but you can bet your mama's cornbread recipe that when it comes time to settle charges like these, the FTC will be a lot more lenient if its staffers believe that the dealer was making a real effort to do things right.

July 2012
A Visit with the CFPB's Rick Hackett

The National Automotive Finance Association was meeting in Ft. Worth at the end of May, and I had been assigned the honor of "interviewing" Rick Hackett, an assistant director of the Consumer Financial Protection Bureau, in charge of the Bureau's Installment and Liquidity Lending Markets section. The "interview" wasn't really an interview—Jack Tracey, the NAF

CHAPTER 5

executive director, had solicited questions from the NAF's Board of Directors. My job was simply to put the questions to Rick. In order to make sure that Rick would be able to give his answers some thought, we submitted the questions to him in advance.

In any event, it was going to be a fun assignment. I've known Rick for 30 years or so as a lawyer in private practice who represented creditors, and I count him as a friend. I'd seen him in similar situations and knew that he'd be very informative. I was excited.

Then I had a better idea.

Our firm had just acquired a new partner. Joel Winston had been with the Federal Trade Commission for 30-some years and had traded in his regulatory hat for a private practice hat. Who better to interview a fellow who had just become a regulator after 30-some years in private practice? Here was a black-hat guy now wearing a white hat and vice versa (I'll leave it to you to assign colors to the guys).

That scenario was way too good to miss, so I asked Rick and Joel if they were OK with me bowing out and Joel stepping in. They were, and the result was one of the best and most informative industry sessions I've seen at any industry conference in recent years.

Here's a recap of Joel's questions and my best recollection of Rick's answers.

Q1. How did a lawyer who has spent a career representing creditors end up as the top credit cop for installment credit at the Bureau?

A1. After a thanks for the flattery, Rick did his standard government disclaimer that he wasn't speaking for the Bureau. He then explained that his unit of the Bureau isn't a "cop," but is more of an intelligence-gathering group to support the cops and other parts of the Bureau, combined with an outreach function to creditors. The "cops," he explained, are in the Supervision, Enforcement, and Fair Lending Division. Rick pointed out that at least one of the Bureau's "cops" was in the audience.

Rick described the SEFL Division's mission in more detail. The Division, he said, will supervise companies within the CFPB's jurisdiction and will couple the supervision with enforcement actions when appropriate. The Division has an enforcement office and two other tightly coordinated offices for supervision of large banks and certain nonbanks. The Division's office of fair lending will monitor lending by both large banks and nonbank institutions for prohibited practices. Rick noted that the large bank supervision effort is already underway, with examinations conducted at several institutions. He noted that the Bureau has published a basic exam manual with product-specific exam guidelines and that more such guidelines are on the way.

Rick then discussed the Bureau's examination of nonbank institutions in those industries Congress named in the Dodd-Frank Act, particularly payday lending and nonbank mortgage lending. He pointed out that the Bureau has proposed a rule to define additional markets and their "larger participants" who will be subject to supervision. So far, those "additional markets" are consumer reporting agencies and debt collectors—other industries may be added later.

Q2. Tell us where the Bureau is, so far as the process of "staffing up" is concerned? How many staffers? How many of those are lawyers? How much will the Bureau spend this year?

A2. Rick responded that the Bureau's staff now numbers over 800, against the FY 2012 staffing goal of 1,095. He discussed the areas of the Bureau where staff is being added—bank and nonbank supervision—and described the Bureau's

CHAPTER 5

efforts to hire more personnel. He wasn't able to pinpoint the number of lawyers at the Bureau, but pointed out that many of the supervisors and some others have legal training but nonlegal jobs.

As for budget numbers, Rick referred Joel to the Bureau's website, which shows that the Bureau spent $102 million in the first quarter of FY 2012. Rick said the expenditures were for people, technology, and vendor support for the Bureau's consumer call center. Rick noted that the Dodd-Frank Act gives the Bureau an "up to" number of 11% of the Federal Reserve System operating budget from 2009, which is a bit more than $500 million. Rick said that the Bureau's budget justification filed with Congress estimated $329 million for FY 2012.

Q3. Does the Bureau have any sort of priority schedule for addressing various types of credit? Will you focus on housing credit, credit cards, auto credit, military credit, student loans, etc. in any particular order, or should we expect to see the Bureau moving on multiple fronts at the same time?

A3. Rick's rather lengthy answer to Joel's multi-faceted question boiled down to "yes" as to the last part of the question. He said that if you take all of the direct mandates in the Dodd-Frank Act together with the grant by Congress of enforcement authority, you could say fairly that Congress told the Bureau to move on multiple fronts in multiple ways.

Q4. Automobile creditors require physical damage coverage to be maintained on the collateral during the life of the credit obligation. What are the Bureau's acceptable guidelines to allow for the creditor to protect its interest in the vehicle by using creditor-placed insurance when the consumer fails to maintain this requirement?

2012: A FULL FRONTAL ASSAULT

A4. I suspected that Rick wasn't going to get into a discussion of such a nitty-gritty question, but he surprised me with the scope of his reply. He noted that the requirements for insurance disclosures in the federal Truth in Lending Act don't really address the practice of force-placing insurance, pointed to a new rule in Dodd-Frank on force-placed insurance in the mortgage world, mused that there were, to his knowledge, no specific rules in the "enumerated statutes" that addressed the issue, and noted that he was unaware of any activity by the FTC to deal with these practices through its "unfair and deceptive" authority.

Q5. *In an effort to identify consumer credit problems, the Bureau is soliciting consumer complaints. As it collects consumer complaints, what process, if any, will the Bureau use to determine which complaints are valid?*

A5. Rick described the Bureau's consumer response system by saying that the Bureau, upon receiving a consumer complaint, forwards it to the creditor for a response. The creditor then has a given time within which to acknowledge the complaint and then 60 days to close the complaint. When the complaint is resolved, the creditor reports the resolution to the Bureau. He said that the Bureau doesn't try to judge the validity of the complaint and that when the consumer is satisfied, the Bureau's participation is over. If the consumer isn't satisfied, the Bureau then assigns the matter to an investigator, who will begin a dialogue with the creditor. That, he noted, is the current system, which he expects the Bureau will modify as it gains experience with the system.

CHAPTER 5

Q6. Assuming that the aggregate number of valid consumer complaints will constitute some sort of rough numerator, how will the Bureau go about determining the appropriate denominator to go with the numerator to come up with data about the frequency of particular consumer credit problems?

A6. Rick responded that the Bureau's "numerator" isn't limited to the complaints it receives but includes the FTC's Consumer Sentinel—Bureau offices that serve particular constituencies such as servicemembers, students, older Americans, and the underserved—as well as information received from state AGs and other federal agencies.

He then pointed out that the Dodd-Frank Act instructs the Bureau to monitor for risks to consumers using means beyond complaints. Specifically, the Bureau is to gather and compile information from a variety of sources, including examination reports concerning covered persons or service providers, consumer complaints, voluntary surveys and voluntary interviews of consumers, surveys and interviews with covered persons and service providers, and reviews of available databases. He noted that the Bureau will be able to require covered persons and service providers who participate in consumer financial services markets to file with the Bureau reports, or answers in writing to specific questions, that furnish specified information.

Q7. As far as auto finance issues go, has the Bureau engaged in any fact finding, other than receiving consumer complaints, that has identified problem areas? If so, what problem areas are you seeing? If not, how do you intend to go about identifying problems?

A7. Before launching into an answer of this question, Rick pointed out that the auto finance market consists of many parts, from subvented prime financing to buy-here, pay-here, and that consumer experiences in the various parts of the market are different. He said that the Bureau would look at those different markets separately where that makes sense in identifying problems and setting priorities. With that warning, he identified military credit, rate participation, and prohibited discrimination as three areas of likely Bureau interest.

Q8. Consumer advocates have pressed for an "all-in" formula for the determination of finance charges and APRs. Is that a likely approach? If so, will such a change require congressional action?

A8. Rick deftly dodged this question, stating that he personally would want there to be more evidence gathered, chiefly by those who are expert in how consumers perceive and behave, before this issue results in changes in the law.

Q9. Is the Bureau going to give any further guidance on what constitutes an "abusive" practice in the auto finance field, or are you investigating possible enforcement proceedings on this issue in auto finance to do so?

A9. Rick noted that the definition of "abusive" in Dodd-Frank was pretty descriptive, and that the term is used in the context of two other words—"unfair and deceptive"—as to which the FTC has provided a lot of law over time. That being the case, he suggested that it makes sense to look at the development of law under section 5 of the FTC Act. He concluded by noting that the Bureau has not currently given advance guidance that certain practices are abusive but that such guidance might become a more obvious option after the Bureau gains more experience.

CHAPTER 5

Q10. How would you characterize the nature and extent of the Bureau's sharing of information on auto financing practice complaints with the FTC and state attorneys general? What degree of information and analysis does the Bureau share? Does the Bureau make a recommendation to the FTC or state AGs when sharing complaints on auto financing?

A10. Rick recapped the Dodd-Frank requirement that the Bureau have a close working relationship with the FTC and state AGs on a wide range of issues, including auto finance, and pointed to formal written agreements with some of those entities that govern the sharing of information and the manner of cooperation. He noted that although he had not yet been involved in many conversations with other agencies on auto issues, the conversations he has been involved in resulted in a cooperative exchange of information.

Q11. Who has the primary regulatory enforcement authority for claims involving auto financing abuses of servicemembers, assuming the dealer in question is a franchised dealer?

A11. After clarifying the meaning of "franchised dealer," Rick replied that the FTC has primary enforcement authority over such a dealer under the federal consumer financial laws, but warned the audience not to forget that state AGs also have parallel authority and have state laws to enforce as well. He pointed out that primary rule-writing authority for TILA and other federal consumer financial laws that have rules and are applicable to installment sales of vehicles would remain at the Federal Reserve Board for those dealers. The Bureau will still have influence over franchised dealers, he noted, because it has primary regulatory enforcement authority of the federal consumer financial laws, as well as rule-writing authority with respect to the auto finance companies that buy retail installment contracts from exempt dealers.

Q12. Does the Bureau have a projected timetable for its report and rulemaking on mandatory arbitration clauses in pre-printed consumer contracts?

A12. Rick noted that the Bureau had just published a detailed Request for Information (RFI) on this issue that signaled some of the issues that the Bureau is interested in. He warned that the RFI seeks guidance on data sources, but does not seek advocacy on the ultimate issue of where any rulemaking should go. He pointed out that a rulemaking is not mandatory, only the study is, so it would be premature to speculate about a schedule for something that might not happen.

Q13. When does the Bureau expect to complete its investigation of buy-here, pay-here dealers, and what can we expect as an outcome?

A13. Rick took the Fifth Amendment on this one, making it clear that it was Bureau policy not to comment on or confirm the existence of a pending investigation. He took a drink of water and called for the next question.

Q14. Is it a fair assumption that the Bureau will gather input from many interested participants in the auto finance field prior to enacting rules?

A14. In response to this one, Rick pointed to the Administrative Procedures Act (APA) process that the Bureau would be required to use in connection with most rulemaking and explained that the APA process was designed to get widespread public input on proposed rules. He said that part of his job is to have a continuous, nonsupervisory dialogue with the industry, providing a means for input before any rulemaking is formally started.

CHAPTER 5

Q15. Are there plans to override existing state regulations dealing with licensing of finance companies, usury rate statutes (where they exist), or repossession regulations?

A15. Rick responded to this question by observing that Dodd-Frank does not promote expanded use of federal law to pre-empt state law and, if anything, tends to lean in the other direction, giving states more power to deal with federally chartered institutions and their affiliates. Further, he observed that Congress specifically kept the Bureau out of the usury business and that he was not aware of any context in which the Bureau would be counteracting state usury laws. He noted that state licensing is unlikely to conflict with federal consumer financial laws.

Q16. Will the Bureau be collecting financial performance information from finance companies as some states do with annual reports to regulators?

A16. After responding that the Bureau has not yet taken a position on whether it will seek to define nonbank auto finance companies under the "larger participant" rules, Rick noted that the Bureau has authority to issue rules with respect to registration of companies, which might include information gathering, but that it has not moved in that direction. He wouldn't predict what the examination or registration of auto finance companies would entail, but noted that states often have responsibility to look after safety and soundness, as well as consumer protection, and that, in the former role, they often gather and need financial performance information.

Q17. What types of depository institutions and affiliates can the Bureau supervise, including nonbank affiliates?

A17. Rick explained that the Bureau has supervisory authority over banks with over $10 billion in assets and any of their bank and nonbank affiliates, and thus has supervisory authority over those banks with $10 billion or less in assets that are affiliates of banks with over $10 billion in assets. He noted that the Bureau also has supervisory authority over subsidiaries of small insured depository institutions that are nondepository covered persons.

Q18. Can you comment on the Bureau's general predisposition toward auto finance? Are there perceived problem areas that are considered to be serious? Are there plans to focus on independent finance companies more strongly than banks, credit unions, or captive finance companies? Are dealer-related finance companies of any special interest?

A18. Rick replied that the Bureau was "data driven," and he hoped it would not be motivated by a predisposition regarding any industry. He pointed out areas where we know there are historical issues—dealer participation and concerns regarding servicemembers. The Bureau's objective, he said, is to promote a level regulatory playing field regardless of charter, and that, in carrying out its duties, the Bureau should be expected to focus its energy based on risks of harm to consumers, not charter type.

Q19. At a recent meeting, Richard Cordray stated that he expects financial institutions to be more transparent and that the required loan documentation needs to be more easily understood by the consumer. Does the CFPB understand how much of the current documentation is government mandated?

A19. I could have answered that one for Rick. He's been in private practice, and I know that he has crafted many a consumer credit form that contains a great deal of federally mandated stuff. Rick didn't disappoint. He confirmed that the Bureau understands the problem and pointed to the Bureau's chore of tackling the TILA-RESPA simplification effort on the mortgage side. He also referred to the fact that the state-regulated vehicle installment sale business is subject to many state disclosure rules on top of the federal requirements and that there is always room for regulators to think about how the historical accumulation of disclosure practices may have produced disclosure overload.

On the other hand, he noted, there may be room for the language of installment sale contracts to be simpler, and he expressed his personal concern that very long combined contract and disclosure forms may make it hard for consumers to understand what they are getting into. He reiterated that virtually any change in TILA regulatory requirements for auto financing would be conducted under the APA, with plenty of opportunity for input, including from the forms automation folks, and said that, to his knowledge, no effort along these lines was in the works yet.

[Author's note: I'm pleased to report that Rick has become a Hudson Cook, LLP partner.]

July 2012
Oops

Every couple of years, I have to write an article 'fessing up to something I've gotten wrong. It's that time again.

This one deals with the Consumer Financial Protection Bureau. If you've got a good memory, and if you were paying attention, you will recall that as the Dodd-Frank Act was working its way through Congress, and as it became more and more evident that the thing might actually pass, the National Automobile Dealers Association and others worked hard to get car dealers exempted from the Bureau's jurisdiction. The effort was only partly successful for the industry as a whole (not all dealers were included in the exemption) but was very, very successful for NADA, whose members all qualified for the exemption, unless they held their own retail installment contracts.

Congress agreed to the exemption of the dealers but extracted a price, insisting on beefed-up powers for the Federal Trade Commission, which would remain the federal cop-on-the-beat for the exempted dealers. And, the Bureau retained its jurisdiction over the sales finance companies that buy retail installment contracts and leases from the exempted dealers, giving the Bureau a way to affect the exempt dealers by doing indirectly many things that it couldn't do directly.

When the dust settled, my conclusion was that NADA hadn't gotten much for the expenditure of treasure and political capital that it spent in order to obtain the exemption. I'd have been fine if I'd stopped right there and kept my conclusion to myself. But I like to write these "'fessing up" articles, and nothing short of putting my conclusions in print would do.

That earned me a shot across the bow from Andy Koblenz, a friend who happens to be NADA's general counsel.

You don't want to argue with Andy. He's a bright guy, the kind who could hold a Mensa chapter meeting while taking a shower, and he's articulate and convincing as well. His performance at the FTC's Roundtables last year showed that he's also a born teacher, the kind who could explain quantum physics to a gerbil. But I digress.

Andy took me to task, pointing out the many ways that the exempted dealers were better off than the nonexempted dealers

CHAPTER 5

and especially pointing out that the exempted dealers were not subject to the Bureau's reporting, registration, and supervisory authority. At the time, I wasn't convinced.

Over time, and after getting some feel for the Bureau, its personnel, and its announced and apparent objectives, I think that, on balance, Andy has the better side of the argument. And that's despite the FTC's Roundtables and the several enforcement actions against dealers that seem to have been spawned by them.

So, that's my most recent goof. Stay tuned—there'll be more.

August 2012
Unregulated?

I really get my nose out of joint when politicians intentionally distort the facts to bolster their positions. I don't like it when Obama does it, and I don't like it when Romney does it. The politicians seem to think that if they say something loudly enough and often enough, a public that consumes news in 20-second sound bites will believe them. I know that's just "politics as usual" in America today, but it still puts a knot in my shorts.

The most recent example of this Pinocchio tendency came from Ted Lieu, the California legislator who is pushing a piece of legislation that will drive a number of buy-here, pay-here dealers out of business. The legislation was evidently inspired by a piece of journalism written by a reporter who knows little about the industry and who appears to have engaged in only the skimpiest of research before concluding that all buy-here, pay-here dealers were bad actors. The legislator justified his measure by saying that California's buy-here, pay-here dealers were unregulated. That isn't a joke—here's his quote: "Senate Bill

956 seeks to regulate an industry that is currently unregulated under state law."

Unregulated?

Buy-here, pay-here dealers are regulated by the same state laws and regulations that govern all car dealers. These include the Automobile Sales Finance Act (ASFA; also called "Rees-Levering"). The ASFA applies to any contract for the credit sale of a motor vehicle between a buyer and a seller. The ASFA has extensive disclosure and other information requirements that drive the content of every credit sale document used by every dealer in the state, including buy-here, pay-here dealers, in such transactions. In certain instances, foreign language disclosures are required. The ASFA requires extensive warnings to the buyer in connection with these transactions and provides for a right of rescission for the buyer in some circumstances. It renders some provisions in a credit sale agreement unenforceable and prohibits other provisions. The ASFA prescribes how finance charges must be computed, limits late charges, and imposes a grace period within which late charges may not be imposed. The ASFA regulates pre-payments, deferrals, and extension of credit contracts and grants significant rights to buyers who have defaulted on their obligations and whose vehicles have been repossessed. The ASFA's penalty provisions are onerous.

Most states have laws that regulate the credit sale of motor vehicles. Most lawyers who are familiar with such laws in the various states will tell you, I think, that the California law is one of the toughest in the country.

Unregulated?

It would be bad enough if the ASFA were the only statutory scheme that California buy-here, pay-here dealers had to worry about. But there are more.

CHAPTER 5

Used car dealers, including buy-here, pay-here dealers, must be licensed in California. Licensing requires a $50,000 surety bond. Salespeople are also required to be licensed. I assume that California licensing authorities have the authority to revoke the licenses of car dealers and salespeople who prey on the public.

Unregulated?

California, like every other state in the union, has enacted a version of the Uniform Commercial Code. The UCC's Article 2 provides the rules for transactions between buyers and merchants. These rules offer substantial protections to a car buyer (they apply to all car buyers, not just those buying on credit).

The UCC's Article 9 deals with the rights and duties of secured creditors (that's what buy-here, pay-here dealers are) and debtors. It has a number of protections for defaulting debtors, one of which is a requirement that a secured creditor (that includes a buy-here, pay-here dealer) sell repossessed collateral (cars) in a commercially reasonable manner, and another of which is that a creditor is not permitted to repossess collateral if doing so would breach the peace.

Unregulated?

California, like most states, has an "unfair and deceptive acts and practices" law. These laws generally prohibit fraud and deception in transactions that involve car buyers and apply to buy-here, pay-here dealers. So-called "UDAP" laws are favorites of attorneys general and plaintiffs' lawyers because they are broad-reaching and not very specific—they can be used in a lot of ways and serve as a sort of Swiss Army knife for those attacking the practices of dealers, including buy-here, pay-here dealers. California lawyers who represent consumers do not have the reputation of being reluctant to use California's version of a UDAP law.

Unregulated?

California has more in the way of consumer protection laws and regulations that apply to all car dealers' credit sales activities. Advertising and anti-discrimination laws come to mind. But the California regulatory scheme pales when you consider the federal rules and regulations that apply to the credit sale operations of car dealers, including buy-here, pay-here dealers. Consider that these dealers are subject to the requirements of the federal Truth in Lending Act and Regulation Z, the Equal Credit Opportunity Act and Regulation B, the Fair Credit Reporting Act, federal privacy laws and regulations, Federal Trade Commission regulations dealing with warranties, the sale of used cars, odometer disclosures, and credit practices, Internal Revenue Service cash reporting rules, Treasury Department anti-terrorist rules, and federal "do-not-call," "do-not-fax," and "do-not-email" rules. And all of these federal requirements were already in place before Congress enacted the Dodd-Frank Act, creating the very powerful Consumer Financial Protection Bureau, with its prohibition against unfair, deceptive, and "abusive" (whatever that means) acts and practices.

And the laws and regulations cited above are ones that deal only with the credit sale of vehicles. These buy-here, pay-here dealers have to comply with the same environmental, labor, tax, and general business laws and regulations that many other businesses have to comply with.

Unregulated?

I read those newspaper articles that outlined the abuses of a very few buy-here, pay-here dealers. I noted that the author of the articles offered not a whit of evidence that the practices he described were either representative or widespread.

I have no doubt that there are some bad actors in the buy-here, pay-here world. But nearly all of the bad acts cited by the reporter, if true, would have violated one or more of the laws and regulations mentioned above, or one or more of the laws or regulations would have provided redress to an aggrieved consumer. California doesn't need more laws—it needs to enforce the ones it has.

Lieu is either badly misinformed or is willing to ignore the facts in order to enact yet another law that would burden or drive out of business buy-here, pay-here dealers who play by the rules.

Unregulated? Makes you wonder what Senator Lieu thinks a regulated industry would look like.

August 2012
Passing Acquisition Fees Along to the Buyer?

This year's National Independent Automobile Dealers Association Conference featured lawyers everywhere you looked. That really wasn't surprising, considering the Dodd-Frank Act, the newly created Consumer Financial Protection Bureau, a newly invigorated and strengthened Federal Trade Commission, and state attorneys general stirred up by the 2012 FTC Roundtables. So, I suppose we should have expected the place to be flush with lawyers and legal presentations.

At one of the legal sessions at the conference, I presented with my partner, Patty Covington. Our topic was titled, "Hello, I'm Your Federal Regulator, and I'm Here to do a Compliance Audit," and our session was well attended.

After our prepared remarks, we turned, as planned, to Q&A from the many dealers in attendance. The dealers asked a lot of questions, but we got the same question, phrased in slightly different ways, from at least three dealers. After Patty and I were finished, I attended other legal sessions and heard the same, or nearly the same, question at least three more times. By my informal count, that made it the most frequently asked legal question at the conference.

The question went something like this: "My dealership sells some of its retail installment contracts—those involving buyers with less-than-stellar credit—to sales finance companies that charge acquisition fees. Can we pass those acquisition fees along to the customer, either by increasing the car's price or by showing the fee as a disclosed part of the Itemization of Amount Financed?"

For some dealers, the context was slightly different, but the issue was the same. They sold their contracts to sales finance companies at a discount to the amount financed. They had the same question: "Can I make the customer pay for the hit I'm going to take when I sell his installment contract at less than face value because he's got bad credit?" For the sake of simplicity, I'll limit this article to the acquisition fee version.

The short answer to the question of whether or not you can pass acquisition fees along to the customer is, "Probably not." Here's why.

Under the federal Truth in Lending Act, the general rule is that any amount a dealer charges for a vehicle in a credit transaction that exceeds the amount charged in a cash transaction, and any amount charged in credit transactions and not charged in cash transactions, is treated as a finance charge and included in the contract's APR. Under federal law, the amount would be treated as a "prepaid finance charge" for disclosure purposes. It cannot be added to the vehicle's selling price.

That actually isn't a big deal, though. TILA deals only with disclosure and does not limit the finance charges that a car dealer selling a car on credit may charge. Disclosing a prepaid finance

CHAPTER 5

charge can be difficult since not all retail installment contracts will accommodate a prepaid finance charge, but that problem could be overcome by using a form of contract that does.

The big deal arises under state law in the form of limits on the types and amounts of finance charges that can be assessed. Most state laws do not permit the imposition of a prepaid finance charge. Some of these laws, for example, permit only a finance charge that is calculated "on the declining balance of the contract." That rules out a prepaid finance charge.

In the states that do permit a prepaid finance charge, the amount or percentage of the charge may be limited, sometimes severely. For example, many states have a maximum permitted rate for motor vehicle retail installment sales transactions. If a prepaid finance charge is involved, it must be added to the other finance charges assessed to determine if the total exceeds the state's maximum rate.

Then there are the states that have no maximum limits set forth in their retail installment sales laws but that have criminal usury laws that set a limit on finance charges. These criminal usury limits also apply to dealers and credit sales. Because the finance charge rates for subprime credit are usually high to start with, it isn't hard to exceed a maximum rate cap or a criminal usury cap if the acquisition fee is more than nominal.

For federal disclosure purposes, there is a solution, of sorts. Dealers do not like it, and we get all sorts of pushback when we mention it.

Here it is: A dealer paying acquisition fees in connection with the sale of its contracts with its poor credit customers should determine (estimate) the aggregate amount of such fees that it will pay and should spread that aggregate amount over all cars it sells, including cars sold in cash transactions and cars sold to "good credit" customers. The aggregate amount of the fees should then be treated as an item of dealer overhead, like the light bill or the phone bill, and not allocated in any way to any particular transaction.

A dealer may object that the acquisition fees that he pays are so high that increasing the cost of all the cars in his inventory makes all the other cars too expensive, rendering his prices not competitive for customers with no credit problems. I understand that problem, but I have no solution that dealers will accept. Maybe there are some deals that, as a practical matter, simply cannot be financed.

We think the "spread the acquisition fees over the entire inventory" fix works for federal purposes. Any dealer who contemplates actually following this advice should not do so without consulting an experienced credit lawyer. For one thing, that lawyer might not agree with our analysis. For another, there may be state law problems lurking as well, and you'll need to have someone knowledgeable to give you the green light for those.

By the way, the second most frequently asked question was, "Can I give a discount when a buyer offers cash on the barrelhead?" That sounds like a good topic for my next article.

August 2012
Push it, Pull it, Drive it, or Drag it? Watch it!

Long ago (actually, in 1965), in a land far, far away (actually, the state of Georgia), I was selling mobile homes, mostly to the hill country folks from the rural areas around Gainesville. At age 21, I had dropped out of the University of Georgia to support my new wife and baby and was doing pretty well with this selling stuff. I was the "manager" of the lot where I worked, and my management duties involved one other salesman and a lot guy who doubled as a delivery driver.

CHAPTER 5

One day, a young fellow drove in and showed some interest in buying one of the 20 or so homes on my lot. He was driving a pickup but asked if I'd be interested in taking in trade a '53 Chevy convertible.

When I told him that we took anything in trade, he left and soon returned with a pretty yellow convertible with a white top. I had plenty of gross in the home he was interested in and gladly gave him $500 for the Chevy (don't snicker—in 1965, you could actually buy a decent ride for $500). The trade-in allowance was an amount that was about equal to the discount he could have bargained for. In effect, I "cleared" the trade, ending up with nothing in it, and, with my boss's approval, bought it from the mobile home dealership for a nominal sum as a gift for my 16-year-old brother.

I think about that yellow drop-top every time I see a dealer's ad screaming that the dealer will give $2,500 (or some amount) for any trade-in that the customer can "push, pull, drive, or drag" to the dealership. Call me cynical, but I think that what the dealer is actually doing is puffing the price of the car he's selling so he can inflate the amount he credits to the consumer for his nearly worthless trade-in sled. Duh.

You'll recall that a couple of months back, the Federal Trade Commission landed on five dealerships, alleging that the dealerships' negative equity ads ("we'll pay off your trade no matter what you owe") were unfair and deceptive. That may be just the beginning. The FTC has been focused on car dealers ever since their three Roundtables churned up a lot of criticisms about dealer practices.

Also, I think the FTC is feeling some competitive heat from the new Consumer Financial Protection Bureau. Not wanting to seem wimpy when it comes to protecting car buyers, the FTC has found new energy.

So, where will the FTC staffers go next? I don't think it's any sort of leap from challenging the practice of burying negative equity in an inflated cash price to burying a trade-in over-allowance in the same way.

So, the next time the ad guys come to you and ask you to bless a "push, pull, drive, or drag" ad, you might want to tell them they can push it—into the round file.

September 2012
Free Legal Advice on the Internet?

The Internet has us all spoiled. If you want to know who co-starred with Cary Grant in "North by Northwest," you just go to Google and type in a few key words. That should work just as well for legal research, right? Just find the right key words, and up pops your answer. Who needs law school?

A few weeks go by without my getting a call or an email from a frugal dealer who has a legal question that he has tried, unsuccessfully, to answer by doing research on the Internet. The dealer frequently isn't a client but assumes that we'll answer his question for free, which makes me wonder what his response would be if I asked him for a free car, but I digress.

The dealer has tried online search engines but has found that the Internet is filled with answers that don't quite fit the question. Many of the answers are from sources that are of questionable accuracy or from sources that have some ax to grind. A researcher who is aware of these problems will stick to primary sources—the actual laws and regulations that apply to the question at hand.

Finding those laws and regulations can be a challenge for those with legal training, much less for those without. If, for example, you don't know the difference between a "loan" and a

CHAPTER 5

"retail installment sale contract," you might end up finding the state laws and regulations that govern the activity of making a loan secured by an interest in a motor vehicle, but those provisions usually will have no application to the retail installment transactions that most dealers engage in when financing their car sales.

And even if you are able to find the laws and regulations that apply to your situation, you still need to know some of that law school stuff to decipher what you are looking at. Legal training teaches you that determining the meaning of the terms you are looking at is key to understanding a law or regulation. Knowing legal principles such as rules of statutory construction and preemption of state law by federal law can mean the difference between the right answer and the wrong answer. Also, courts often interpret laws and regulations in ways that are, shall we say, unexpected. Unless you are skillful enough to find the reported court cases that have interpreted the provisions you have found and to correctly analyze those cases, you may be missing the difference between "correct" and "oops."

All of which is not to say that the Internet can't be helpful in your compliance efforts (pardon the double negative). For years, we have suggested to dealers whose budgets simply don't permit them to hire lawyers to do compliance work for them that there are some inexpensive (sometimes free) resources available to them. Many of these resources can be found on the Internet.

We tell dealers to bookmark sites for the Federal Trade Commission, the Federal Reserve Board, the new Consumer Financial Protection Bureau, their state attorney general, their state consumer protection agency, their motor vehicle administration, and their state dealer association and to check them regularly. All of these sites are free, and some (particularly the FTC's site) contain a great deal of helpful, authoritative legal help.

But Internet legal research by people with no legal training? Reminds me of do-it-yourself brain surgery.

P.S. The co-star to Cary Grant in the Alfred Hitchcock film "North by Northwest" was Eva Marie Saint.

September 2012
Secret Agent Man (or Woman)

What if that next "up" is an undercover investigator working for the Consumer Financial Protection Bureau or the Federal Trade Commission who is posing as a car buyer? An article in the August 12 issue of the *Washington Times* reported that the Consumer Financial Protection Bureau is recruiting investigators in ads that suggest the agency may go undercover to pursue cases against companies that fall within its broad jurisdiction. And last year, the Federal Trade Commission hired a mystery shopper company.

The ad said that investigators may have to arrange for and oversee contracts with private investigators. The ads said that these private investigators "may know the players, culture, history in a specific geographic area in which a case is centered."

If that struggling single mother with marginal credit is in fact a Fed, maybe it's a bad idea to tell her that you've got to increase the price of the car she's landed on because you've found out that the only company that will buy the contract from you is a deep discounter.

If that young steelworker you are trying to get financed is really James Bond in disguise, maybe it would be a bad idea to tell him that he can't get credit unless his wife co-signs with him.

If that mild-mannered and seemingly gullible schoolteacher is really one of Elliot Ness's deputies, maybe telling her you can't

CHAPTER 5

get her financed unless she buys a service contract isn't a career-enhancing move.

Ditto telling the servicemember that you can't find financing unless she agrees to pay by allotment.

Or maybe you've advertised for a new F&I manager, and the applicant across from you is wearing a wire because he's really an undercover investigator. You probably don't want to describe for him the various not-quite-legal ways that he can get rich in your dealership by ripping customers' heads off.

You should be getting the idea by now.

If your dealership engages in these or other illegal or sleazy practices, every word in every encounter with someone who seems to be a customer or a potential employee could end up appearing in Exhibit One to the complaint the Bureau files against you. And, "encounter" includes face-to-face meetings, phone conversations, email chats, tweets, messaging, and any other form of communication.

And if, on top of those bad practices, you're training your sales and F&I employees to do things that violate the law, remember that the Consumer Financial Protection Bureau announced last fall that it wanted to hear from employees who were willing to "blow the whistle" on employers engaged in bad acts.

The lesson here? For the first time in a long time, the federal cops are on the dealership beat. If you're an independent dealer without a service department, or if you are a dealer and you or your related finance company hold and collect the retail installment sale contracts resulting from your sales, the Consumer Financial Protection Bureau is the enforcement agency you need to worry about. If you are a dealer with a servicing department and you don't hold your own contracts, your cop is the FTC.

Not that it matters which one you answer to—either one could ruin your entire day.

By the way, if you're looking for a really interesting job, the Bureau said the investigators would earn $98,000 to $149,000 per year.

October 2012
Do You Know the Risks of Not Knowing the Rules?

A recent court opinion illustrates the mischief that a dealer's advertisements can cause and the expense a dealer is likely to incur if the authorities decide to yank the dealer's chain over advertising content.

A New Jersey-based used car dealership has been ordered to disclose damage to and prior use of the vehicles it is offering for sale, after the attorney general and the New Jersey Division of Consumer Affairs sued the dealership.

The state alleged that Lencore Leasing, Inc., which does business as North Jersey Auto Mall and DCH Motors, and Lenny Belot, the owner/operator of the dealership, violated the Consumer Fraud Act, Used Car Lemon Law, and Motor Vehicle Advertising Regulations in their advertisement, offering for sale, and sale of used motor vehicles.

A superior court judge recently granted the state's request to stop the dealership from advertising and selling used vehicles without disclosing prior damage and/or prior use, pending a hearing on the state's request for preliminary injunctive and other relief. The judge also granted the state's request for the appointment of a temporary monitor for the dealership.

"Used cars are not inexpensive. Consumers who are spending thousands of dollars for a used vehicle are legally entitled to be told if the vehicle has sustained prior damage or if

CHAPTER 5

it's been used as a fleet or rental vehicle," Attorney General Jeffrey S. Chiesa said.

The state's complaint identified 51 used vehicles that the defendants allegedly offered for sale that, by the state's calculation, had a cumulative $213,758 in undisclosed damage. The state also alleged that, in some instances, consumers were told that vehicles were "absolutely mint in and out" or were "in pristine condition" when that was not the case.

The opinion dealt only with a motion by the state to regulate the dealer's actions pending a hearing on the state's motion for injunctive relief. So, it is possible that, as the matter proceeds, we'll find out that there are facts more favorable to the dealer, but that's down the road a bit.

Right now, we're looking at a dealer who has been hauled into court and ordered to stop doing things that the attorney general characterizes as being illegal. The dealer has had his reputation impugned and, presumably, has incurred the cost of hiring a lawyer and going to court to defend against the state's claims. Before the matter is resolved, it's likely that the AG will seek to recover for consumers the estimated dollar amount of the undisclosed damage and will attempt to impose monetary penalties, as well. To add insult to injury, the AG may also seek to stick the dealer with the AG's own costs of litigation, as well as court costs. The aggregate sum of all of these amounts would be an expense that would put a lot of smaller dealerships out of business.

What do you do to avoid these dire consequences? Well, you could have a lawyer review all your ads (keep in mind that this includes anything you are doing on the Internet, as well as through social media, and it especially includes anything an outside advertising or promotion company tries to sell you). You might choke at the idea of paying for such a professional review, but the amount you'll pay pales in comparison with the recent hits dealers have taken in AG advertising enforcement actions—fines of $250,000 are not unusual.

If you aren't convinced that having a lawyer review your ads is the way to go, or you simply don't have the resources for that, how about creating an internal advertising checklist and implementing it?

Determine what advertising laws and regulations apply in your state. Go to your state auto dealer association and/or independent auto dealer association, and ask if they have advertising guidelines. Many associations have such materials, and some are very good. Go to the Federal Trade Commission's website, and glom onto the excellent advertising guideline material there. Then go to the principal federal regulations that govern advertising for credit sales and leases, Regulations Z and M, and add the advertising materials from those regulations to your pile.

When you have gathered everything you can find, ask your lawyer if you've correctly identified all the applicable provisions, and ask if you've missed any (I know, you're trying not to spend bucks on lawyers, but sometimes you just have to bite the old bullet).

Train someone at your dealership to be your advertising specialist. Provide that person with all of the materials you have been able to locate, and give him or her enough of a budget so that when questions arise over the advertising requirements, he or she can call the lawyer for help.

Remember that the world turns. Nothing stays the same, and that's true for the laws and regulations that affect advertising. Schedule a periodic update of your advertising requirements. Your lawyer can help you decide how frequently the updating should take place.

CHAPTER 5

Another time-consuming, pain-in-the-rear compliance requirement? Absolutely.

More expense? Yup.

But there is no alternative, unless you count closing the dealership before the AG does it for you, taking the money, and opening that bait shop.

December 2012
Dumpster Diving

One of the first things that we do when we conduct an on-site dealer or finance company compliance audit is go dumpster diving to see if we can find confidential customer information protected by federal law tossed in a circular file accessible by the public. OK, we don't actually put on our garbage man overalls and crawl in the dumpster, but we do ask a lot of pointed questions about what goes into the trash cans, and we ask for a copy of the dealership's federally required disposal policy. We also peek in the trash cans that sit beside the desks of salespeople and F&I folks.

The whole process usually elicits a blank stare, which is a bit odd. It's odd because, for a number of years, federal law has required creditors to safeguard and properly dispose of protected consumer information.

Maybe the recent news that the Federal Trade Commission tagged a company with a $100,000 civil penalty will make dealers pay attention. According to the FTC's press release, here's what happened.

A company that provides management services to more than 300 payday loan and check cashing stores and an affiliated company that owns and operates several stores agreed to pay $101,500 to settle FTC charges that it violated federal law by allowing sensitive consumer information to be tossed into trash dumpsters.

The FTC charged that PLS Financial Services, Inc., and The Payday Loan Store of Illinois, Inc., failed to take reasonable measures to protect consumer information, resulting in the disposal of documents containing sensitive personal identifying information—including Social Security numbers, employment information, loan applications, bank account information, and credit reports—in unsecured dumpsters near several of their retail loan and check cashing locations. PLS Group, Inc., which owns PLS Financial Services and The Payday Loan Store of Illinois, was also named in the lawsuit.

According to the FTC's complaint, PLS Financial Services and The Payday Loan Store of Illinois violated the FTC's Disposal Rule by failing to take reasonable steps to protect against unauthorized access to consumer information in the disposal of credit reports. They also allegedly violated the Gramm-Leach-Bliley Safeguards Rule and Privacy Rule, which require financial institutions to develop and use safeguards to protect consumer information and to deliver privacy notices to consumers.

If the FTC's allegations are correct, the companies failed to properly protect consumer information. That would have been bad enough, but the FTC also charged that all three defendants violated the FTC Act by misrepresenting that they had implemented reasonable measures to protect sensitive consumer information. The apparent translation of this charge is that the companies had privacy policies, or at least gave consumers notice of their privacy policies, but then ignored their own policies.

The FTC alleged that PLS Group owns approximately two dozen operating companies, such as The Payday Loan Store of Illinois, that in turn own and operate more than 300 retail stores in nine states under the names PLS Loan Stores and PLS Check Cashers. These stores offer a variety of products and services, including payday loans, check cashing, automobile title loans, debit cards, phone cards, and notary services. PLS Financial Services provides management services to the PLS Loan Stores and PLS Check Cashers locations, including establishing their policies and procedures for the handling and disposal of consumer financial information.

In addition to the $101,500 civil penalty imposed on PLS Financial Services and The Payday Loan Store of Illinois for violation of the Disposal Rule, the settlement bars all of the companies from violating the Disposal, Safeguards, and Privacy Rules and from misrepresenting the extent to which they maintain and protect the privacy and integrity of personal information.

The order also requires that the companies implement and maintain a data security program with independent third-party audits every other year for the next 20 years and imposes bookkeeping and recordkeeping provisions to allow the FTC to monitor compliance with the order.

The consent judgment, by its terms, is for settlement purposes only and does not constitute an admission that the law has been violated. Consent judgments have the force of law when approved and signed by the district court judge.

This is the third time the FTC has charged a violation of the Disposal Rule, which requires that companies dispose of credit reports and information derived from them in a safe and secure manner. What lessons do actions like these have for dealers and finance companies?

First, it's evident that the FTC is serious about enforcing the privacy rules. Second, you can't comply with the privacy rules by crafting a policy and then putting it on a bookshelf and ignoring it. Finally, the policy needs to be one that the organization's privacy officer (also required by federal law) is charged with implementing and maintaining, and the privacy officer needs to be fired if something like this happens.

At least that's what would happen if he or she worked for me.

December 2012
Cheese Moving

Who Moved My Cheese? An Amazing Way to Deal with Change in Your Work and in Your Life is the title of a 1998 motivational book written by Spencer Johnson. The book deals with the reaction of the book's characters, two mice and two miniature humans who live in a maze, to the disappearance of a supply of cheese that they had come to rely on for sustenance. It's a parable that deals with change and the reaction that people have to change. One of my favorite points in the book occurs when one of the characters writes on the wall, "If You Do Not Change, You Can Become Extinct."

I thought about cheese, change, and extinction as I pondered a recent release by the Consumer Financial Protection Bureau titled "Supervisory Highlights: Fall 2012." It is evident from that document that the CFPB is involved in some pretty hefty cheese-moving. If you haven't read the full report, you should, but I want to share with you a couple of particularly interesting parts.

The report announces that a "critical component of a well-run financial institution is a robust and effective compliance management system (CMS), designed to ensure that the financial institution's policies and practices are in full compliance with the requirements of Federal consumer financial law." The

CHAPTER 5

CFPB describes a CMS program as including internal controls and oversight, training, internal monitoring, consumer complaint response, independent testing and audit, third-party service provider oversight, recordkeeping, product development and business acquisition, and marketing practices.

It is clear that the CFPB is moving the compliance cheese. If it was ever sufficient for a creditor to simply avoid violating the law, it is clear that "nonviolation" will no longer suffice. Now, an institution that is subject to the CFPB's supervision will have to be able to demonstrate that

- it has a compliance playbook subject to internal controls;
- its employees, officers, and directors understand the playbook, abide by it, and receive continuing training regarding its contents;
- the playbook is independently tested and audited;
- consumer complaint processes are in place and followed;
- there is third-party service provider oversight;
- it maintains appropriate recordkeeping; and
- it exercises appropriate consideration during product development, business acquisition, and marketing practices of compliance issues and ramifications.

The Bureau will require each entity it supervises to develop and maintain a sound CMS that is integrated into its overall framework and applied to its entire product and service lifecycle.

The CFPB says that it understands that compliance management will be handled differently by big and complex financial organizations at one end of the spectrum and by small entities with a narrow range of financial products and services at the other end. Whether or not the institution is big and complicated or small and focused does not matter; the CFPB expects compliance management activities to be a priority and to be appropriate for the nature, size, and complexity of the institution's consumer business and expects the institution to establish an effective CMS to ensure legal compliance.

The CFPB's pronouncements regarding CMS have come in connection with discussions about entities that the CFPB will supervise. In the car finance field, that will mean the "larger participants" in auto financing. Auto creditors that find themselves outside the "larger participants" supervised group shouldn't assume that they will receive a free pass from the CFPB. Even a smaller participant with a bucketful of consumer complaints can find itself in the "directly supervised" category.

The Bureau's opening enforcement salvos have not been aimed at the auto finance market, although its actions that deal with credit card marketing service providers offer some lessons to auto creditors and dealers regarding their responsibilities. Don't be fooled into thinking that the CFPB won't be interested in auto finance.

You'll see some serious cheese-moving in 2013. Remember, "If you do not change, you can become extinct."

December 2012
The Feds Prowl for Advertising Violations

Because our law firm represents all sorts of creditors, not just those involved in auto credit, I have the advantage of being able to look over my partners' shoulders and see legal developments in other credit markets. That happened a few days ago when I picked up a development that my car folks need to know about. Here's what happened.

The Federal Trade Commission staff has just fired a few shots, in the form of warning letters, across the bows of 20 real estate agents, home builders, and lead generators, warning them that their ads may be deceptive. The FTC urged the companies to review their advertisements for compliance with the Mortgage Acts and Practices Advertising Rule and the FTC Act.

The FTC sent the letters in coordination with the Consumer Financial Protection Bureau, and the Bureau also issued warning letters to approximately a dozen other companies. The CFPB sent its warning letters to mortgage brokers and lenders. Both agencies have opened nonpublic law enforcement investigations of other advertisers that may have violated federal law.

The agencies reported that they had reviewed approximately 800 mortgage ads from a wide variety of media, including websites, Facebook, direct mail, and newspapers. The agencies seek to spur compliance with the Mortgage Acts and Practices Advertising Rule, since rule-making authority for it transferred from the FTC to the CFPB. The rule prohibits material misrepresentations in advertising or any other commercial communication regarding consumer mortgages. The FTC and the CFPB share enforcement authority over nonbank mortgage advertisers, such as mortgage lenders, brokers, servicers, and advertising agencies. Mortgage advertisers that violate the rule may be required to pay civil penalties.

The agencies' review revealed several types of troubling claims that could be misleading to consumers. The agencies' review found, for example:

- advertisements offering a very low "fixed" mortgage rate, without discussing significant loan terms;
- advertisements containing statements, images, symbols, and abbreviations that suggest that an advertiser is affiliated with a government agency; and
- advertisements "guaranteeing" approval and offering very low monthly payments, without discussing significant conditions on these offers.

If these ads sound familiar, it's because very similar ads appear in the car finance world every day, especially in the buy-here, pay-here world. Many dealer ads talk about "low rates" without mentioning important conditions that apply to such rates, such as substantial downpayments or strong credit ratings.

I've reviewed many a direct mail piece that is dummied up to look like a piece of government correspondence, complete with the "government brown" envelope and a reference to some nondescript department that sounds vaguely like a governmental entity, festooned with enough eagles to start an aviary.

And as for the third ad referenced above, how many dealer ads have you seen that say something like "We finance everyone" or "Nobody walks"?

If you haven't been diligent about having the content of your ads reviewed for legal compliance and rooting out any statements that the regulators could claim are unfair or deceptive, then you should treat these warning shots as ones aimed directly at you. If you need any encouragement in this regard, note the language above that the advertisers "may be required to pay civil penalties."

And if you think that you don't need to worry about enforcement actions regarding your ads because you farm your ads out to some direct mail house or other ad provider that has "never been sued," think again. The Bureau and the FTC will hold you responsible for your ads' content just as if you had drafted them yourself.

CHAPTER 5

Chapter 6

2013: Rolling Out the Heavy Artillery

CHAPTER 6

In 2013, the CFPB hit its stride. No longer a fledgling agency, it took on creditors, including car dealers, in ways that made it clear that it was no longer "compliance enforcement as usual" in Washington, D.C. The FTC was not content to let the CFPB hog the spotlight, and turned to fruit that was so low hanging it was on the ground—dealer advertising violations—and proceeded to cut a swath through a host of widespread dealer advertising violations. Dealers were "shocked, I tell you, shocked" to find out that ad campaigns that they had been running for years were filled with blatant federal disclosure violations or were unfair or deceptive. For the FTC, the enforcement headlines were easy to come by.

And just to throw a little hot oil on the fire, a legislator took aim at a dealer practice called "spot delivery." The legislative effort fizzled, but the attempt to prohibit or severely limit the practice provided a fitting backdrop for all the other federal anti-dealer fire coming from D.C.

January/February 2013
Playing with Fire

I'm a reformed arsonist. At about age six or so, a neighbor kid my age and I were, quite literally, playing with matches at the edge of a line of pine woods bordering the family property in north Georgia. You know the result—fire, sirens and fire trucks, three blackened acres, and, for me, a very sore rear end.

I thought of this episode from my misspent youth when an item crossed my desk recently. Except that, this time, it was dealers playing with fire. And this time the fire was the Federal Trade Commission.

The FTC announced that its Southwest Region Office warned 11 used car dealerships in Jonesboro, Arkansas, that their sales practices violate the FTC's Used Car Rule, which requires used car dealers to display a "Buyers Guide" detailing warranty and other important information on the cars they sell.

The FTC staff found that eight dealers failed to display Buyers Guides on almost all used cars offered for sale, and three dealers failed to display the guides on a significant number of used cars. The FTC sent warning letters urging the 11 dealers to come into compliance by properly displaying the guides in a clear and conspicuous location on all used cars.

Ten other dealers were apparently doing it correctly, properly displaying the guides on all or nearly all of the used cars offered for sale. We could not confirm the rumor that all the dealers doing it correctly were *Spot Delivery* subscribers.

"We are glad to see that a significant number of used car dealers in Jonesboro, Arkansas, are in substantial compliance with the Used Car Rule by properly displaying Buyers Guides on their used cars offered for sale. We believe these Rule requirements are important to consumers in determining to purchase a used car," said Deanya Kueckelhan, director of the FTC's Southwest Region in the FTC announcement. "We hope the rest of the Jonesboro's used car dealerships will be in full compliance shortly."

The FTC makes ongoing efforts to enforce the Used Car Rule, in conjunction with state and local officials. The FTC has brought more than 80 actions since the rule took effect in 1985, with civil penalties totaling more than $1 million. Hundreds of state actions also have been brought to enforce the rule.

On December 4, 2012, the FTC announced that it is seeking public comment on proposed changes to the Buyers Guide. The FTC also issued a final rule that makes technical corrections and revises the Spanish translation of the guide. The FTC last reviewed and amended the Used Car Rule in 1995.

CHAPTER 6

The Used Car Rule requires that Buyers Guides be displayed at all times on each vehicle offered for sale, stating

- if the vehicle comes with a warranty and, if so, whether it is a "full" or limited warranty;
- which systems are covered by the warranty and the duration of the warranty period;
- if it is a limited warranty, what percentage of the cost for covered parts and labor the dealer will pay for;
- if the car is sold with no written or implied warranty or, in other words, the car is sold "as is;" or
- if the car is sold with no written warranty, but with implied warranties. (Some states and Washington, D.C., do not allow dealers to sell cars without implied warranties.)

The Used Car Rule also provides that the Buyers Guide becomes a part of the sales contract and overrides any contrary provisions contained in the contract. The Buyers Guide also contains important warnings and suggestions for consumers, such as asking the dealer if they can have a mechanic inspect the car they are considering. The guide warns consumers not to rely on spoken promises, which may be impossible to enforce. Instead, consumers should ask the dealer to put any promises in writing on the guide and in the sales contract. If the sales negotiation for the vehicle is in Spanish, a Spanish-language version of the guide must be used, and the contract language referencing the guide must be in Spanish.

Why do I say that these dealers were playing with fire? First, the FTC is a powerful federal agency with essentially an unlimited budget and strong enforcement powers. You don't want to give the FTC the idea that you don't much care about one of its rules that has been around for decades.

Second, this announcement is likely to be picked up by the plaintiffs' bar. If that happens, we won't be surprised to see lawsuits alleging that the violation of this federal regulation constitutes an unfair or deceptive act or practice under a state's UDAP law. That's an argument we've seen used successfully before.

Finally, the FTC's announcement of its actions in this case stated, "The FTC appreciates the assistance of Legal Aid of Arkansas in this matter." So, not only is the FTC chewing on these dealers, it appears that the local Legal Aid office is aware of their compliance shortcomings regarding the Used Car Rule. The Legal Aid and plaintiffs' lawyers are likely to conclude that if these dealers are ignoring a fairly simple, decades-old rule like this one, the rest of their compliance efforts are likely to be slipshod, too.

Maybe it's time to call the fire brigade.

March 2013
Don't Look Now, But Things Have Changed

Sometimes things change in Washington, D.C., and sometimes they don't. For all the recent talk about gridlock and nothing getting done in the nation's capital, there are some extremely broad-reaching changes in the works for any business that offers a financial product or service to a consumer.

If you've been doing a "Rip Van Winkle" for the past few years, and you just woke up, you'll find that the regulatory scenery has been drastically altered. Dominating the scene is the Consumer Financial Protection Bureau (CFPB), a creation of the Dodd-Frank Act.

The CFPB, created in 2010, actually came into being in July 2011. The young agency is beginning to make some waves. As it does, we're beginning to see how this new sheriff thinks.

I've been slow to recognize one of the biggest changes from the previous federal regulatory regime. It has only dawned on

CHAPTER 6

me in the last few weeks (as I have spoken to several industry groups about how they need to prepare themselves for a visit from the new sheriff) that it is no longer enough for a creditor or lessor to say, "I have not violated the law." For the last several decades, a creditor or lessor that had not violated the law had little to worry about from federal or state regulators.

Those days are over. Gone like yesterday.

Now, a creditor or lessor must be able to demonstrate that it is not violating the law—but that will be just the first step in satisfying the new Bureau. The Bureau's response to your "I'm not violating the law" statement will be something like, "That's interesting, but show us how you go about making sure that you don't violate the law."

It's a bit like being stopped by a traffic cop when you were not speeding and receiving a ticket for not having a recent eye examination or not reading the car's owner's manual.

The Bureau's early examination efforts have created a phrase that we didn't have before. The Bureau expects to see a "Compliance Management System" in place. That CMS, as we'll call it, will be your evidence that your company is taking active steps to identify all the laws and regulations that apply to it and is conforming its operations to comply with them. The Bureau is also very keen on evaluating the risk of harm that creditors and lessors pose to consumers. The Bureau sees a well-done and well-run CMS as a means of reducing the risk of harm to consumers.

A CMS will have several key elements. First, a CMS will be the subject of board and senior management oversight. This isn't one of those pesky chores you can push down the chain of command in hopes that you don't hear about it again.

The CMS will revolve around a written compliance program that will cover the financial products that you offer from product design through the final contact with the customer. The CMS will incorporate a robust complaint resolution program designed to identify problem areas and satisfy consumer complaints. The company will be expected to have auditable compliance processes and procedures to reduce or eliminate harm to consumers and to frequently conduct compliance audits to determine if those processes and procedures are working as designed. The CMS will also incorporate risk management measures to identify and reduce or eliminate the risk of compliance violations.

A year ago, I don't think I had ever heard the term "compliance management system." Now I'm telling clients who are or may soon be subject to the CFPB's supervisory authority that they need to have a CMS in place sooner rather than later. And I'm telling clients who aren't subject to the Bureau's supervisory authority that a CMS is now an industry "best practice."

The country voted for "change." Looks like we got some.

April 2013
Complain, Complain, Complain

Car dealers don't have to worry about one of the Consumer Financial Protection Bureau's examination teams appearing at the door any time soon. Indeed, franchised dealers who don't hold their own retail installment contracts or leases will probably never have that concern.

But even a dealer that isn't likely to be subjected to the Bureau's examination process should pay attention to the Bureau's examination materials. There is a treasure trove of information to be found there. A good example is the Bureau's discussion of how its supervised entities are expected to handle complaints.

CHAPTER 6

The Bureau summarizes its overall view of the handling of consumer complaints as follows: "An effective compliance management system should ensure that a supervised entity is responsive and responsible in handling consumer complaints and inquiries. Intelligence gathered from consumer contacts should be organized, retained, and used as part of an institution's compliance management system."

The Bureau then instructs its examiners on what to look for in an entity's consumer complaint response process. Examiners are to determine if

- consumer complaints and inquiries, regardless of where submitted, are appropriately recorded and categorized;
- complaints and inquiries, whether regarding the entity or its service providers, are addressed and resolved promptly;
- complaints raising legal issues involving potential consumer harm from unfair treatment or discrimination, or other regulatory compliance issues, are appropriately escalated;
- complaint data and individual cases drive adjustments to business practices as appropriate;
- consumer complaints result in retrospective corrective action to correct the effects of the entity's actions, when appropriate; and
- weaknesses in the compliance management system exist, based on the nature or number of substantive complaints from consumers.

The Bureau instructs its examiners to review records, interview management, and contact consumers, if needed, to evaluate this consumer response component of the compliance management system.

It further admonishes the examiners to

- obtain and review records of recent consumer complaints and inquiries received by the CFPB about the entity and

its service providers;
- review industry or other benchmarking complaint data collected by the CFPB;
- to the extent available, obtain and review records of recent consumer complaints against the entity from the entity's regulators, from state attorneys general offices or licensing and registration agencies, and from private or other industry sources;
- request and review from the entity its policies and procedures for receiving, escalating, and resolving consumer complaints and inquiries;
- request and review the record of consumer complaints and inquiries received by the entity for a specific recent period of time;
- identify complaints alleging deception, unfair treatment, unlawful discrimination, or other significant consumer injury, and review some or all of those complaints for handling, timeliness, disposition, and any prospective and retrospective corrective actions;
- determine if corrective action is offered or taken for any complaint resulting in a conclusion of violation of law or regulation;
- determine if complaints involving service providers or other third parties referring business to the supervised entity receive prompt and appropriate handling and follow-up by the entity;
- if the entity maintains multiple consumer response centers or units, determine if it employs a common set of best practices, as applicable;
- determine if evaluations of consumer contacts are shared within the entity and included in compliance management reporting to the Board and senior management and if

CHAPTER 6

such information is used in modifying policies, procedures, training, and monitoring; and
- draw preliminary conclusions regarding the strength, adequacy, or weakness of the entity's response to consumer issues and concerns, and identify business conduct areas, specific regulations, or organizational units for more detailed review.

Where am I going with all of this? I'm suggesting that if your dealership does not have a written, well-thought-out, and robust complaint system, you should consider instituting one. The system should, at a minimum, record and categorize inquiries and complaints, require that they be addressed and resolved promptly, and require that they lead to adjustments in business practices and corrective action where appropriate.

The system should include a process for analyzing the complaint data and the periodic reporting of complaint data and analysis to management. The analysis does not have to be sophisticated. For example, if the complaints are categorized, that information alone can be instructive. If a dealership is getting multiple complaints about a particular product, there may be some consumer confusion surrounding that product. The complaint data can reveal patterns that management should carefully consider. Maybe salespeople or F&I managers need to be re-trained (assuming they were initially trained) on the product.

Or the dealership may be getting multiple complaints about a particular employee—say, that the employee told the customer X, but the customer later learns Y. That pattern might indicate that the employee might be engaged in unfair or deceptive trade practices. This information should prompt management to investigate and, if a problem is discovered, address the problem and remediate with respect to affected customers.

For complaints received, any that appear to involve consumer harm or violations of consumer protection laws should be moved to the front burner, and the entire complaint process should be reviewed from time to time.

The dealership should approve the complaint process at the highest management level, and management should designate someone to manage the complaint process. In order to provide the oversight such a program will require, that person should take the role of the "examiner" as outlined in the second set of bulleted points on the previous pages.

Are you required to take these or similar steps under current law? Whether you are or are not, consider doing so anyway. That way, when your regulator comes calling and asks to see your complaint process, you'll be ready.

April 2013
The CFPB Fires a Warning Shot on Fair Lending

Before I say a word about the Consumer Financial Protection Bureau's recently released fair lending guidance, I have to rant.

It frustrates me to see the Bureau mischaracterizing the dealer-assisted financing business by referring to "loans," "lenders," and "borrowers." In a typical dealer financing transaction, there are no "loans," there are no "lenders," and there are no "borrowers." Credit buyers sign retail installment sale contracts in which they promise to pay for their cars over time. Dealers then sell these contracts to banks and sales finance companies.

There are important distinctions between loans and retail installment sales—a very obvious difference is that loans and retail installment sales may be subject to different maximum finance charge limits, late charges, grace periods,

CHAPTER 6

and repossession remedies. The Bureau has announced that it believes that educating consumers about credit is important. Why not set an example by correctly describing these transactions?

But let's forget my rant and move on to the release itself.

The introductory paragraph indicates the scope of the bulletin's guidance. "This bulletin provides guidance about compliance with the fair lending requirements of the Equal Credit Opportunity Act . . . and Regulation B, for indirect auto lenders that permit dealers to increase consumer interest rates and that compensate dealers with a share of the increased interest revenues." That might make you think that banks and finance companies that don't permit dealers to increase a "buy rate" to determine the consumer's finance charge rate are not subject to the "guidance." You need to keep reading.

The Bureau release then discusses the background of dealer financing for a page or so, mostly accurately except for the aforementioned incorrect characterizations regarding loans and lenders.

For the better part of a page, the Bureau holds forth on why "indirect lenders" are creditors under the ECOA and Reg. B. The Bureau then offers an unconvincing explanation of why Reg. B's language providing that one creditor isn't responsible for the ECOA violations of another creditor in the same transaction doesn't always apply. The guidance then gratuitously points out that the provision gives a creditor no cover with regard to its own violations.

Finally, the guidance gets around to the meat of the matter. If you are going to engage in a program of buying retail installment contracts and permitting dealers to "mark up" your buy rate, then, says the Bureau, you need to impose controls on dealer markup and compensation policies or revise your existing

2013: ROLLING OUT THE HEAVY ARTILLERY

policies, and you need to monitor and address the effects of those policies.

Don't want to hire a bunch of lawyers and statisticians and otherwise increase your expenses by riding herd on your dealers' pricing polices? No sweat, says the Bureau. Just stop giving dealers discretion to mark up the rate, and compensate them some other way, like paying a flat fee for each contract.

You'll have to hire those lawyers and statisticians anyway, though, because the guidance goes on to describe the sort of fair lending program it expects to see. Such a program involves an up-to-date fair lending policy, regular training for employees, officers, and board members, compliance monitoring, and review of credit policies for potential violations, including potential disparate impact. It would also involve, depending on the size and complexity of the organization, regular analysis of account data to identify potential disparities in pricing, underwriting, or other aspects of your transactions.

In addition, the Bureau will expect to see regular assessments of your marketing and, finally, oversight by your management of your fair lending practices. All of these steps will be necessary, says the Bureau, regardless of whether or not you retain a dealer participation model.

If you decide that you'll keep your participation model, plan on taking on some additional burdens. The Bureau will expect you to communicate with your dealers, educating them on the ECOA, stating your compliance expectations, and reminding them of their obligation to price in a nondiscriminatory manner. You'll also need to analyze your accounts for pricing data, both on a portfolio-wide basis and on a dealer-specific basis, to look for problems resulting from dealer markup and compensation policies. You'll need to take action against any problem dealers you identify and promptly remunerate affected customers.

CHAPTER 6

It would have been nice if the Bureau, more in keeping with its "transparency" mantra, had elected to proceed by rulemaking rather than by issuing this "guidance." The rulemaking process might have provided a forum for the discussion of the Bureau's supporting research and conclusions regarding discrimination. As it is, we don't get to see the Bureau's methodology, findings, and conclusions.

There's a lot more to this debate, I expect, than appears from this guidance, and all the participants who have an interest, including dealers and the regulators who oversee dealers, should have a chance to offer competing views before the government starts making policy decisions.

May 2013
They Don't Care!

I admit I'm a Tommy Lee Jones fan. I'd buy a ticket to watch him read the phone directory. His recent appearances in "Lincoln" and "The Emperor" have made my movie year, so far.

But it was one of his earlier works that came to mind recently as I contemplated some of the stories circulating about the supervisory and enforcement actions of the Consumer Financial Protection Bureau.

In the 1993 movie "The Fugitive," Jones appeared with Harrison Ford. Ford played the part of Richard Kimble, a wealthy doctor wrongfully convicted of murdering his wife (who was really killed by a mysterious one-armed man, but you knew that). On his way to prison, Kimble escapes. Deputy Samuel Gerard, played by Jones, doggedly pursues Kimble.

Kimble is apparently cornered when the ambulance he has stolen as a getaway vehicle is trapped in a long tunnel that is part of a huge hydroelectric dam. Kimble slides into the drainage

2013: ROLLING OUT THE HEAVY ARTILLERY

system underneath the road, with Gerard hot on his heels. In my favorite scene, Gerard catches up with Kimble just as the tunnel Kimble has been following ends in a several-hundred-foot drop down the waterfall at the front of the dam.

"Stop," says Gerard. Kimble turns and, facing Gerard, shouts, "I didn't kill my wife."

Gerard, using words that could be the motto of the CFPB, responds, shouting, "I don't care!" Kimble then turns and takes a pretty swan-dive header down the face of the dam, escaping yet again.

That's the phrase that got me thinking about the Bureau. When I listen to my clients complain about the CFPB's latest activities, I can hear Deputy Gerard, as the Bureau's spokesperson, repeatedly responding, "We don't care."

So, for instance, when my industry friends bemoan the fact that they're being steamrolled by regulation when the car finance business had little or nothing to do with the recent financial meltdown, the Bureau says, "We don't care."

When my car finance friends complain that they never intentionally discriminate on a prohibited basis when extending credit, but that the Bureau has stated that intent doesn't matter—"disparate impact" is all they need—the Bureau says, "We don't care."

When dealers and finance companies complain that the Bureau's new prohibition on "abusive" practices rests on a term, "abusive," that the Bureau is unable or unwilling to define, and that they are unable to determine what is and isn't prohibited, the Bureau says, "We don't care."

And, finally, when our clients tote up the cost of developing a compliance management system, hiring compliance personnel, reworking policies and procedures, preparing for examinations, and actually undergoing examinations and object that all those

CHAPTER 6

costs result in very little benefit to consumers, the Bureau all but screams, "We don't care."

The Bureau's indifference to these complaints should not be surprising. The Bureau was created to protect consumers. That is its legislative mandate. It makes no effort to follow an even-handed approach to the problems it finds in the credit marketplace. It identifies those problems and sets out to protect the interests of its designated protectees—consumers.

Got a problem with that?

They don't care.

May 2013
To the CFPB: Thanks for the Non-Guidance

A few weeks ago, the Consumer Financial Protection Bureau created a big stir in the world of dealer financing, firing a shot across the bow of any company that buys retail installment contracts from dealers. In the last few days, dealers have been receiving communications from such companies that indicate that the companies intend to do much more to supervise the dealers' discretion in setting financing rates for their customers.

What's going on here? The Bureau has been rattling its sabers about fair lending for many months, but this is the Bureau's first foray into discrimination in auto finance.

There's a logical disconnect between the CFPB's world view on what it calls "fair lending" and the reality of the process of dealer financing. There are multiple models, even within a single dealership, for determining how installment contracts get sold. By its public statements, the Bureau perceives that dealers take a credit application, collect "buy rates" from interested finance companies, then mark up those rates and present them to consumers. That is one model, but it is not necessarily the predominant model.

Take, for example, the spot delivery. The dealer has pulled a credit report on the customer and sees he has a 770 Beacon score. The dealer negotiates the transaction (including the setting of the rate), and the customer drives off before a finance company has had a first look. Why? Because the dealer knows that one of his finance companies will buy that transaction at the rate the customer agreed to (and, presumably, was perfectly happy with).

The Bureau's vision of how the business works is flawed. The model the Bureau seems to envision is but one way the messy world of dealer financing operates. A typical dealer will have arrangements with several contract buyers—finance companies, banks, and credit unions—to sell them retail installment contracts entered into between the dealer and consumers. It isn't unusual for a dealer to sell contracts to a half-dozen such contract buyers, and many dealers deal with many more than that. A dealer with a number of potential contract buyers may sell his contracts to many different contract buyers, so a single contract buyer may end up buying only a small percentage (sometimes single digits) of the dealer's contracts. Each such contract buyer will have its own "buy rate." Each will also impose a maximum rate for contracts it is willing to buy.

Negotiations between the dealer and the consumer will determine the rate to be imposed in connection with a particular transaction. That rate will be at least as high as the buy rates of the dealer's contract buyers, but will not exceed the maximum rates that the dealer's contract buyers specify.

The dealer will have a good idea of which rates are offered by each of the various entities he deals with (as well as the rates of local competing banks and credit unions) and will know the

197

CHAPTER 6

credit risk tolerance of each of the entities. He will typically send the consumer's credit application to a number of potential contract buyers. Typically, several will respond with an approval of the deal, indicating that if the dealer completes the deal with the consumer, they would be willing to buy the retail installment contract from the dealer. Note that none of the approving contract buyers will have any obligation to buy a contract once they have approved the deal. The dealer, in effect, has a "put" option; an approving company does not have a "call."

If Bank A's buy rate is 6%, Finance Company B's buy rate is 5.5%, and Credit Union C's buy rate is 5.75%, and the dealer and the consumer agree to a rate of 7%, the dealer may elect to sell the contract to A, B, or C. The amount the dealer earns on the contract will depend on which entity buys the contract. The dealer might elect to sell the contract to Bank A because Bank A provides floor plan financing to the dealer. The dealer might elect to sell the contract to Finance Company B because Finance Company B's buying process is not as rigorous as the buying processes of other potential contract buyers—in effect giving up a little revenue in exchange for less hassle. Or the dealer might decide to sell the contract to Credit Union C because the sales rep for Credit Union C is his next door neighbor, and he likes her.

Note that the dealer's decision about which contract buyer to sell the contract to does not affect the 7% finance charge rate that the consumer pays. Also note that the potential contract buyers do not know how many other potential contract buyers there may be or the buy rates and caps of the other potential contract buyers.

How, under these real-world facts, does the Bureau impose liability for credit discrimination on companies buying retail installment contracts?

How, indeed. The Bureau employs a disputed legal theory called "disparate impact." Under the disparate impact theory, intent to discriminate is not a requirement. The Bureau looks at the aggregate pricing imposed by the dealer and looks for patterns of illegal discrimination, primarily in the areas of race, ethnicity, and gender. When the target of the Bureau's inquiry is a contract buyer, the Bureau looks at the contract buyer's data on a dealer-by-dealer basis and on a "portfolio-wide" basis.

Because there is presently no requirement for dealers financing vehicles to collect data on each consumer regarding race or ethnicity, the Bureau employs certain "proxies" in looking for prohibited discrimination. For example, if the consumer's zip code is one in which 80% of the residents are African American, the Bureau might assume that consumer is African American for the purposes of its analysis.

If the Bureau's analysis reveals that consumers in a protected class are paying more for credit than are consumers who are not in a protected class, even by a very small margin, it may then engage in supervisory action (for entities that it supervises) or enforcement activities (for other entities). The Bureau has been unwilling, thus far, to reveal the amount of margin it deems significant for these purposes. It has also refused to reveal the proxies that it uses in place of actual hard data about race, ethnicity, and gender.

Contract buyers are scratching their heads over how to comply with the Bureau's unhelpful guidance. It is almost as if the Bureau is saying, "Don't exceed the speed limit, and, by the way, we aren't going to tell you what it is." Contract buyers that wish to continue to permit dealers to exercise their discretion in setting rates to be charged to consumers will be expected to engage in close supervision and monitoring of the dealers in order to police the dealers' rate-setting activities to avoid illegal discrimination.

CHAPTER 6

Contract buyers trying to avoid "nannying" their dealers may instead decide to abandon such programs and instead compensate dealers by paying a flat fee for each contract. Chances are that dealers will end up working with contract buyers who compensate them the best, regardless of the compensation method.

Because the Bureau's view of dealer financing seems to be so limited, the only possible way for all parties to avoid a claim of unintended discrimination is to charge everyone, regardless of dealer or finance company, the same rate, just like utility companies do.

It's really capitalism at its best, don't you think?

July 2013
Are You Ready for the Money Man?

I hear two recurring themes at the car dealership and finance conferences I attend.

The first involves liquidity—dealers and finance companies burn through a lot of money as they start doing business and ramp up to a size that permits them to fund themselves on an ongoing basis. Companies in this situation need to borrow money, find more equity, or sell assets, usually their retail installment contracts.

The second involves what the business consultants refer to as an "exit strategy." Most folks I know in this business enjoy what they do, but not many of them still want to be doing it when they are 120 years old. When the call of the golf course or the fishing hole becomes insistent, business owners start thinking about how to escape the daily grind.

Both of these situations lead business owners to the door of the Money Man.

2013: ROLLING OUT THE HEAVY ARTILLERY

We are presently going through another of those cycles in the car business when money is chasing investment opportunities. Compared with even the recent past, money is relatively easy to come by.

Funny thing about the Money Man, though. Even though he is easier to find and easier to deal with than he has been in the past, he's still no pushover. And even though there's a lot of new money coming into the sector, there also are a lot of potential businesses in need, so the Money Man can be careful about the companies he deals with.

"Careful," in this case, is spelled "d-u-e d-i-l-i-g-e-n-c-e." That's what the investor and banker communities call the process of checking out a potential investment or purchase before doing the deal. It's basically "kicking the tires," looking for weaknesses and soft spots—and for reasons not to write that check.

We represent a number of Money Men. A typical assignment starts with a phone call identifying the company that is the potential investment target. Sometimes the Money Man wants to buy a portfolio of retail installment contracts. Sometimes the Money Man intends to lend money and take the contracts as collateral. And sometimes the Money Man is contemplating buying part or all of the company that holds the contracts.

You'll quickly see that the common thread running through these three possibilities is those retail installment contracts. For that reason, a lot of the due diligence process focuses on them.

First and foremost, are the contracts enforceable? Has the consumer granted the seller a security interest in the vehicle identified in the contract? Is that security interest "perfected"? Do the contracts comply with state and federal law? Are the finance charge rates and other fees and charges shown in the contract permitted by state law?

201

CHAPTER 6

Does the consumer have any claims or defenses against the original creditor (the dealer) that can be asserted against a subsequent holder of the contract? The answer to this question will require an examination of other documents in the deal jacket to make sure that, for instance, there are no violations of the Equal Credit Opportunity Act, the Fair Credit Reporting Act, the Federal Trade Commission's rules, and all of the other federal and state laws that govern vehicle credit sale transactions.

Is the Money Man done yet? Nope.

He'll ask what licenses the company holds and will want to know about the license renewal process and timing. He'll want to know what the underwriting and collections manuals look like. He'll want to see all of the collection letters and notices that the company sends to defaulting consumers. He'll check the company's internal customer complaint file and will go beyond the company's own records to see if the company has had any difficulty of record with the regulatory agencies. He will check out the background of the company's owners and top management.

If all of this sounds like the Money Man is picking the company up by its feet and shaking it to see what falls out of its pockets, that's probably not far off the mark.

So, how do you get ready for the Money Man? I think the best strategy is to step back and pretend that you are the Money Man and that you are thinking of forking over some of your hard-earned money to your own company. Then, go through this kind of formal due diligence process, probing for every weakness and problem you can identify. When you're done, fix every problem you've discovered.

Then, maybe you'll be ready for the Money Man.

August 2013
Washington, D.C., and Rabbit Disaster Recovery Plans

I couldn't make this stuff up if I tried.

One day recently, I took my cup of coffee and copy of *The Washington Post* to the screen porch, took a sip of my coffee, and unfolded the paper. On the front page was a story about Maury the magician and Casey the rabbit.

It seems that Maury, a 54-year-old professional magician, used Casey in his magic act that he performed mostly for kids. Some time ago, as Maury concluded his act, a woman flashed a badge and said she was with the U.S. Department of Agriculture. "Where," she asked, "is your federal license for Casey?"

A federal rabbit license? Yep, that's right. A 1966 law, later amended, requires most people who "exhibit" animals to get licenses for their animals. So, Maury got the license.

The rules that come with the $40-per-year license require Maury to periodically take Casey to the vet and also allow USDA inspectors to make surprise visits to Maury's home to make sure that Casey is OK. When Maury and Casey go on the road, Maury must submit their itinerary to the feds.

Recently, Maury got a letter from the USDA telling him that if he wanted to keep the bunny, he needed a "disaster recovery plan" setting forth what he would do to keep Casey safe in the event of a flood, hurricane, tornado, ice storm, or other form of catastrophe.

The front-page newspaper story, or the threat of it, resulted in some furious backpedaling over at the USDA, with the secretary of the agency ordering a review of how the disaster recovery rules were to be applied to small operations like Maury's.

By now, you're wondering what on earth this has to do with the car business.

CHAPTER 6

Here's the connection. As the new Consumer Financial Protection Bureau has started its examination of the car finance operations of banks and other consumer finance businesses over which it has examination authority, we've learned what the Bureau expects when it does a compliance examination. In the process, we've learned a new "buzz-term": "compliance management system."

A compliance management system, or program, is the mechanism by which those banks and businesses regulated by the Bureau will meet the new compliance standards imposed by the Bureau. What are those new standards? How has the compliance burden changed?

Here's how. Before the Bureau came into existence, for the most part, a dealer and others regulated by the Bureau could stay out of trouble by not violating the law.

That is no longer sufficient. Dealers and those others must not only avoid violating the law, they must also be able to show that they have programs and systems in place to avoid violating the law. Those programs and systems comprise that "compliance management system" previously noted.

If you review the Bureau's published expectations about what a compliance management system should look like, you will find that creating and managing a system will take much money and effort—not unlike that rabbit disaster recovery plan.

You'd be forgiven for thinking about Maury and Casey, but for one saving part of the Bureau's description of these required systems. According to the Bureau, a compliance management system can be based on the size, complexity, and scope of activities of the regulated entity.

Will the Bureau enforce its mandate regarding a compliance management system in such a way that a three-person dealership can comply without breaking the bank?

Hmmm . . . a government agency exercising sensible discretion? That would be almost like magic—a bit like pulling a rabbit out of a hat.

September 2013
Legal Advice from Yogi Berra

A friend of mine teaches pre-licensing classes to dealers. His curriculum contains a good bit of compliance material, so we occasionally share war stories. He recently emailed me about an experience he'd had with a dealer pupil. Here's what he said:

I just finished a private new dealer class for a fellow from Tennessee. He has over 19 years of experience as a GM, independent dealership owner and began his career some 19 years ago in (of course) a franchise dealership. He knows all the "lingo," truly has a grip of his subprime customers (says his average credit score in Memphis is 480). His current dealership has sold nearly 600 units so far this year with most being BHPH. He's looking to open up in my state, so is taking my class.

Of course, being from Tennessee, where there is no mandatory dealer training, he knew nothing about my state's DMV rules, thus no surprises that I'd spend a considerable amount of time coaching him on the regulatory environment here. But then we moved into Fed rules and regulations such as TILA, ECOA, FCRA, FDCPA, FTC, privacy notices, safeguards, red flags, risk-based pricing, adverse action notices, OFAC'S SDN list, yada, yada.

Well by golly . . . guess what? Other than the FTC's Buyers Guides, he'd never heard of ANY of this. While he currently pulls credit bureau reports that include (or should) an OFAC check and indicate if Red Flags are present . . . he told me he'd seen that "stuff" on the bureau reports but didn't know what they were!!

CHAPTER 6

He did use a retail installment contract supplied by a national vendor, but, otherwise, he was probably as compliant as I am as a 747 pilot, and I assure you that you wouldn't want to be a passenger on any plane I'm flying!

This is one of the gazillion examples I've experienced [involving] a man whom I take to be willing to be compliant but . . . he's never been forced to stick his nose in a book (such as the esteemed Mr. Hudson's F&I Legal Desk Book) *or plop his butt in a chair in a classroom, [so] he simply cruised along thinking what he was doing was just hunky-dory. While there are plenty of "bad actors" in this business, my general experience is that they aren't all bad by design or intent.*

It once again reaffirms my notion that one solution to "consumer protection" in the retail automotive arena is MANDATORY dealer education . . . both initially and at least once every year or two.

. . . [H]e had never heard of the CFPB and was "all ears" when I explained the Bureau's who, what, when, where, and why to him.

After receiving his email, I called my friend to chat. I asked him to guess, based on his experience, the percentage of dealers he comes in contact with who are in about the same compliance shape as this dealer. My guess was 25%. His was 50%.

Yogi Berra said, "When you come to a fork in the road, take it." If the description of the dealer above fits you, you've come to a fork in the road.

Your choice is, on the one hand, to exit the car business or, on the other hand, to educate yourself on the legal requirements that will apply to you if you stay in the business.

If you own a dealership and you don't know what the Consumer Financial Protection Bureau is, don't have a privacy safeguarding policy, don't have a privacy statement, don't know what an adverse action notice is, don't have your forms and policies periodically reviewed by counsel, don't belong to your state independent auto dealers association, don't subscribe to as many updating periodicals as you can, and have never been trained in your F&I responsibilities by the Association of F&I Professionals or some other reputable training source—you're living on borrowed time. You should get out of the business before the feds or the state enforcement authorities put you out of business.

September 2013
"This Lawyer Walks into the F&I Office ..."

I broke down and bought a new car recently. Because we spend a bit over half of our time in South Carolina, I decided to do business with a dealer in Myrtle Beach. The sales guy, the F&I guy, and I all did our little dance, and pretty soon it was time to sign on the dotted line. The buyer's order was the first document I looked at, and I instantly saw two problems with it. When you look at as many buyer's orders as I do, you get a pretty good feel for the sorts of mistakes that the drafters of the things make when they don't do their homework. Sure enough, the drafter of this form had made a couple of common mistakes.

I signed it anyway because no one was paying me to fix the thing and because both of the problems worked in my favor or could be used for leverage if I had problems with the deal, the dealer, or the car. I won't identify the dealer, by the way, because I'd just as soon not tip off some plaintiffs' lawyer to the dealer's problems.

The first problem that jumped off the page was a violation of the Federal Trade Commission's Used Car Rule. That rule requires that a certain notice appear in the contract of sale and further requires that the notice be "conspicuous." The dealer's form contained the required notice, but it appeared in the same type size and font that was used in most of the rest of the document. The failure to use a "conspicuous" notice violates the Used Car Rule, exposing the dealer to the FTC's tender mercies.

The second "jump off the page" problem was similar to the first. The Uniform Commercial Code provides that a sale of goods (that includes vehicles) is subject to certain "implied warranties." These warranties apply whether the buyer and seller expressly agree to them or not. The UCC, however, permits a seller of goods to "disclaim" any implied warranties, provided any such disclaimer is conspicuous. This dealer's disclaimer, like his used car notice, was not conspicuous. You can bet that a car buyer would argue that the failure to use a conspicuous disclaimer results in the disclaimer being ineffective.

When I arrived home with my new ride, I sat down and perused the paperwork more closely. That turned up an additional issue. One of the documents I had signed was an arbitration agreement. I read through the arbitration agreement and concluded that it wasn't in bad shape, except for one little problem. The drafter had provided in the arbitration agreement that South Carolina's arbitration law would apply.

That's a bad idea. When we draft arbitration agreements, we specifically state that arbitration under the agreement will be pursuant to the Federal Arbitration Act (FAA). The reason we reference the FAA is that a number of business-friendly published court decisions say that the FAA trumps, for the most part, state judicial and legislative attempts to prohibit or limit the ability of businesses to use arbitration agreements to defend themselves against class action lawsuits and potentially large "runaway" jury verdicts. Electing the state's arbitration law, instead of the federal law, to govern the document deprives the dealership of the benefit of these favorable precedents.

After thinking some more, I decided that it would be a waste not to at least mention these problems to the dealer. So I called up the nice F&I man and explained what I'd found. I'm sure that right away he alerted the owner of the dealership to the forms deficiencies and then immediately called the dealership's lawyer to fix the problems. Then he sent a nice "thank you" letter for my free legal advice.

Sure he did.

October 2013
Are the Prices in Your Ads Based on Multiple Possible Discounts?

If so, read on.

In an April 2012 article, I tried to outline where I thought the Federal Trade Commission's next advertising enforcement action might come from. Here was my prediction:

> *Some dealers run ads that show prices that assume that the buyer can and will qualify for every dealer and finance company discount and special offer that exists, even when very few (or no) buyers will qualify for all of them. So, if your ads show a price that has been computed by subtracting the senior citizen discount, the first buyer's discount, the loyal customer discount, the college student discount, the returning war fighter discount, and the Girl Scout discount (all right, I made that one up), you might want to begin to assemble your sales records so that you can show the FTC that you occasionally have a customer who qualifies for all those discounts at the same time. Good luck with that.*

CHAPTER 6

Well, maybe the FTC staffers read that article, because dealers advertising a price based on multiple discounts recently found themselves in the FTC's crosshairs.

Car dealers from Maryland and Ohio recently agreed to settle FTC charges that they falsely advertised the price or available discounts for their vehicles. The settlements prohibit the dealers from advertising prices or discounts unless the ads clearly disclose any qualifications or restrictions.

The FTC charged that Timonium Chrysler, Inc., of Cockeysville, Maryland, violated the FTC Act by advertising discounts and prices not available to a typical consumer. Timonium Chrysler's website touted specific "dealer discounts" and "Internet prices," but allegedly failed to disclose adequately that consumers would need to qualify for a series of smaller rebates not generally available to them. The complaint further alleged that, in many instances, even if a consumer qualified for all the rebates, the cost of the vehicle was still greater than the advertised price.

Ganley Ford West, Inc., in Cleveland, was charged with misrepresenting that vehicles were available at a specific dealer discount, when in fact the discounts only applied to other more expensive models of the advertised vehicles. Ganley advertised its discounted vehicles on its website and in local newspapers and allegedly failed to disclose that its advertised discounts generally only applied to more expensive versions of the vehicles advertised.

The FTC said that its proposed orders settling the charges against the two dealerships are designed to prevent them from engaging in similar deceptive advertising practices in the future. The two auto dealers cannot advertise prices or discounts unless accompanied by clear disclosures of any required qualifications or restrictions. The auto dealers also are barred from misrepresenting

- the existence or amount of any discount, rebate, bonus, incentive, or price;
- the existence, price, value, coverage, or features of any product or service associated with the motor vehicle purchase;
- the number of vehicles available at particular prices; or
- any other material fact about the price, sale, financing, or leasing of motor vehicles.

The dealers must maintain and make available copies of all advertisements and promotional materials to the FTC for inspection upon request for the next five years, and they are required to comply with the FTC's order for 20 years. Yes, 20 years.

I see advertising enforcement actions like this and am reminded of a quote from the Illinois Attorney General in 2004. In announcing an advertising enforcement action by her office, she said, "Car dealerships are not allowed to make up whatever they think will lure consumers to the lot."

A word to the wise.

October 2013
We Violate the Truth in Lending Act

Would you lease a billboard at the edge of town and plaster a sign on it that identifies your dealership and says "WE VIOLATE THE TRUTH IN LENDING ACT"? How stupid would that be?

Yet, believe it or not, some dealers are doing the equivalent of that on the Internet. A friend of ours from South Carolina sent us this Internet ad posted by a local dealer:

CHAPTER 6

> 2004 Toyota Camry Solara SLE, 149,672
> OMG!!! THIS IS ONE SHARP RIDE!!!
> JUST $7995 AND ONLY $2500 DOWN
>
> AND
>
> $250 A MONTH.....NO INTEREST!!!!
> WOW!!! WOW!!!! WOW!!!! WOW!!!!!!!!!!!!
> OR IT CAN BE YOURS FOR JUST $5800
> CASH.....OUR SPECIAL WHOLESALE
> PRICE.....AND HAVE NO PAYMENTS!!!
> EVEN BETTER WOW!!!!!!!!!!!!!!!

Check them out! Not one, not two, but three Truth in Lending violations! Failure to state the cash price, claiming no interest, and failing to comply with federal advertising rules. A trifecta.

Listing two different figures for the cash price of the vehicle doesn't work. It's clear that the car can be bought for cash for $5,800. That, then, is the "cash price" for TILA purposes. The price of $7,995 for an installment purchase clearly contains a hidden finance charge—the difference between $5,800 and $7,995. Only in this case, it isn't exactly "hidden" because the dealer has been kind enough to leave the equivalent of a signed confession by saying the cash price is $5,800.

The dealer might be under the mistaken impression that the so-called "no interest" transaction is not subject to TILA. That would be wrong because it is clear as a bell that the difference between $5,800 and $7,995 is a finance charge, and because TILA applies to any credit transaction repayable in more than four installments, whether interest is charged or not. If TILA applies, those provisions of TILA that regulate advertising apply.

Those advertising provisions say that if an ad contains a "triggering term," as the above ad does, additional disclosures are required that are not in this ad.

Dealers, and especially dealers away from the large metropolitan areas where the federal enforcement agencies often have offices, were once able to fly under the radar when it came to strict compliance with federal consumer protection laws. No more.

All those young, idealistic enforcement lawyers who work for the Consumer Financial Protection Bureau, the Federal Trade Commission, the Department of Justice, state attorneys general offices, and other enforcement agencies have computers. They can sit at their desks in the home office and cruise the web looking for advertising violations like this one. The radar keeps getting lower.

Maybe the dealer who put this ad together should contemplate other ways to make money.

I know! Maybe he could sell exclamation points! WOW!!!!!!!!!!!

November 2013

Senator Takes Aim at Dealer Participation and Spot Delivery Practices, but Misses

An October 23 letter from Massachusetts Senator Edward J. Markey to Federal Trade Commission Chairwoman Edith Ramirez urged the FTC to take action regarding dealer participation and spot deliveries, practices discussed in the FTC's 2011 Roundtables. The letter, which looks like it could have been authored by the National Consumer Law Center, and likely was, conveniently ignores the fact that neither practice, done correctly, violates the law. The FTC's Roundtables turned

CHAPTER 6

up anecdotes, all of which involved violations of existing law, but no reliable data indicating that there were problems in either area.

I will address the rate participation issue first. I'll get to spot deliveries later, after I've scraped myself off the ceiling.

Senator Markey's letter reflects a profound ignorance of the facts and the law in the area of dealer-assisted finance. For example, the letter asserts that dealers "collude with third-party lenders" to engage in "secret" markups. Consumer advocates love to throw around words like "collude" and "secret," even when the practices they refer to are legitimate business practices that are fully disclosed to car buyers.

The letter claims that dealers make "loans." In fact, dealers engage in retail installment sales transactions, not loans. The contracts are between car buyers and dealers. Under the contracts, the dealers are entitled to all of the fully disclosed finance charges imposed in the contracts. Most dealers elect not to hold these contracts and collect the finance charges, but rather sell the contracts to finance sources. Nearly all forms of retail installment contracts in use today contain a disclosure to the buyer that the dealer may retain a portion of the finance charge. Secret? Hardly.

The practice of dealer-assisted financing has been around for decades. The National Auto Dealers Association (NADA) and the American Financial Services Association (AFSA) jointly authored a consumer education booklet on the topic that accurately describes the process and the dealer's role in it, including the retention by dealers of a part of the finance charge. NADA and AFSA asked the Federal Trade Commission to review the document before printing, and the FTC did so. The pamphlet bears the FTC's mark on the last page. Secret? Hardly.

The Federal Reserve Board has pondered the issue of whether dealers should be required to disclose the amount of the finance charge they retain in dealer-assisted finance transactions, and has determined that disclosing the full financing charge, without breaking out the dealer's portion, was a more useful approach. A consumer needs to know the amount of finance charge the consumer is paying—the identity of the party retaining it doesn't vary the amount. The FRB's discussions on this topic arose during its rule-making process and appeared in the Federal Register. Secret? Hardly.

Finally, several reported court opinions have dealt with the practice of dealer-assisted financing. Plaintiffs' lawyers have asserted that the retention by the dealer of part of the finance charge violates the law under a number of theories, including fraud, unfair and deceptive trade practice violations, and disclosure violations. Nearly all of the published opinions in these cases have rejected these attacks. Secret? Hardly.

The letter also conveniently ignores the fact that most vehicle financing in this country is done on a so-called "simple interest" basis on contracts that impose no pre-payment penalties. A consumer who feels that he has agreed to an above-market rate and who has found a less expensive source for his financing can refinance to obtain the more favorable rate. Rates offered by these other sources of financing are available in mailers, print ads, and on the Internet. Secret? Hardly.

Turning to spot delivery transactions, Senator Markey follows the NCLC's line like a bloodhound on a scent. Everybody in the car business knows that an abusive spot delivery (what NCLC and the senator call a "yo-yo transaction") violates a number of laws. A spot delivery, however, can be conducted in a manner that does not involve such abuses and that offers significant advantages to consumers and dealers alike.

215

CHAPTER 6

Senator Markey heaves the baby out with the bathwater. It would have been much more constructive for him to simply second the 2012 letter from the state attorneys general to the FTC urging the FTC to propose a regulation that reflected industry best practices in spot deliveries.

But that wouldn't have garnered a headline.

Chapter 7

2014: The Campaign Continues

CHAPTER 7

By 2014, it had become evident that car dealers' hopes for congressional action to de-fang the CFPB were futile. No Republican House committee was going to come up with anything that would seriously weaken the CFPB and still stand any chance at all of clearing the entire House, the Senate, and overriding the president's veto. It also became evident that the CFPB's agenda, if allowed to go unchallenged and unchanged, would dramatically change the way that dealers sell, finance, and lease vehicles.

The CFPB was operating with one hand tied behind its back because franchised and many independent dealers (those with vehicle repair facilities that did not retain their retail installment sale contracts) were exempted from the CFPB's jurisdiction. That fact did not handicap the Bureau much, though. It still had authority over the banks, credit unions, and finance companies that bought the retail installment contracts from dealers, and it proved adept at "deputizing" those within its regulatory control to exert pressure on those who were not.

"So," you say, "Why don't those companies subject to all these punitive regulatory enforcement actions take on the Bureau and challenge its aggressive interpretation of the laws and regulations that govern the extension of consumer credit?"

Why indeed? It might have something to do with the reluctance of these companies to challenge their federal regulator, possibly incurring retaliation that would result in harm for years down the road. And don't forget that taking the federal government to the mat isn't like engaging in litigation with some private party. Private parties don't have their own mints. They can't print money.

All-in-all, challenging the fed isn't for sissies.

March 2014
Nap Time?

Rip Van Cardealer nodded off for a short nap in 2010. As evidently happens with some people named Rip, he didn't wake up until 2020. Rip was a hard-working sort, so rather than puzzle over why his beard was two feet long, he shaved, took a shower, and went to work at his dealership.

Luckily for Rip, his kids were in business with him, so while he'd been snoozing, the kids had been running the dealership. At first glance, Rip didn't see that much had changed. On second glance, though, he noticed that all the cars had price tags on them like the ones you'd see on refrigerators at Sears.

"What's with the price tags?" he asked his daughter.

"Oh," she replied. "The Consumer Financial Protection Bureau and the Federal Trade Commission decided that car dealers must put price tags on their cars and cannot deviate from the price on the tag."

"I remember the Federal Trade Commission, but what is the Consumer Financial Protection Bureau?" asked Rip.

About four hours later, Rip's eyes were glazed over, but he had the inside skinny on the CFPB. Then he asked, "What's with the prices on those tags? They aren't set at $9,995; $14,995; or any other 'close-to-the-next-thousand' number we used to use to make buyers think they were getting a bargain."

"Oh," said his son. "We can't do that anymore. The CFPB says we can't mark up a car that we finance more than 20% above the amount we paid for it. Markups higher than that, they say, are 'abusive.' So in order to get all the profit we can, we just use a straight 20% markup, and that results in numbers that are all over the map."

CHAPTER 7

"Well," Rip replied, "that's no big deal. We'll just goose the profit on our F&I products to make up for what we can't make on the cars."

"Sorry, Dad," his daughter answered. "We can't do that either. The government says we can't keep part of the finance charge like we used to. We also can't mark up our F&I products more than 20% either because they say that would be 'abusive.' And some products we can no longer sell at all. The Bureau says there's so little value in them that no consumer should have to pay for them. But that doesn't matter much anyway—we aren't selling enough in the F&I office to make a difference in the bottom line."

"Why not?" asked Rip. "We used to get a substantial part of our profits from there."

"Not anymore," the son groaned. "The Bureau says that we cannot even mention things like service contracts, GAP, tire and wheel protection, dent repair, and other products until 10 days after the sale of the vehicle. By that time, we aren't face-to-face with the buyer, and that really cuts down on our penetration rate. The Bureau says that making us wait until the vehicle sale is completed eliminates the danger of payment packing."

"I've never heard such socialistic tripe in my life," Rip thundered. "We need to go right to the top of the federal government and raise hell."

"You can try that, Dad, but I don't think you'll get much of a reception from President Warren," said the son.

"Well," Rip asked, "what are we going to do? And anyway, why are you two packing all these boxes?"

"Oh, Dad," the daughter responded. "We're closing the business. You can go back to sleep now."

March 2014
Job Security

Somewhere, there's a line of work that offers more job security than being a dealer compliance lawyer. Undertaker, maybe, or garbage collector. Those folks will always be needed, right?

Well, I will always have a job, too. Here's why.

In January, the Federal Trade Commission announced that nine vehicle dealers agreed to settle deceptive advertising charges and that it is taking action against a tenth dealer in "Operation Steer Clear," a nationwide enforcement sweep that focuses on the sale, financing, and leasing of motor vehicles.

Dealers settling with the FTC were from California, Georgia, Illinois, Michigan, North Carolina, and Texas. The remaining action involves a Massachusetts dealer.

The FTC claimed that the dealers made misrepresentations in print, Internet, and video advertisements that violated the FTC Act. Among other charges, the FTC said that some of the dealers ran ads falsely leading consumers to believe they could make no upfront payments to lease vehicles.

Fast forward 30 days or so, and my email inbox lights up with a note from a friend who sees a lot of dealership ads. The ad, from a Florida dealership, screamed in very large, brightly colored type:

"NO MONEY DUE. ZIP, ZERO, ZILCH!"

Other parts of the ad (which I have doctored lightly to avoid identifying the dealer) went on to name the dealership, followed with:

CHAPTER 7

"Where you get the 2014 [car make and model] for only $249 per month or the 2014 [car make and model] for only $299 per month with absolutely NO MONEY OUT OF POCKET!"

The ad continued:

"That's Right! ZERO MONEY DOWN!!!

At [Dealership name] you can choose from 2 of the Hottest [car makes and models] for 2 of the LOWEST PAYMENTS anywhere in Florida with NO MONEY DOWN! ZIP, ZERO, ZILCH!

Drive away today with....

ZERO OUT OF POCKET!"

At the bottom of the ad, in type that wouldn't be visible if it were smaller, appeared the following:

"Prices and payments include $598.50 Pre-delivery service fee. Plus tax, license and title fees.*"

What was this dealership thinking? The FTC has made it perfectly clear: You cannot giveth with big, hulking fonts and taketh away with teeny-weeny type. It has announced a national campaign to clean up dealer advertising. It has nailed dealerships in an enforcement action for misleading customers by falsely claiming that cars can be leased with no money up front. And after all that, only a month later, this Florida dealership runs this ad?

2014: THE CAMPAIGN CONTINUES

How does "no money out of pocket" square with writing a check for $598, plus taxes and license and title fees? Even a cursory review of this ad by anyone at the dealership in a position of responsibility should have revealed the internal inconsistency of the screaming big print and the sly small print.

We've often said that Rule No. 1 in advertising is "Tell the truth." There are two statements here—"zero out of pocket" and "$598 plus tax, license and title fees." One of those statements is patently not true.

I will mention again one of my favorite admonitions on dealer advertising. Illinois Attorney General Lisa Madigan said something like, "You can't just say anything you want to in an ad to get people into your dealership."

But, evidently, a lot of dealers out there disagree with AG Madigan and will run anything in their ads, true or untrue, to attract buyers. And that's why I'll always have a job.

April 2014
No Haggle. No Problem—Or Not

Fads, by definition, come and go. Sales methods can be faddish, too.

One method that has been around a couple of times and seems to be coming around again is "no-haggle" pricing. Recently, the editors at a dealer magazine called me as they planned an issue that would focus on this topic. They asked, "Can a dealer get into trouble using no-haggle pricing?"

Hmm.

Let's assume that the dealer's no-haggle advertising is splashed all over billboards, the Internet, print, radio, and TV and that the advertising doesn't say anything about pricing other than the bald no-haggle statement. Then let's assume that the dealer haggles.

CHAPTER 7

My first thought was to wonder what the Federal Trade Commission might think about this scenario. Fortunately, the fellow who, for ages, headed up the FTC unit responsible for advertising violations, Joel Winston, is now my partner, so I put the question to him.

Joel's reply? "I suppose it could be considered deceptive, but it depends on how reasonable consumers interpret 'no-haggle pricing.' It could mean we never negotiate with anyone, but there are other interpretations possible. In any event, the consumer injury would appear to be very low, and it's not a very appealing case for the government."

OK, so the feds wouldn't get their knickers in a twist over the practice, but what about the possibility of a suit by one of the dealer's customers?

I promptly took off my dealer lawyer white hat and reached for my customer lawyer black hat. Pretending that I was looking for any way possible to sue a dealer that my client had a beef with, I started thinking about possible ways I could attack a dealer's no-haggle pricing strategy.

Here's how I'd analyze the facts. My client went to the dealership to buy a car. Based on the dealer's stated no-haggle policy, my client cheerfully paid $29,995 for his new Belchfire V-6, thinking that he had no choice but to do so. After all, that's what "no-haggle" means, right? Two days later, my client's brother-in-law goes to the same dealership, picks out the same car, and says, "I'll take it, but my top offer is $29,500." The dealer takes the offer. He haggled.

"So what?" you ask.

So this: Most states have a law with a title like "unfair and deceptive sales practices" or "unfair and deceptive acts and practices." The laws are usually general, with the terms "unfair" and "deceptive" not defined or very broadly defined. These laws are favorites of plaintiffs' lawyers because, with broadly defined terms, it's hard to get a case dismissed in its early stages, favoring suing consumers over defending dealers. The laws also frequently provide that a successful plaintiff can recover a multiple (double or triple) of his or her actual damages and attorneys' fees.

So, staying in character, I take off my black hat for a moment and scratch my head. "Hmm," I say. "This dealer said he doesn't haggle, but he does, and I can prove it. Maybe I'll bring a class action lawsuit against the dealer on behalf of all of those buyers who relied on the dealer's no-haggle claim and bought without attempting to haggle."

So I file the lawsuit on my client's behalf and then get into what lawyers call "discovery." Modern court rules, in an effort to minimize surprises at trial, permit the parties to "discover" the facts of the other party's case by demanding documents, taking depositions, asking for admissions of facts, and the like. As part of my discovery, I'll be looking at the dealer's pricing practices for cars, finance rates, service contracts, GAP, and all the other F&I products, looking for instances in which the dealer and the customer engaged in haggling.

You get the idea. My answer to the editors was that a determined plaintiffs' lawyer can come up with ways to attack a no-haggle policy if, in fact, the dealer haggles.

Would such a lawsuit be successful? That would depend on lots of facts that we haven't yet considered. What if the dealer's advertisements said, "We cater to buyers who don't want to haggle"? That's a different claim from "no-haggle" and makes the buyer's case harder. Or the dealer might hope that a court would agree that saying "no-haggle" was just a harmless form of "puffery" that buyers didn't take literally.

So, go no-haggle if you want, but unless you intend never to haggle, talk the program over with your lawyer before you do.

CHAPTER 7

April 2014
Undertakers, Garbage Collectors, and Credit Lawyers

I wrote an article for last month's *Spot Delivery* about how my job security ranked right up there with undertakers and trash collectors. The article was inspired by a Florida dealer's advertisements—ads that were exactly like the ads of a dealer who had been nailed by the Federal Trade Commission a month earlier for advertising violations. If dealers were that cavalier about enforcement risk, I mused, I'd never lack for work.

Then another month goes by, and a report sails across my desk of a dealer whose actions were so bizarre that I could scarcely believe the report. Here's what happened.

On March 14, the FTC charged an Arkansas auto dealer, Abernathy Motor Company, and its two principals with failing to display Buyers Guides on used vehicles offered for sale, as required by the FTC's Used Car Rule. Each violation could result in a civil penalty of up to $16,000.

The Used Car Rule has been around since before the invention of fire. The window sticker requirement is about as easy to comply with as any regulatory requirement anywhere. You simply buy forms that meet the FTC's regulations for content, font size, and type style from a reputable vendor, complete them properly (there's plenty of help on the FTC's website), place the forms in or on your cars as required by the rule, and you're done. If you negotiate deals in Spanish, you'll need two forms—one in English and one in Spanish.

"Used car dealers are required to post a Buyers Guide providing warranty and other important information on the cars they offer for sale. That's the law," said Jessica Rich, Director of the FTC's Bureau of Consumer Protection. "Consumers have a right to receive this information up-front to help them make an informed buying decision."

The FTC's Used Car Rule specifically requires used car dealers to disclose whether the car comes with a dealer's warranty or is being sold "as is." If the car is sold with a dealer's warranty, the rule requires the Buyers Guide to list the warranty's basic terms and conditions, including the duration of coverage, the percentage of total repair costs to be paid by the dealer, and the exact systems covered by the warranty.

OK, so maybe this dealer is new to the business and hadn't gotten around to doing his compliance homework. That's a bit like going off the high dive before filling the pool, but it can happen.

But no. This dealer had been in business for awhile, so that would make you wonder. But what would make your jaw drop is that the dealer had been an FTC target before, and fairly recently. In January 2013, the FTC announced that its Southwest Region Office had warned 11 used car dealerships in Jonesboro, Arkansas, that their sales practices violated the Used Car Rule. All but Abernathy Motor Company subsequently came into compliance.

Abernathy Motor Company has four used car sales locations in Arkansas. The FTC's complaint also names the company's owners, Wesley and David Abernathy, and an affiliated dealership, Ab's Best Buys AMC Inc., as defendants.

According to the complaint, the FTC visited an Abernathy dealership in November 2012 and found that none of the vehicles for sale displayed a Buyers Guide. The agency informed the dealership of that fact and forwarded a copy of the Buyers Guide along with A Dealer's Guide to the Used Car Rule, an FTC publication. In May 2013, the FTC revisited the Abernathy dealership and visited Ab's Best Buys and found both dealerships were offering used vehicles for sale that did not display Buyers Guides.

CHAPTER 7

Dealers like these are why credit lawyers will never lack for work. Here, the FTC accused these folks of violating the law and fired a shot across their bow, only to have the dealership ignore the warning. Now it looks like the FTC will be firing for effect.

And before I leave this topic, note Ms. Rich's comment, "That's the law." The FTC's Used Car Rule is the law, as are the Red Flags Rule, federal privacy rules, the risk-based pricing rule, and several others, yet we frequently review dealer operations, only to find that some dealers have not complied with these laws, even those that have been in place for years.

April 2014
Broader FDCPA in the Works

So far, car dealers who sell their retail installment contracts to sales finance companies don't have to be concerned by the prohibitions and limitations of the Fair Debt Collection Practices Act. They don't collect consumer obligations, so they're beyond the scope of the FDCPA.

Buy-here, pay-here (BHPH) dealers don't have to be concerned about the FDCPA either because it doesn't apply to companies attempting to collect obligations that are initially owed to them, as is the case with a BHPH dealer collecting from its own customers.

A BHPH dealer's related finance company doesn't have to be concerned with the FDCPA because the Act doesn't apply to the assignee of an original creditor if the assignment takes place when the obligation is not in default.

All of this may be about to change.

The Consumer Financial Protection Bureau, purportedly acting under authority of the Dodd-Frank Act, has proposed to apply the FDCPA to all original creditors and their assignees.

As long as the limitations and restrictions contained in the FDCPA are not extended (and more on that in a moment), the CFPB's expansion of the FDCPA will not impose many significant new burdens on those companies that have previously enjoyed exemptions from the FDCPA. That's because many of these companies have long since implemented FDCPA compliance as a "best practice," even though they were not required to do so.

The proposed CFPB action has the support of the state attorneys general. Attorneys general in 30 states plus the District of Columbia have urged the Bureau to adopt strong new debt collection rules that will better protect consumers and military servicemembers.

Among other recommendations, attorneys general urged the CFPB to

- give states co-enforcement authority to address violations of new debt collection rules;
- apply debt collection rules to original creditors as well as to debt buyers;
- require those who sell debts to transfer detailed original account information;
- ensure that collectors possess credible supporting evidence before initiating collection or litigation activity;
- require collectors to extend traditional collection tactics protections to new modes of communication, such as cell phones and text messages;
- implement rules to address the collection of time-barred debts; and
- better protect servicemembers by limiting collectors' contacts to servicemembers, particularly those in combat zones.

With this urging, and with the natural inclination of the CFPB to fill every regulatory vacuum, you can bet that the

CHAPTER 7

FDCPA rules will be extended and strengthened. Companies that have so far ignored the FDCPA altogether will now face a significant new compliance burden. Companies that have considered voluntary FDCPA compliance as a "best practice" will have new compliance burdens, the extent of which will depend on the degree of the extension and strengthening of the FDCPA requirements.

The CFPB is in the earliest stages of its rulemaking. You can expect the credit industries to weigh in to try to limit the damage, but odds are that we'll end up with a lot more regulation than we want.

April 2014
Operation Speed Trap

If the police chief in your town announced that he was arming all of his officers with radar guns and ordering them to enforce the 25-mile-per-hour speed limit on Main Street, you'd think that maybe, just maybe, folks would dial it down a bit while going through town. Maybe not, though. The Federal Trade Commission has essentially pointed its radar guns at dealer advertising, yet dealers still keep the advertising pedal to the metal.

In January, the FTC announced that nine car dealers agreed to settle deceptive advertising charges and that the agency was taking action against a tenth dealer in Operation Steer Clear, a nationwide sweep that focuses on the sale, financing, and leasing of motor vehicles. The dealers settling with the FTC are from California, Georgia, Illinois, Michigan, North Carolina, and Texas. The remaining action involves a Massachusetts dealer.

The FTC claimed that the dealers made misrepresentations in print, Internet, and video advertisements that violated the

FTC Act, falsely leading consumers to believe they could buy vehicles for low prices, finance vehicles with low monthly payments, and/or make no upfront payment to lease vehicles. One dealer misrepresented that consumers had won prizes they could collect at the dealership.

The FTC's allegations varied by dealer, but included charges that

- the dealers deceptively advertised that consumers could buy vehicles at specific low prices when, in fact, the price was higher;
- consumers could pay nothing up front to lease a vehicle when, actually, substantial charges were involved;
- dealers advertised that cars could be bought for low monthly payments when later payment amounts turned out to be higher;
- consumers had won sweepstakes prizes when, in fact, they had not;
- consumers could buy cars at specific low monthly payments without disclosing that the consumers would face a large final balloon payment; and
- leases were misrepresented as sale transactions.

The advertisements also allegedly violated the Consumer Leasing Act and Regulation M by failing to disclose certain lease-related terms. One dealer's advertisements allegedly violated the Truth in Lending Act and Regulation Z by failing to disclose certain credit-related terms.

If stroking big checks to the FTC and to your defense lawyers is your idea of a good time, then just ignore the FTC's push to clean up dealer advertising. However, if I am a dealer, I can think of better ways to spend my money.

With that in mind: I am going to match the FTC's blitz with my own internal blitz for my dealership. I'm going to

CHAPTER 7

instruct my Compliance Officer (if you don't have a Compliance Officer, you have some preliminary steps to take) to
- move advertising compliance to the top of his or her list;
- implement a review of all federal and state advertising requirements;
- put in place a process for ad review; and
- confer with my advertising guru(s) to
  o review all media contracts to ensure that they comply with all the laws that apply to my business;
  o require that all advertiser employees be aware of and trained in implementing the legal requirements that apply to my advertising; and
  o indemnify my dealership in the event the ad people screw up and create liability for me.

I'm also going to make sure that my Compliance Officer has the budget and other resources to make these things happen. And (pardon the pun), I'm going to drive home to him or her the consequences of getting me in trouble with the FTC.

And I'm going to hold it under 25 when I drive through town.

May 2014
Can You Be Held Responsible for Your Company's Actions?

You incorporated your car dealership or your finance company in order to protect the individual assets of you and your employees, right? Isn't that one of the principal advantages of operating a business in corporate form? If the corporation gets sued, you and management aren't individually liable for its actions.

But is that true? Under some circumstances, business

232

2014: THE CAMPAIGN CONTINUES

owners and executives can find themselves exposed to the dreaded risk of individual liability. Here's an example.

Kristy Ross, an executive at Innovative Marketing, Inc., participated in the development of an online marketing campaign that displayed pop-up advertisements stating that a scan of the consumer's computer had been performed and had detected a variety of dangerous files. In reality, no such scan was ever performed.

The Federal Trade Commission sued Innovative Marketing, Inc., and several of its high-level executives and founders, including Ross, for engaging in deceptive Internet advertising practices. The trial court entered summary judgment for the FTC on the issue of whether the advertising was deceptive, but it set for trial the issue of whether Ross could be held individually liable. The trial court found that Ross satisfied the standard for individual liability because she had actual knowledge of the deceptive advertising scheme. Ross appealed, and the U.S. Court of Appeals for the Fourth Circuit affirmed.

On appeal, Ross argued that the trial court lacked the authority to award consumer redress under the Federal Trade Commission Act. The appellate court rejected Ross's argument, concluding that—even though the FTC Act does not expressly authorize courts to exercise their equitable jurisdiction—by authorizing courts to exercise their injunctive power, Congress intended that courts be able to exercise the full measure of their equitable jurisdiction.

Ross further argued that the trial court applied the wrong standard in finding her individually liable under the FTC Act. The appellate court rejected the standard proposed by Ross and reiterated that a person can be individually liable under the FTC Act if she participated directly in the

CHAPTER 7

deceptive practices or had authority to control those practices and had or should have had knowledge of the deceptive practices.

Finally, Ross challenged the trial court's evidentiary findings that she had control of the company, that she participated in the deceptive acts, and that she had knowledge of the deceptive advertisements. But the appellate court again rejected Ross's arguments, finding that the trial court did not clearly err in making its findings.

The appellate court's discussion in this case should give you pause. Do you participate in an activity of your company that the federal regulators might deem to be deceptive? Do you have knowledge of those deceptive acts? If so, there just might be room for the FTC or the Consumer Financial Protection Bureau to argue that you, along with the corporation, are liable for the deceptive acts.

If the feds can get past your corporation defenses and get their mitts on your personal assets, maybe it's time to rethink those early retirement plans.

Federal Trade Commission v. Ross, 2014 U.S. App. LEXIS 3476 (4th Cir. (D. Md.) February 25, 2014).

June 2014
The Cost of Compliance

We are frequently asked about the cost of dealer compliance with federal and state laws that regulate the sale, lease, and financing of vehicles. Usually these questions come in the form of requests for fee estimates for compliance work, but sometimes the questions are broader than that.

The answer depends, of course, on how much of a compliance effort the dealer is willing to make or can afford. The answer is also different for the 30-car-per-month dealership and the 300-car-per-month operation.

If the dealership asking the question is a mid-sized, independent (nonfranchised) dealer, I'll usually estimate $25,000 to $50,000 as an initial annual compliance budget. My estimate isn't much more than an educated, experienced guess, and it is easy to spend a lot more than that for a real crackerjack compliance effort.

A franchised dealership with any volume, or a multi-rooftop franchise operation, would, of course, need an even bigger compliance budget. Just hiring and training a compliance officer, monitoring legal developments, developing and maintaining a compliance management system, and subscribing to *Spot Delivery* (sorry, couldn't resist) could drive the budget into six figures. But so far, all we've been able to offer are "guesstimates" when we're asked about compliance costs.

Now comes a study on compliance costs from the Center for Automotive Research in Ann Arbor, Michigan. The study, commissioned by the National Automobile Dealers Association, concluded that franchised new-car dealers in the United States spent a combined $3.2 billion in 2012 to meet federal regulations. The study looked at one dealership in Maryland and seven in Michigan and Ohio. Dealers were asked to estimate costs and were "encouraged to substantiate costs, where appropriate," the study said.

When we worry about compliance costs, we focus on the couple of dozen federal laws that regulate the sales and F&I process. The CAR study was broader, however, covering 61 major federal rules. CAR concluded that consumers paid more for their cars and that the U.S. economy also paid in the form of 10,550 fewer dealership jobs, 75,000 fewer total jobs, and $10.5 billion in lost economic output.

CHAPTER 7

CAR says that, in 2012, the average dealership spent $182,754 to comply with federal mandates governing employment, business operations, vehicle financing, sales, marketing, vehicle repair, and maintenance. The regulatory costs equaled about 22% of the average dealership's pre-tax profits, or about $2,400 per dealership employee. The report concluded that the average dealership needed to sell 106 vehicles in 2012 to recoup its regulatory compliance costs. Regulations on employment, accounting, and vehicle financing made up nearly two-thirds of the estimated federal regulatory compliance costs, the study said.

The study did not analyze the cost of mandates, such as fuel economy and safety rules, on manufacturers, nor did it include in the estimate the compliance cost associated with the Affordable Care Act. Also, it did not consider state and local regulatory mandates.

The CAR study produced compliance cost estimates that would make any dealer frown, but we think those cost estimates are on the low side. In the short time between the period addressed by the study and today, the Consumer Financial Protection Bureau, the Federal Trade Commission, and the Justice Department all have been active in the dealership space. That has led to increased compliance efforts at most dealerships, and we suspect an identical study based on 2014 data would produce higher numbers.

August 2014
Dealers Scolded for Advertising Missteps

When it comes to dealer advertising, the Federal Trade Commission has been on the warpath. Recently, its national program, Operation Steer Clear, has gotten a lot of press coverage.

The FTC isn't the only lawman in the posse, though. State authorities also have jurisdiction over dealer advertising. Because state authorities are more familiar with what dealers in their states are doing, often they are attuned to questionable advertising practices.

A good and recent example comes from Oregon. A July 24 release from the Oregon Department of Justice starts with the following warning:

It has come to the attention of the Department of Justice that dealers have been failing to accurately disclose the offering price of vehicles. Motor vehicles are generally a negotiable price item and dealers do not need to advertise a set price for vehicles offered for sale. However, when a dealer advertises a vehicle at a certain offering price, it must disclose that offering price to prospective customers and permit customers to purchase the vehicle at that price. Additionally, any reference prices used by the dealer must be accurate.

The DOJ release flagged several specific practices that it identified as "violations of the law." Readers of *Spot Delivery* will recognize some of the bad practices as ones we've harped on for years.

The DOJ's first example involved a dealer advertising an "Internet price" on its website. Sometimes, noted the DOJ, the "Internet price" is accompanied by a statement that a consumer

CHAPTER 7

must print a copy of the price or a coupon to receive the advertised price. This special deal for Internet buyers runs afoul of Oregon law, which requires that when a dealer advertises a sales price for a vehicle, that price must be posted on the vehicle, and all consumers must be able to purchase the vehicle for that price.

The DOJ's second gripe involved dealers who advertised a "cash price." The DOJ pointed out that offering a different sales price to cash customers than the price offered to "financed" customers violates the federal Truth in Lending Act and Oregon rules.

Finally, the DOJ targeted what it called "reference pricing," in which a dealer states a "market value" either in comparison to an offering price or as the offering price. This "market value" price is typically wholly unrelated to a price guide value (such as Kelley Blue Book) for used cars, MSRP for new cars, or the average sales price of a similar vehicle. More specifically, the DOJ appears to be going after dealers who falsely claim, for example, that a car's price "was $12,000" but "is now $10,995." That sort of pricing can be done under Oregon law, but only by following the strict guidelines set forth in the regulations.

The DOJ went on to scold dealers like an angry schoolmarm: "It is simple to follow the law and there are no excuses for failing to do so. When a dealer advertises a sales price for a vehicle, that price must be posted on the vehicle and all consumers must be able to purchase the vehicle for that price."

Dealers everywhere should take note of this release. Oregon is just the latest state to zero in on dealer advertising practices. Make sure you know the rules, and don't depend on some ad company for your compliance.

Good sources of help for advertising compliance? Your first stop should be a visit with your lawyer. In addition, many state new car and independent dealer associations have compiled advertising guides. The FTC provides some useful material on its website, www.ftc.gov. Smart dealers designate someone to be responsible for dealership advertising, learn the rules, and review all this helpful advice, and they give that person a hotline to the dealership's lawyer for difficult questions.

Not-smart dealers don't.

October 2014
12 Steps to Get You Started

I have spoken at several buy-here, pay-here dealer conferences over the years. Federal enforcement actions are a popular topic.

Afterward, dealers line up to ask me this paraphrased question: "Can you give me a basic playbook to help me set up a compliance program that will keep the Federal Trade Commission and the Consumer Financial Protection Bureau from flogging me in the public square and throwing me in jail?" Evidently, these dealers have taken the compliance message to heart.

That oft-asked question is usually accompanied by a caveat that the compliance program must be one that won't break the bank. This article outlines some steps you can take toward establishing a serious compliance program, followed by a guesstimate of the "hard costs" involved, not including management time, implementation time, and the time your employees spend studying, training, and researching.

Here goes.

CHAPTER 7

Step 1: Make the decision to become a squeaky-clean operation.

Without this step, none of the rest of the stuff we recommend will work. The decision needs to come from the top of the organization, and, if your organization has had compliance problems, all hands need to understand that it is a real sea change and not just window dressing. Your people need to be told that anyone who does not treat customers honestly and ethically will be fired. Anyone who doesn't buy into the new compliance culture should be told to hit the road. Cost: $0.

Step 2: Appoint a privacy officer.

While you're at it, make that same person your compliance officer and the administrator of your Red Flags program. If your organization is large enough, this person may need help in the form of a small committee. The privacy/compliance officer should report to the highest-ranking person in the organization. Have signs made for your dealership showroom that identify that person. Cost: $5 for the signs.

Step 3: Give your privacy/compliance officer a real budget so that he or she can actually get some stuff done.

No budget for privacy and compliance will assure that you will have a privacy/compliance program that's not worth a hoot. Several of the tools that the privacy/compliance officer will need, such as copies of the federal Truth in Lending Act and Regulation Z, the federal Consumer Leasing Act and Regulation M, the federal Equal Credit Opportunity Act and Regulation B, the federal Gramm-Leach-Bliley Act, the Federal Trade Commission's privacy regulation, the FTC's Used Car Rule, the Red Flags Rule, and the Risk-Based Pricing Rule, can be found online, although your privacy/compliance officer might need some training to access them. As part of that privacy/compliance budget, allocate enough money to send as many people as you can possibly afford through a compliance certification course (your mechanics are trained—your F&I people need training, too). One such program is offered by the Association of Finance and Insurance Professionals (www.afip.com). Have your privacy/compliance officer obtain and read all the books on F&I compliance that he or she can find. Likewise, have the privacy/compliance officer subscribe to online legal compliance services. Cost: Start with at least $5,000, but you easily can spend a lot more.

Step 4: Train, train, train.

Dealers tend to have high turnover of sales and finance personnel, and this compliance stuff can be less than riveting. So, you need to train your revolving sales and finance force and periodically re-train the ones who stay with you. There are third-party trainers, some of whom are quite good, but if your privacy/compliance officer turns out to be a crackerjack, he or she might well be able to handle the training. Cost: $0 in-house, $10,000 for outside training twice a year.

Step 5: Download and print copies of "Understanding Vehicle Financing."

This consumer education pamphlet is free on the National Automobile Dealers Association website and is available in English and Spanish. It provides an overview of how car financing at dealerships works and bears the seal of approval of the FTC. Everyone in your organization will benefit from reading it. Make copies to display around your dealership, and put a copy into each customer's packet of papers as you close each deal. Cost: The download is free, plan on $1,000 for printing.

Step 6. Download and print copies of "Keys to Vehicle Leasing."

This is another consumer education pamphlet. It's from the FRB and is a good overview of closed-end auto leasing. It also is available in English and Spanish, and you should use it just like you use "Understanding Vehicle Financing." Cost: The download is free, plan on $1,000 for printing.

Step 7: Require everyone in the sales and financing process to read carefully your buyers order, retail installment sales agreement and lease forms, privacy policy, arbitration agreement, and all other documents that you ask the customer to sign or give to the customer.

This should include credit life and accident policies and certificates, GAP addenda, service contracts, "etch" agreements, and anything else the customer sees. Make up a test to determine how much of what each employee has read he or she actually understands. Cost: $0.

Step 8: Adopt a true, transparent "menu" process for the sale of additional products through the F&I office.

Work with your lawyer to prepare the menu and the script. Dealers who use a menu say that the transparent sales process costs them some sales that they might otherwise make, but that offering every product to every customer every time through a menu results in more sales. Follow up with your employees to make sure that they're actually using the menus you've adopted in the way they are supposed to be used. Cost: $0.

Step 9: Appoint a person to help customers if they have a complaint.

Sometimes referred to (using a $10 word) as an "ombudsman," such a person helps the customer work through a complaint with the dealership. You don't want customers resolving complaints with the dealer representatives that they originally dealt with—and who often caused the complaint—and get defensive as a result. You want someone who did not take part in the sales and financing process who can look at the customer's complaint dispassionately. Having a formalized complaint-resolution process might deter some customers from taking their gripes to a lawyer or to the CFPB. Cost: $0.

Step 10: Have your privacy/compliance officer periodically search the web.

He or she should check the site of your state's attorney general so that you'll know what the AG's current hot buttons are. Another site to check is that of your state's motor vehicle dealer regulatory body. Also, on a regular basis, check the CFPB's and the FTC's websites, the NADA website, your state and local ADA's or IADA's website, and any other sites you've discovered that are useful. Use your Microsoft Outlook program to set up a weekly or monthly reminder to do these searches. (Confession: I stole the Outlook tip from Gil Van Over). Cost: $0.

Step 11: If your dealership isn't using a mandatory arbitration agreement in its sales, leasing, and financing transactions, consider doing so.

The CFPB has announced that it is studying the use of arbitration agreements in consumer transactions, and the Bureau may eventually ban their use. Until that happens, using an arbitration agreement can be an effective defense against those

CHAPTER 7

predatory class action lawyers. Some state association-produced buyers orders contain arbitration language, or you can buy free-standing arbitration agreements off the shelf from vendors like Reynolds and Reynolds (but make sure your state permits the use of additional documents and doesn't have a so-called "single document rule"). Regardless of which way you go, have a lawyer who is really knowledgeable about consumer arbitration agreements look over the agreement you intend to use. Cost: $2,000, plus any ongoing printing costs.

Step 12: Have a forms and procedures review and a written compliance program.

All of your sales and F&I forms and procedures, underwriting procedures, and servicing and collections procedures should be reviewed by a lawyer who is knowledgeable about compliance law. All of these procedures should be documented and maintained in a compliance manual. You and your lawyer should periodically review your manual because laws and regulations change. Use your Microsoft Outlook program to schedule a review at least every six months. Cost: $10,000 to $20,000.

So, there you are. If you implement those 12 steps, you'll spend about $30,000 to $40,000. You still won't have a first-class compliance program, but you'll be miles ahead of where most dealers are. Once you get these measures in place, we can start talking about how to bring the program to the next level.

Not willing to invest serious money in compliance? Maybe it's time to think about closing the dealership and opening a bait shop.

October 2014
Apples and Pomegranates

"Apple" is a five-letter word. "Pomegranate" is an 11-letter word. If your goal is to write in such a way that your reader understands you, would you use "apple" to refer to a "pomegranate"?

Of course not. And why not? Because pomegranates are not apples, right?

However, the Consumer Financial Protection Bureau makes just this sort of mistake. The Bureau uses the term "loan" in many instances when it is referring to a retail installment contract. Bureau staffers I have talked to justify the mistake on the grounds of writing "simply."

I support any effort by the federal government to write in a way that makes text more readable. I fear, however, that the Bureau has gone too far in its "simplification" efforts. Misusing these terms harms consumers.

A "loan" involves borrowing money. A consumer who borrows money signs something titled a "note" or a "promissory note." If the loan is a secured loan (the security might be a vehicle), the consumer signs a "promissory note and security agreement." The parties to these instruments are called the "lender" (often a bank) and the "borrower." A borrower receives money from a lender and agrees in a note to repay it.

A retail installment contract (RIC) is used to evidence the sale of goods on credit. The parties to a RIC are called the "buyer" and the "seller" of the goods. A buyer receives goods from a seller and agrees in a RIC to pay for those goods over time.

RICs are commonly used for dealer financing of vehicles. Many dealers sell the RICs that result from car sales on credit to finance companies. The sale of a RIC by a dealer to a finance company is a commercial transaction between two businesses.

CHAPTER 7

The buyer of a RIC is not a *lender* but is, rather, a *purchaser* of the RIC.

Semantics? Pointy-headed lawyer distinctions?

Hardly.

Loans and RICs are regulated differently. Federal disclosure laws and other federal laws, such as the Equal Credit Opportunity Act and the Federal Trade Commission's Credit Practices Rule, treat the two transactions differently. Indeed, after a recent action by the federal banking regulators, there is no Credit Practices Rule for "loans" made by depository institutions—but there is a Rule for RICs.

Many state laws also treat the transactions differently. In some states, a "lender" may be required to have a license, while a credit seller does not. The transactions may be subject to different maximum finance charge rates, late charges, grace periods, bounced check fees, limitations on events of default, consumer rights upon repossession, etc.

So when the Bureau calls a RIC a "loan," it misleads the consumer or at least points the consumer in the wrong direction in determining his or her rights and consumer protections. A consumer who bought a car by signing a RIC and who follows the Bureau's releases may believe that he or she has a car loan when in fact he or she is a credit buyer. The consumer may decide to look at state laws and state regulatory guidance to determine what his or her rights are and might consult the loan law instead of the law regulating retail installment sales. More likely, perhaps, a consumer might seek help from consumer protection agencies and mischaracterize the transaction as a loan rather than a RIC, resulting in incorrect advice from the agency—or even advice from the wrong agency.

Isn't an accurately informed consumer worth a little extra text?

Misuse of the term "loan" also misleads car dealers, especially smaller independent dealers and buy-here, pay-here dealers who struggle with legal compliance and who typically do not have lawyers to assist them. The confusion of these dealers can result in consumer harm. Many of these dealers use industry jargon already, referring to RICs as "loans" or "notes." The Bureau's misuse of the terms perpetuates this mistake by dealers.

I know of many dealers intending to sell cars on credit who have applied to the state for a "loan" license when they either did not need a license at all or should have applied for the license required for credit sale transactions. I have seen many instances of dealers going to office supply stores and buying pads of promissory notes to use when selling cars on credit because they erroneously believed that the transactions they were entering into were loans. That mistake can result in significant harm to consumers when the document used by the dealer does not conform to a state's retail installment sales act, which typically contains many consumer protections. The same mistake will result in consistently erroneous Truth in Lending disclosures, which is presumably bad for consumers. Again, the Bureau's misuse of the terms perpetuates this mistake by dealers.

A little more text—three words instead of one—would help educate dealers about their obligations to consumers.

I understand why the Bureau's press releases need to be written in language that the media will understand. But the Bureau's over-simplification efforts in this case mislead consumers and the businesses that deal with consumers. If a business used language in its ads that misled consumers, and tried to justify its actions on the grounds that the misleading words were easier to understand than words that were not misleading, what would the Bureau's response be? In a market where 80% of all financing is made through RICs, it should not be all that hard to use an accurate term such as "auto finance contracts" in lieu of the misleading and inaccurate term "loan."

Now, pass me one of those pomegranates, will you?

October 2014
Dealer Advertisements:
Low-Hanging Fruit for Enforcers?

I admit that I'm a bit quirky. Quirky Exhibit One is what I do when I travel. Whenever possible, at breakfast, I try to find a local paper. When I do, I sip my coffee and go immediately to the car dealership ads to see how many disclosure and "unfair and deceptive acts and practices" violations I can find and if dealers have found new ways to violate the advertising laws. Dealership ads are a source of entertainment for me that beats the comics, hands down.

Federal and state enforcers, however, are threatening to end my fun. The Federal Trade Commission's Operation Steer Clear has announced a number of advertising enforcement actions against dealers, and now state attorneys general are joining the posse. The latest AG to get a dealership in the crosshairs is New Jersey's.

On August 5, Acting Attorney General John J. Hoffman and the New Jersey Division of Consumer Affairs announced the filing of a complaint against Bergen Auto Enterprises, LLC, d/b/a Wayne Mazda and Wayne Auto Mall Hyundai, for repeated deceptive advertising practices. The complaint alleges that the dealerships (1) advertised vehicles for sale without disclosing to consumers that used vehicles had previously been used as rental vehicles and/or had sustained significant prior damage and (2) failed to publish statements to consumers about applicable purchase costs, as required by New Jersey law.

2014: THE CAMPAIGN CONTINUES

The five-count complaint alleges that the dealerships committed multiple violations of both the New Jersey Consumer Fraud Act and the state's motor vehicle advertising regulations. The state of New Jersey wants restitution for consumers and the imposition of civil penalties, among other remedies.

Additionally, the complaint alleges that certain new vehicles offered for sale or lease had been sold months before but remained featured in the dealerships' advertisements. The AG claims that a 2013 Mazda advertised for lease had actually been sold almost 11 months before the advertisement was published. In another instance, the Hyundai dealership allegedly advertised for at least 175 days a 2013 Hyundai Genesis for lease that it did not possess and that was, in fact, located and titled in Pennsylvania.

"The alleged actions of Bergen Auto Enterprises demonstrate contempt for consumers and their rights under the law. The Wayne Mazda and Wayne Auto Mall Hyundai dealerships allegedly offered vehicles and terms that were not attainable, and concealed important details about other vehicles for sale and lease, all in a calculated effort to profit at consumers' expense," said Division of Consumer Affairs Acting Director Steve Lee.

Newspaper advertisements for Wayne Mazda and Wayne Auto Mall Hyundai also allegedly failed to include legally required statements that explain to consumers what costs the advertised price included and what additional costs consumers would need to pay. The complaint also alleges that the dealerships advertised prices of new vehicles that reflected dealership discounts but failed to properly explain the qualifications necessary to obtain those discounts. For instance, Wayne Mazda advertised prices and included a footnote—

"Available to qualified buyers on select vehicles"—but did not specify the vehicles to which the discount applied or the conditions necessary for the consumer to qualify for the discount.

Keep in mind that, so far, all we have here are allegations—the AG still has to convince a court that the dealerships did what they are charged with doing. If the AG's allegations are true, though, I really have to wonder who at the dealerships is responsible for the legal compliance of these ads and what the advertising compliance review process looks like.

My bet is on "nobody" and "nothing." If that describes your dealership, you need to know that the federal and state enforcers are in an absolute lather about dealers' ads. If your ad process isn't up to snuff, it's time to get to work.

December 2014

Dealers, Related Finance Companies, and the Fair Debt Collection Practices Act

The federal Fair Debt Collection Practices Act imposes a number of requirements on debt collectors. Buy-here, pay-here dealers without related finance companies don't have to worry about the FDCPA because it does not apply to a creditor collecting obligations originated by that creditor. Dealers with related finance companies also enjoy an exemption from the FDCPA if the finance companies acquire credit contracts from their dealers at a time when the contracts are not in default. The RFCs enjoy another exemption from the Act, however, and a court in a recent case used that exemption as the basis for dismissing FDCPA claims against the finance company.

Kimberly Golden bought a used car from Automotive Restyling Concepts, Inc. d/b/a Automotive Concepts.

The security agreement Golden signed indicated that she made a $2,000 down payment and agreed to finance the remaining balance.

Golden and Automotive Restyling also executed a Check Pledge and Note stating that if Golden's $2,000 down payment check was not negotiable, Golden would make immediate payment in full. The parties disputed whether Golden made the down payment.

The law office of William H. Henney later sent a letter to Golden on behalf of John W. Prosser and Prosser Holdings, LLC d/b/a A.C. Financial regarding the alleged past due down payment amount. About a month later, Prosser—chief manager of A.C. Financial and president of Automotive Restyling—wrote to Golden on behalf of A.C. Financial regarding the debt.

Golden sued A.C. Financial, Automotive Restyling, and Henney's law office for violating the FDCPA and Minnesota law. The parties cross-moved for summary judgment.

The federal trial court first dismissed the FDCPA claims against Henney. Golden argued that Henney violated Section 1692e because she did not owe the $2,000 at issue. The court found that an allegation that a debt is not owed cannot form the basis for a false and misleading practices claim under the FDCPA.

Golden also argued that Henney's letter was false and misleading because Automotive Restyling, not A.C. Financial, was her original creditor. The court found that even if the letter misstated the name of the creditor, it was not a material misrepresentation because the letter stated that the debt was related to Golden's recent purchase of a vehicle. This information was sufficient for Golden to understand the letter and submit a response. The court also found that Henney did not use unfair or unconscionable means to collect the debt.

CHAPTER 7

With respect to the FDCPA claims against A.C. Financial, A.C. Financial argued that it was acting as a creditor and not a debt collector. A.C. Financial handled Automotive Restyling's in-house financing needs and was thus responsible for handling Golden's down payment. The court found that even if A.C. Financial was a debt collector under the Act, acting on Automotive Restyling's behalf, A.C. Financial would still be exempt from the FDCPA under Section 1692a(6)(B)'s "affiliate exemption" because it was affiliated with Automotive Restyling. The court noted that both entities were managed by Prosser.

Many buy-here, pay-here dealers and their related finance companies comply with most of the parts of the FDCPA, like restrictions on when consumers can be called, as a "best practice." But adopting FDCPA provisions as a best practice doesn't negate the liability for a violation if the creditor doesn't quite get it right, so having this additional exemption is handy.

But the exemption won't mean much if the Consumer Financial Protection Bureau is successful in its efforts to apply the FDCPA to "first-party" creditors. It has issued a proposed rule to do exactly that, so stay tuned.

Golden v. Prosser, 2014 U.S. Dist. LEXIS 128423 (D. Minn. September 15, 2014).

December 2014
Ready, Fire, Aim!

Over the last couple of decades, more and more businesses have adopted pre-dispute mandatory arbitration clauses in their consumer agreements as a first line of defense against class action claims. A well-drafted arbitration agreement specifically precludes class actions. Indeed, without such a preclusion, there would be little incentive for businesses to use arbitration agreements.

2014: THE CAMPAIGN CONTINUES

Consumer advocates and trial lawyers have ranted and raved about the evils of arbitration agreements for years. The consumer advocates' protests and frequent challenges to the enforceability of arbitration agreements by private litigants have resulted in an evolution of arbitration agreements from those in the '90s, which were slanted toward business interests, to today's agreements, which bend over backward to favor consumers.

The Dodd-Frank Act reflects the consumer advocate and trial lawyer influence. It directs the Consumer Financial Protection Bureau to study the use of pre-dispute mandatory arbitration agreements in consumer financial services contracts. That survey is underway, and while the Bureau has issued a preliminary report, it has announced no conclusions.

Clearly carrying water for the consumer advocates and trial lawyers, 16 state attorneys general (all Democrats) have submitted a letter to CFPB Director Richard Cordray urging that the Bureau "protect the public interest by imposing prohibitions, conditions or limitations on the use of pre-dispute arbitration agreements for consumer financial products or services." The recommendation comes before the Bureau has reached any final conclusions on the subject. For anyone who has followed developments in this area over the past couple of decades, the letter elicits nothing but painful groans.

I don't think that it is very likely, but it's possible that the Bureau might adopt the common-sense regulatory approach we frequently recommend—to find out what responsible businesses in the marketplace are doing and determine whether the forms and practices of those businesses are fair to consumers. If the Bureau decides that such "best practices" are fair to consumers, it could fashion any rules it implements around those best practices.

If the Bureau looks at the best practices of the responsible users of pre-dispute mandatory arbitration agreements, it will see

CHAPTER 7

that the evils that consumer advocates and these attorneys general rail about largely disappear.

The AGs' letter argues that high arbitration costs and inconvenient venues "deter injured individuals from pursuing their rights." You have to wonder if the AGs bothered to collect even a small sample of arbitration agreements from major businesses. If they had, they would have seen that modern arbitration agreements have very generous (and sometimes very, very generous) provisions for payment of arbitration costs by the business. As for inconvenient venues, the arbitration agreements that I see (and write) call for arbitration to occur in the federal judicial district where the consumer lives or, sometimes, simply in a place convenient to the consumer. So much for those two concerns.

As another example, the letter cites "repeat-player bias," where, supposedly, an arbitration organization's arbitrators will be more likely to favor the company over the consumer because such favoritism will result in repeat business from the company. If the AGs had bothered to sample the arbitration agreements in use today by responsible businesses, they would, I believe, find that most of the arbitration agreements name an arbitration organization, but further permit the consumer to select a different organization if the named organization is not acceptable to the consumer.

Yes, there are some trade-offs to permitting arbitration. Class action prohibitions inflame trial lawyers and consumer advocates, but I have seen way too many class action settlements where the consumers involved get "awards" that are sometimes so worthless they don't bother to claim them, while their lawyers rush down to the nearest yacht dealer to order new toys.

And yes, arbitration decisions don't serve as precedent. The AGs point this out in their letter, but for some strange reason fail to mention that the arbitration decisions favoring businesses do not have precedential value either. In the real world, though, plaintiffs' lawyers have networks that spread the word of successful and unsuccessful arbitration claims. Word gets around.

Finally, perhaps close to a half of the AGs' letter consists of citations, at least two of which are to products of Public Citizen, a Washington, D.C.-based pro-consumer organization. Conspicuously absent is any mention of the several contrary academic and industry studies on the fairness of the arbitration process in connection with consumer transactions. Surely this omission was unintentional. Riiiiiiiiiight.

So, here's my advice to Director Cordray: Do what the wise old college dean did when new campus dormitories were built. He postponed sidewalk construction until he could identify the walking paths of students to and from the dorms. If Director Cordray and the Bureau take the time and effort to see what the "best-in-class" companies are doing with mandatory pre-dispute arbitration, and fashion any regulation of arbitration agreements around those best practices, they will protect consumers while retaining the ability of businesses to avoid the high cost of class litigation, a cost that consumers end up paying in the form of higher prices.

The only ones who will suffer from this approach will be the yacht dealers.

CHAPTER 7

December 2014
The Time to Prepare for an FTC Investigation Is Before it Happens

My email mailbox lit up recently with the rumor that the Federal Trade Commission had dropped Civil Investigative Demands (essentially subpoenas) on a number of dealers. The CIDs, said the rumors, dealt with the dealers' spot delivery practices.

Dealers who read *Spot Delivery* and who are not doing spot deliveries correctly have no one but themselves to blame if the FTC hammers them for bad acts. We have featured several articles on spot delivery "best practices," outlining steps dealers can take to avoid trouble.

After its Roundtables on auto finance, the FTC asked interested parties to submit additional comments on the Roundtables' topics. In May 2012, the attorneys general of Alaska, Arizona, California, Colorado, Connecticut, Delaware, District of Columbia, Georgia, Hawaii, Idaho, Illinois, Iowa, Maine, Maryland, Massachusetts, Minnesota, Mississippi, Missouri, Nevada, New Hampshire, New Jersey, New Mexico, New York, Ohio, Oregon, Pennsylvania, Rhode Island, Tennessee, Utah, Vermont, Washington, and West Virginia got together and submitted comments for the FTC's further consideration.

The AGs urged the FTC to regulate spot deliveries to prohibit abusive practices. Their recommendations read very much like "best practices" that dealership lawyers have been urging dealers to institute in connection with these transactions. Here are the specific practices that the AGs urged the FTC to regulate by rule:

- Require dealers to retain consumers' trade-in vehicles until financing is approved.

- Preclude dealers from threatening to repossess or repossessing vehicles in a manner that does not comply with state law and from threatening to file or filing a theft or other police report due to the consumers' refusal to return the vehicle to the dealership if financing is not approved.
- Bar dealers from charging consumers for mileage, for wear and tear, or for any other reason, pending approval of financing.
- Require dealers to offer consumers either a complete unwinding of the deal or credit under other terms, with the consumers having the choice to decide which of the two alternatives to accept, and bar dealers from making any representations to the contrary concerning the consumers' obligations or rights.
- Bar dealers from retaining portions of down payments or deposits when a deal falls through.
- Require dealers to disclose to consumers that if the first finance agreement is rejected, the consumer has the right to walk away from the deal and has no obligation to the dealer.
- Prior to completing a spot delivery, require dealers to clearly disclose to consumers that financing has not been finalized and the responsibilities and potential consequences for consumers.

With a couple of exceptions, these recommendations echo those that I and other lawyers have been making to dealers for several years. Compare the previous AGs' list with the following list from my "Pitch the Bathwater, Save the Baby" article from two years ago (arguing that spot deliveries, done correctly, are not abusive):

- Allow for mutual rescission until the contract is assigned.
- Require a dealer to keep the customer's trade-in until the customer's retail installment contract is assigned.

CHAPTER 7

- Provide a reasonable period (say, 10 business days) for the assignment of the retail installment contract, beyond which the deal could not be unwound.
- Prohibit a dealer from imposing any fees on the consumer other than charges for excess wear and use or damage to the car.
- Prohibit a dealer from requiring a customer to re-contract if the retail installment contract could not be assigned.
- Prohibit any unwinding of a deal unless the customer has agreed in writing to the unwind (this last one, in my view, isn't necessary, since a dealer generally has no unwind rights absent the customer's written agreement, but the prohibition might still serve a useful educational purpose for dealers and consumers alike).

I'll add a couple suggestions to those above.

Your spot delivery practices should be in writing and reviewed by your counsel to assure that they reflect best practices like the ones above and that they comply with state laws and regulations. This written spot delivery manual should be updated periodically to make sure that it reflects any changes in the laws and regulations applicable to spot deliveries. Your personnel responsible for handling spot deliveries should be trained on the procedures, and periodically re-trained, to make sure that they know what the dealership's obligations are.

I haven't seen one of the rumored CIDs yet, but I'll bet you my Mama's fried okra recipe that one of the things the FTC demands in those CIDs is a copy of the dealership's spot delivery procedures. Those dealers who can produce one that reflects the best practices outlined above will do better than dealers whose response to such a request is, "Say what?"

Chapter 8
2015: Manning the Ramparts

CHAPTER 8

By 2015, as illustrated by the articles that follow, the feds have the dealership castle of "the way we've always done things" surrounded, and they are draining the moat. The enforcement victories that have led to this situation have emboldened the attackers, and dispirited the defenders.

The auto sales, finance, and lease industry's generally "ho-hum," "fly under the radar" approach to federal compliance will change, because those players who can't or won't toe the line will be exiting the business. Expect a steady drumbeat of enforcement actions, mostly against smaller players who will not fight back, that will establish by enforcement what the agencies could never accomplish through regulation.

Despite the best efforts of those manning the battlements, this castle is history.

January/February 2015
A Wake-up Call for Dealers on Spot Deliveries

We've written frequently about spot delivery practices, including a May 2012 article discussing comments submitted by a number of state attorneys general urging the Federal Trade Commission to adopt rules to regulate abusive spot delivery practices. The allegations of a consumer referenced by the court in a recent opinion illustrate some of the dealer activities the AGs were concerned about.

Joann Hester's son, Ryan, had a phone conversation with an employee of Hubert Vester Ford, Inc., about buying a used Jeep. Joann agreed to be the co-signer for the purchase. The next day, Joann and Ryan went to Vester Ford and agreed to buy the Jeep for $22,000 with a trade-in credit of $1,000. The monthly payments were in the $300 to $350 range.

Vester Ford contended that it sold the Jeep to Joann and Ryan on September 30, 2009. However, evidence showed that someone saw Ryan driving the Jeep several weeks before that date. A credit application was submitted on Joann's behalf to finance the purchase of the Jeep and was dated September 24, 2009. The credit application allegedly inflated Joann's income. Evidence also showed that the Jeep was transferred to Joann's insurance on September 28, 2009.

Joann alleged that an employee of Vester Ford contacted her in early October 2009 and stated that her financing had fallen through and that she needed to sign a new purchase contract for the Jeep with new financing. The employee also allegedly stated that if she did not sign the new contract, the Jeep would be repossessed.

A Vester Ford employee then went to Joann's residence and presented her with the new contract, which was backdated to September 30, 2009. The employee allegedly told Joann that the contract terms were the same.

Joann alleged that the employee physically obscured the top half of the contract when she signed it. The second contract required monthly payments of approximately $614 with an interest rate of 14.69% for 60 months, almost doubling the monthly payments allegedly required under the original contract. The credit application submitted to the new creditor also allegedly inflated Joann's income.

After the Hesters defaulted on the second contract, the Jeep was repossessed. A deficiency judgment was entered against Joann for the rest of the amount owed, but was set aside by a consent order.

Joann sued Vester Ford and one of its employees for unfair and deceptive trade practices, fraud, and common law extortion. Both Joann and the defendants moved for summary judgment.

CHAPTER 8

The trial court granted the defendants' motion and denied Joann's motion. Joann appealed.

The Court of Appeals of North Carolina reversed the trial court's decision in part and affirmed it in part.

The appellate court first addressed the UDTP claim arising from the formation of the second contract. The appellate court, taking into account the circumstantial evidence established by Joann that the original contract was entered into before September 30, 2009, assumed that the original contract existed despite the fact that Joann couldn't produce a copy of it. Therefore, the appellate court assumed that Joann had a property interest in the Jeep before she was presented with the second contract. As such, a material question of fact existed as to whether Vester Ford committed an unfair or deceptive act when it threatened to repossess the Jeep if Joann did not sign the second contract. If such an act took place, the resulting harm would be that Joann was subjected to a subsequent purchase contract on less favorable terms.

The appellate court noted that Joann alleged some actual damages resulting from the alleged unfair and deceptive acts, such as losing the value of her trade-in vehicle after the Jeep was repossessed. Therefore, the appellate court concluded that Joann sufficiently alleged an UDTP claim, and the trial court erred by granting summary judgment to Vester Ford on this claim.

The appellate court also noted that questions remained regarding whether Joann reasonably relied on Vester Ford's assertion that the terms of the second contract were the same as the original contract. If she did reasonably rely on this assertion, her alleged failure to read the second contract would not preclude recovery. There was also a question regarding whether Joann signed the second contract under duress because of Vester Ford's threat to repossess the Jeep.

Next, the appellate court concluded that Joann's claim for fraud should survive summary judgment based on the same evidence that supported the UDTP claim. Joann presented evidence that Vester Ford intentionally and falsely represented to her that it could repossess the Jeep in order to induce her to sign the second contract.

With respect to Joann's common law extortion claim, the appellate court found that extortion is not a cognizable tort under North Carolina law.

The appellate court upheld the trial court's decision in favor of Vester Ford with respect to Joann's UDTP and fraud claims arising from Vester Ford's alleged inflation of her income on the credit applications. The appellate court also concluded that the trial court properly granted summary judgment to the Vester Ford employee on all of Joann's claims against him.

Nothing in the opinion mentions an "unwind" agreement that set forth the terms under which the dealership could require the buyer to sign a second contract. Absent such an agreement, and assuming that the initial agreement was a typical retail installment sales contract, the dealer likely had no right to compel the buyer to sign a new contract and no choice but to accept the buyer's payments under the original contract for as long as the buyer was not in default.

Keep in mind that there has been no trial in this case. All we have had to this point is mostly unsuccessful requests by both parties to grant judgment to them on various claims without a trial. If it ever gets to that stage, we might learn facts that are not evident at this early stage of the proceedings.

It is amazing that many dealers don't know the "rights" and "wrongs" of spot deliveries. If you are one of these dealers, use this article as your wake-up call to institute spot delivery

CHAPTER 8

procedures and documentation that address the concerns expressed by those AGs to the FTC.

Hester v. Hubert Vester Ford, Inc., 2015 N.C. App. LEXIS 2 (N.C. App. January 6, 2015).

April 2015
Look Who Emailed Me!

You've just poured your third cuppa, and you've plopped yourself down in front of your computer to clear the latest crop of emails. After reading and deleting a few, including a notice that you've won the Irish Sweepstakes and that your prize is on the way if you'll just send the $1,000 bank fee to cover the paperwork, you get to this one:

> *Good Morning Mr. [Insert your name here],*
>
> *The Consumer Financial Protection Bureau (CFPB) may have received a consumer complaint about your company, and your company has identified you as the designated point of contact to address your company's complaints. To view and respond to consumer complaints, your company must get access to the CFPB's Company Portal (Portal). The Portal is a secure online system that serves as the primary interface between CFPB and your company. This email provides you with the information you need to get access to the Portal.*
>
> *Complete and return the attached Office of Consumer Response's Company Portal Boarding Form to CFPB_StakeholderSupport@cfpb.gov within 5 business days of receipt. To expedite the boarding process, be as accurate and complete as possible when you complete the form.*
>
> *After you have submitted the completed form, you will receive an email with instructions on how to access the Portal. Keep in*

mind that boarding and accessing the Portal is a time-sensitive process. If your company has received a complaint, your company is required to respond within 15 calendar days of receiving the complaint from the CFPB.

If you have any questions, contact a Stakeholder Support team member at CFPB_StakeholderSupport@cfpb.gov.

Thank you,
Office of Consumer Response
Consumer Financial Protection Bureau

Yikes!

Attached to the email is a seven-page, 20-question (multiple parts to each question) form to be filled out. Ironically, the final page contains a Paperwork Reduction Act Statement. Don't tell me your government doesn't have a sense of humor.

I had not seen one of these nastygrams before, and I sent it along to my partner, Michael Benoit, in case he was also unfamiliar with this process. Both Michael and I have talked with many dealers about the pluses and minuses of signing up for the CFPB's Complaint Portal before they received complaints or a notice like this one, and I knew he'd be interested. Here's his response:

I've not seen the Bureau reaching out to a lot of small players, but I think their MO now is that if they get a complaint, they send an invitation to join the Portal. The upside is that any complaints get forwarded to you to resolve. The downside is that any complaints get forwarded to you to resolve. Most of the clients I've dealt with have chosen to sign up, with the warning that they will need to be responsive to any complaints that get directed to them through the Portal. I expect they keep track of folks who don't sign up, and I suspect that's played a part in their decision to issue CIDs to some of the small business owners we have represented.

CHAPTER 8

So, if you're the lucky recipient of one of these notices from the CFPB about a complaint, check with your lawyer, but we think it's likely that he or she will say, "Forget the pluses and minuses. They've identified you as a target and have you in their sights. Time to sign up." And after you sign up, make sure that you know the CFPB's rules for responding to complaints and that you respond to any complaints in accordance with those rules.

April 2015
Spacemen Abduct Regulators!

Two aliens brought their spaceship down slowly above the California highway, matching their speed to the cars on the highway beneath them. Opening the ship's cargo bay, they positioned themselves over a car traveling below. Activating their magnetic loader, they sucked the car and its two passengers into the cargo bay.

Their mission was a simple one. They had come to Earth for the purpose of capturing a couple of the humans who inhabited this strange planet in order to determine how humans think and how they transmit thoughts from one to another. They quickly put the two humans into a sleep state and did brain scans, reading and recording the contents of their minds. When the aliens were finished, they returned the humans—completely unaware of what had been done to them—to the highway below and sped back to their mother ship.

A month later, the aliens repeated the mission, but this time over a highway in Oregon. And on this second mission, the objective was to see if they could transfer the contents of the two California humans' brains to two humans captured in Oregon. That test, too, turned out to be successful.

Little did they know that the two Californians they had captured were wild-eyed consumer advocates and activists who spent all their time and energy trying to advance as many radical laws and regulations as possible to curb a wide array of evils that only they could identify.

And the Oregonians? They turned out to be two Oregon state employees, working for the Oregon Department of Consumer and Business Services, Division of Finance and Corporate Securities.

Now, I can't say for sure that that's what happened, but it is the only plausible explanation for the appearance of David Tatman, the administrator of DCBS, and his sidekick, Rick Blackwell, identified as a senior analyst, before the Oregon Senate Committee on Business and Transportation to testify on Senate Bill 276, a DCBS bill. Testifying in support of the bill, the first thing Tatman said was that buy-here, pay-here dealers are "unregulated."

That's when I knew the aliens had struck. Surely a state official coming to testify before a Senate committee would know that all BHPH dealers are under the jurisdiction of the federal Consumer Financial Protection Bureau. And he would know that they also are subject to the federal Truth in Lending Act and Regulation Z, the federal Equal Credit Opportunity Act and Regulation B, the federal Fair Credit Reporting Act, the federal Gramm-Leach-Bliley privacy law and Federal Trade Commission privacy regulations, the Magnuson-Moss Warranty Act, the USA Patriot Act, rules of the Office of Financial Assets Control, several FTC Trade Regulation Rules, the FTC's advertising rules, the Servicemembers Civil Relief Act, and several other federal laws. Wouldn't he?

OK, all of those are federal laws. Maybe he thinks that for some reason they don't apply in Oregon. But isn't it true that

CHAPTER 8

BHPH dealers are subject to the Oregon Motor Vehicle Retail Installment Sales Act, Articles 2 and 9 of the Oregon Uniform Commercial Code, Oregon's Unfair and Deceptive Acts and Practices law, the state's advertising laws, and several other state consumer protection statutes?

Unregulated? Only to a radical consumer advocate.

And that was just the start. SB 276 started life as mostly a regulatory housekeeping bill, imposing licensing, examination, and other burdens on BHPH dealers. But the DCBS has proposed several amendments to the bill that were lifted directly from the playbook of the consumer advocates. Among other things, the amendments would

- treat a contract as a BHPH transaction if the dealer holds onto the finance contract for 14 days, instead of 45 days;
- require the interest rate on a loan to decrease with higher down payments;
- impose an "ability to repay" requirement under rules to be promulgated by the DCBS director;
- require that the price of the car be disclosed before any credit checks occur;
- remove disclosure language that directs the buyer back to the dealer to resolve problems;
- prohibit repossession of a vehicle for 30 days after the consumer fails to make a scheduled payment; and
- prohibit the installation of devices that remotely monitor or disable a vehicle's vital systems.

If these two regulators are proposing such a draconian level of regulation, their action certainly was prompted by an extensive study of the business practices of BHPH dealers that produced hard data about BHPH business practices, right? The DCBS surely determined what dealers had adopted as "best practices" in their businesses—things like rates and prices charged, how many months of repayment were required by a typical BHPH retail installment contract, whether credit was being extended to people who were unable to pay, and whether dealers were engaging in other sharp practices, right?

Wrong on both counts. If the DCBS had any actual data about the BHPH business, it was not evident from the testimony of Tatman and Blackwell. It was also evident from their persistent use of the term "loan," instead of "retail installment sale," that they did not understand the legal basis of the credit sales of vehicles.

After Tatman and Blackwell finished testifying, three other witnesses appeared before the committee. Two plaintiffs' lawyers testified, painting BHPH dealers as "payday lenders who use cars as bait," in an effort to link BHPH with payday lending. They then offered as data the sort of anecdotal stories that consumer advocates always put forth—including a baseball bat-wielding BHPH dealer repossessing a car from a woman who was trying to make her delinquent payment. As always with witnesses who are plaintiffs' lawyers, they did not indicate whether their horror stories were typical of the BHPH business or were outlier examples of the sorts of business people who will cheerfully violate any and all consumer protection laws. Nor did they bother to mention that most, if not all, of the dealer actions they were complaining about violated some existing law.

I've had a couple of words with the aliens. I've suggested that the next time they go looking for brains to read, they should scour our planet for the sorts of regulators who actually go the distance to learn about the businesses they regulate and their respective best practices before they propose new laws and regulations.

The aliens said they'd try, but were not optimistic. They contend that such regulators are an endangered species.

CHAPTER 8

You might think, "I don't operate in Oregon, so why do I care about this?" The answer, dear friend, is that this sort of misinformed, uninformed legislative proposal could crop up anywhere—your state included.

If your state auto dealer trade association isn't regularly educating your state regulators and legislators about your business, they should begin to do so.

April 2015
CFPB's Arbitration Report—Balanced or Biased?

The Dodd-Frank Wall Street Reform and Consumer Protection Act directed the Consumer Financial Protection Bureau to conduct a study on the use of pre-dispute arbitration clauses in consumer financial markets. The Act specifically prohibited the use of arbitration clauses in mortgage contracts but gave the CFPB the power to issue regulations on the use of arbitration clauses in other consumer finance markets.

The CFPB conducted a public inquiry on arbitration clauses in April 2012 and released some preliminary research in December 2013. Industry has been waiting since then for the other shoe to drop. Did anyone just hear a big *kerplop*?

If so, it was probably a copy of the CFPB's mind-numbing, 728-page report hitting the doorstep. The report, crammed with charts and numbers, was accompanied by a press release trumpeting the CFPB's interpretations of the study.

According to the release, the report results indicate that

- tens of millions of consumers are covered by arbitration clauses;
- consumers filed roughly 600 arbitration cases and 1,200 individual federal lawsuits per year on average in the markets studied;

- roughly 32 million consumers on average are eligible for relief through consumer finance class action settlements each year (it is not clear how this relates to arbitration);
- arbitration clauses can act as a barrier to class actions (you've really got to love this one—the main reason creditors use arbitration clauses in their agreements with consumers is for the protection those clauses give against class action lawyers, so it's nice of the CFPB to point out the obvious);
- the CFPB found no evidence that arbitration clauses lead to lower prices for consumers; and
- three out of four consumers surveyed did not know if they were subject to an arbitration clause (the report didn't indicate whether this was because the consumers were generally unaware of the contract terms or whether they understood everything in the contract except for the arbitration clause).

The authors of the press release seem to have cherry-picked the study's findings in order to support an anti-arbitration title for their press release. The release did not bother to mention that the report shows that

- in many class action cases, where the principal purpose of seeking class relief is to pressure a settlement, members of the class got nothing or next to nothing;
- class action cases almost never make it to a trial on the merits, while a significant percentage of arbitration proceedings actually resolve the disputes of the parties; and
- arbitration is both faster and more economical than litigation.

And the study had some gaping holes, as well.

There was no discussion about creditor "best practices" reflected in the terms of arbitration clauses. The arbitration

CHAPTER 8

clauses used by creditors have grown more consumer friendly with each passing year. It isn't unusual now to see arbitration clauses that provide for the payment by the creditor of some or all of the costs of arbitration, permit the consumer to pick the arbitration organization, provide a carve-out for claims brought as single actions in small claims courts, and even permit the consumer to opt out of arbitration by notice. Creditors frequently use various means to call attention to the presence of an arbitration agreement by using large type, separately boxing the clause, having it separately signed or initialed, and/or adding "With Arbitration Agreement" to the title of a credit document. The study offers no insight on whether forms featuring these best practices might change any of the study's conclusions.

The study was not limited to auto financing. In fact, the bulk of the report dealt with other sorts of consumer financial services—credit cards, checking accounts, student loans, and the like.

There is very little in the report that specifically deals with auto credit, and what is there is close to useless because of the CFPB's continuing refusal to take the time to understand why auto credit is very different from other consumer financial services.

I think I had put 200 pages behind me before I came upon anything dealing with auto financing. And, sure enough, the CFPB predictably referred to the transactions as "loans."

Now, perhaps the transactions studied by the CFPB were loans, but I strongly suspect that they were instead retail installment contracts, typically used in dealer financing. If I'm right about that, then much of the study becomes really murky in a hurry.

"Why?" you ask. Here's why.

A retail installment sale contract evidences the simultaneous sale of a vehicle and the financing of the vehicle. Disputes involving these transactions can be credit related (perhaps the finance company incorrectly charges finance charges), but they can also be car related (the transmission fails). The type of dispute will have a bearing on the amount of the claim (an engine repair is expensive), the likelihood that a claim would be appropriate for class relief (a claim of fraud in the sales process is unlikely to get class treatment because of the individualized proof required), and the likelihood that a claim will be brought by a consumer (larger claims, it seems, would be less likely to be simply dropped by the consumer). The study makes no attempt to tease out of the data any distinctions regarding credit-related and car-related auto disputes.

So, there's much to dislike about the CFPB's work so far on arbitration. You'd think that arbitration must have some things to recommend it; after all, Congress passed the Federal Arbitration Act, and all or nearly all the states have enacted laws permitting arbitration. The CFPB seems determined not to see any good in the process.

My prediction? The CFPB is staunchly anti-arbitration (pre-dispute, binding arbitration) and has determined to prohibit its use in consumer financial transactions.

May 2015
Pinocchio and the Senator

A recent quote from Senator Elizabeth Warren got a lot of attention from the auto dealer community, and for good reason. Here's what she said: "One study estimates that these auto dealer markups cost consumers $26 billion a year. Auto dealers got a specific exemption from CFPB [Consumer Financial

CHAPTER 8

Protection Bureau] oversight, and it is no coincidence that auto loans are now the most troubled consumer financial product. Congress should give the CFPB the authority it needs to supervise car loans—and keep that $26 billion a year in the pockets of consumers where it belongs."

That statement was the subject of an article by Glenn Kessler, the fact-checking investigator at *The Washington Post*. He gave the statement a grade of "Four Pinocchios" for Sen. Warren's "false claim that auto dealer markups cost consumers $26 billion a year." "Four Pinocchios" is *The Washington Post's* worst rating, awarded for "erroneous claims by political candidates, interest groups, and the media."

Sen. Warren's $26 billion a year claim was taken from the widely criticized findings of an April 2011 "report" by the Center for Responsible Lending. That study, frequently and accurately debunked by the National Automobile Dealers Association, also claimed, among many other inaccurate findings, that the average dealer participation earned in subprime finance contracts is 5.04% (even though the contractual caps on what dealers can earn on such deals are usually well below that amount). Despite the questionable scholarship evidenced by the study, it has been cited over and over again by politicians and their aides, the media, and others since its release.

It's refreshing to see *The Washington Post*—not exactly a fan of the consumer financing industry—call out Sen. Warren on her statement. The article was an excellent effort, reflecting the sort of probing and questioning that reporters seldom seem to bring to the claims of consumer advocates.

Mr. Kessler could have added, by the way, that even the CFPB has conceded that dealers are entitled to compensation for their role in the auto financing process. Although there is an argument about what constitutes fair compensation for dealers, the aggregate amount of such compensation would be quite a big number.

Mr. Kessler also could have pointed out that Sen. Warren offered not one whit of evidence that subjecting car dealers to CFPB oversight, instead of the oversight of the Federal Trade Commission, as is now the case, would make any difference in enforcement efforts.

And Mr. Kessler could have pointed out that Sen. Warren offered no support whatever for her laughable statement that "auto loans are now the most troubled consumer financial product." If there is any truth to her proposition, Mr. Kessler should point out, Sen. Warren should be blasting the FTC for its lack of oversight and enforcement.

As a final quibble, you should note that Mr. Kessler, like most journalists, mischaracterizes the auto finance process as it operates at dealerships. Dealers do not make loans. They engage in credit sale transactions.

Before you scoff at "mere semantics," consider this: Loans and credit sale transactions are almost always governed by different laws, including those related to maximum finance charge caps and disclosures. More importantly, in a credit sale transaction, the dealership is the initial creditor, extending credit by the act of exchanging a car for a contract containing the buyer's promise to pay for the car over time. The dealership, by the way, could keep the credit contract and collect payments (including the full finance charge, not simply "participation" in part of it) directly from the buyer, if it wished.

Most dealers prefer liquidity and do not want to hold and service these contracts, so they sell the contracts to finance companies, banks, and credit unions (not as "brokers," as Mr. Kessler characterizes them, but as primary parties in the credit

CHAPTER 8

sale to the car buyer). Other dealers do keep their credit contracts—they are called buy-here, pay-here dealers (most dealers who keep their contracts are not exempt from the CFPB's jurisdiction).

The role of dealerships in auto finance is accurately described in a publication called "Understanding Vehicle Financing," a consumer education publication produced jointly by the American Financial Services Association and the NADA, in cooperation with the FTC. This pamphlet is a "must read" for any reporter who writes about auto financing. I'm sending Mr. Kessler a copy.

So, good work, Mr. Kessler. I was tempted to give you half a Pinocchio for not calling out Sen. Warren on her other claims and for not correctly describing the business you are writing about, but you did such a thorough job on the $26 billion claim that I decided to give you a pass.

May 2015
FTC Enforcement Actions—Nothing New

The federal agencies most important to the auto sales, finance, and leasing world really like to trumpet their enforcement actions in press releases. The Consumer Financial Protection Bureau has earned an early reputation for saying things in press releases that are not supported by the actions being announced. The Federal Trade Commission's press folks, on the other hand, are becoming known for the catchy names they apply to their enforcement efforts.

In early 2014, the FTC announced "Operation Steer Clear," described as a "nationwide enforcement sweep focusing on the sale, financing, and leasing of motor vehicles." In that action, the FTC announced that nine vehicle dealers agreed to settle deceptive advertising charges and that the agency was taking action against a tenth dealer. The FTC claimed that the dealers made misrepresentations that violated the FTC Act in print, Internet, and video ads, falsely leading consumers to believe they could buy vehicles for low prices, could finance vehicles with low monthly payments, could lease vehicles with no upfront payment, and/or had won prizes they could collect at the dealership. The ads also allegedly violated the Consumer Leasing Act and Regulation M by failing to disclose certain lease-related terms and/or the Truth in Lending Act and Regulation Z by failing to disclose certain credit-related terms.

Evidently, the FTC press folks liked the catchy "Steer Clear" moniker so much that they've done it again.

On March 26, the FTC and multiple law enforcement partners announced the results of "Operation Ruse Control," a nationwide and cross-border enforcement effort focusing on deceptive practices in car sales, leasing, and financing. Ruse Control involved 252 enforcement actions. There were 187 actions in the United States since the FTC's last sweep in early 2014 and 65 in Canada. These actions involved enforcement efforts by the FTC, the U.S. Attorney's Office in the Northern District of Alabama, and other U.S. and Canadian federal, state, and local agencies. The cases include civil and criminal charges of deceptive advertising, financing application fraud, odometer fraud, deceptive add-on fees, and deceptive marketing of car title loans. The FTC has settled six of these cases, obtaining more than $2.6 million in monetary judgments.

The FTC's press release said, "For the first time since receiving expanded authority over auto dealers under the Dodd-Frank Act, the FTC has taken two auto enforcement actions involving add-ons, which is the practice of a dealer or other third party adding to the vehicle sales, lease, or finance agreement

CHAPTER 8

charges for other products or services." That statement may be technically correct, but it's misleading. It implies that Dodd-Frank gave the FTC new powers, but the FTC has had the necessary enforcement authority to bring actions like these since before wheels were invented—long before Dodd-Frank was enacted. What Dodd-Frank did was exempt certain car dealers from the jurisdiction of the CFPB, essentially pressuring the FTC to take up the regulatory slack.

What was striking to me about both Operation Steer Clear and Operation Ruse Control is that the FTC's toolbox for bringing the actions contained nothing new. The laws and regulations that the FTC claimed dealers were violating—TILA, for example—have been around for decades. The FTC has had authority to prohibit deceptive practices since 1938, and since 1914 if it could prove injury to competition. And, no, I wasn't there for either of those.

Not only have the laws and regulations been around for decades, the FTC's actions did not rely on any imaginative or innovative interpretations of those laws. The rules the FTC claims the dealers broke are about as clear as rules get.

What was also striking about the FTC's actions was the apparent complete ignorance (or indifference) of the targeted dealers to the requirements under these long-standing laws and regulations. How many times will it be necessary for the FTC to unlimber its 2x4 and flail more dealers before it finally dawns on the dealers that they have compliance responsibilities they must take seriously?

If your compliance officer has not read all of the documents the FTC released in connection with these operations and adjusted your dealership's advertising and sales practices where necessary, you should do so immediately.

Don't have a compliance officer? I rest my poor, tired case.

June 2015
As We Bid a Fond Farewell to Arbitration Clauses

Since the early to mid-1990s, auto finance companies and car dealers have increasingly incorporated mandatory, pre-dispute arbitration clauses into the documents that consumers sign in connection with credit transactions. "Mandatory," because the consumer and the creditor agree that all disputes will be arbitrated or that, at the request of either party, all disputes will be arbitrated. "Pre-dispute," because the parties agree to arbitration before the dispute arises.

Creditors adopted these arbitration agreements because they could include language that banned class action relief. Creditors had long objected that the class action mechanism gave consumer lawyers an unfair advantage—if a consumer's complaint survived the creditor's motion to dismiss and the court certified a class, the game was over. No creditor wanted to "bet the company" on a class action trial, so the cases quickly settled, usually on terms that mostly benefited the lawyers supposedly representing the class. Arbitration clauses prohibiting class relief took this blackmail tool away from the class action lawyers.

The arbitration agreements generally performed as advertised. The class action lawyers challenged the enforceability of the agreements in case after case, usually arguing that the clauses were "unconscionable" and should not be enforceable. As courts rejected their arguments, the lawyers came up with new theories. Users of arbitration clauses over time revised the terms of the clauses to meet each new theory.

For the most part, courts have upheld the enforceability of arbitration clauses. Frustrated by the inability to successfully challenge the use of arbitration agreements in the courts, the critics of arbitration turned to Congress.

CHAPTER 8

For years, the anti-arbitration crowd has been railing against the use of arbitration clauses in consumer financing contracts. They were successful in having several bills that banned the use of arbitration clauses introduced in Congress, but they had no luck advancing the bills to enactment.

Then along came the steamroller called the Dodd-Frank Act. The trial lawyers and consumer advocates tried to append an outright ban on arbitration to the bill as it plowed through Congress. They were unsuccessful, ending up with only the Dodd-Frank mandate to the Consumer Financial Protection Bureau to study the topic and take action on its findings, up to and including a "license to kill" the use of arbitration altogether.

The CFPB is gearing up to take action on arbitration clauses. So far, the Bureau's activity on arbitration has been limited to issuing two reports of studies it has conducted on the topic, and we haven't yet seen an outright ban on the use of arbitration. But make no mistake; one is on the way.

There was a brief moment of hope that arbitration might survive when the Bureau's second report said that, in many class action cases, when the principal purpose of seeking class relief is to pressure a settlement, members of the class got nothing or next to nothing; class action cases almost never make it to a trial on the merits, while a significant percentage of arbitration proceedings actually resolve the disputes of the parties; and arbitration is both faster and more economical than litigation.

That glimmer of good sense quickly disappeared under the weight of a lot of discussion by the Bureau of the advantages of class action lawsuits. The report also did not discuss the public policy implications of the use of arbitration clauses evidenced by the enactment of the Federal Arbitration Act and of arbitration laws in nearly every state, nor did it dwell on the hundreds of court opinions that rejected the unconscionability arguments of the class action lawyers. Those observations would not have advanced the Bureau's agenda.

A prediction? I'll bet my favorite rod and reel that the Bureau has bought the rope, measured it, tied the noose, found the tree, and dug the grave for arbitration. Now all the CFPB needs to do is give it a fair trial.

July 2015
Advertising Roulette

If you are a dealer and you have not heard that federal and state authorities are launching a serious crackdown on advertising violations, you must be living under a rock. For the last several years, there has been a steady increase in ad violation claims, with the most recent and most attention-getting initiatives being the Federal Trade Commission's "Operation Steer Clear" and "Operation Ruse Control."

With all the publicity about regulatory scrutiny of dealership ads, I find it hard to work up much sympathy for a dealer who hasn't gotten the word and is playing "ad roulette." That was certainly my reaction when I read the latest report of one of these enforcement actions.

The Office of the Attorney General of Tennessee announced on April 20 that it had reached a settlement with a Tennessee auto dealer that the AG and the Tennessee Division of Consumer Affairs had charged with using deceptive business practices to target military families. The dealer, Wholesale Inc., agreed to immediately change its advertising practices and pay the state $50,000.

A county court approved the settlement among the dealer, the Tennessee AG's office, and the Division of Consumer Affairs. The settlement agreement centered around two

CHAPTER 8

advertising mailers sent to would-be customers. One mailer specifically targeted servicemembers living near Fort Campbell.

After reviewing a servicemember's complaint, the state alleged that the dealership made numerous false representations in violation of the Tennessee Consumer Protection Act. According to the state, a fictitious lender called "CreditAble Auto Funding," claiming to be "by military, for military," was offering "a limited amount of loans to military personnel."

Under the settlement, the dealership must maintain proof to support all ad claims and will be required to include the company name on all ads sent to consumers. The dealership also must develop written policies and procedures for reviewing and approving its ads.

Nothing in the settlement agreement mentioned an ad agency, but I'll bet my favorite bass lure that this dealer didn't dream up this ad campaign and that some ad agency has come up with an ad program it sells to dealers located near military bases. Some ad agencies seem to believe that it's OK to say anything in an ad that will bring potential car buyers in the door—I've seen ad packages offered to dealers that seem to have absolutely no regard for the truth of the statements made in the ads. If the dealer bites and buys the ad package, those statements, of course, become the dealer's statements.

If my suspicions are correct, one lesson from this Tennessee action is clear. The authorities will hold the dealer accountable for every ad and every claim in every ad. They will require that the dealer "substantiate" each claim made in the ad. So, if an ad describes a creditor company as "by military, for military," it is the dealer's responsibility to determine if that statement is true. If a creditor named in an ad turns out not to exist, the authorities will hold the dealership responsible for implying or stating in its ad that the creditor is real.

Another lesson is equally clear. Not only must dealerships pay attention to federal laws like the Truth in Lending Act and the Consumer Leasing Act, they must contend with the Federal Trade Commission and state attorneys general—enforcers of prohibitions against unfair acts and practices.

So what should a dealership do to avoid being in the crosshairs of the ad police? I can think of a few things.

First, if a dealership's ads come from an ad agency, the dealership should do a "due diligence" review of the agency to determine if the agency's ads have ever created problems for dealers. The ad agency should be questioned about the level of dealer compliance training, if any, its personnel have received and should agree to stand behind its ads.

Then the dealer should read the ads and confirm that the statements in them are accurate and complete. If the statements make claims, the dealer should assume that those claims may, at some point, be challenged, so all such claims should be substantiated in writing before the ads are used. The dealer should confirm that the ads meet the requirements of federal and state law, including, where applicable, laws regulating merchants generally, dealers specifically, and ads involving a lottery, a game of chance, or other regulated activity. That sort of confirmation may require the advice of counsel, but there are many helpful ad compliance materials available on the FTC's website and on the websites of organizations such as state auto dealer associations.

The dealer's entire ad review process should be in writing and reviewed by counsel and should be updated periodically. All of these chores should be the responsibility of the dealership's Compliance Officer.

Your dealership doesn't have a Compliance Officer?

Oh my! We need to talk.

CHAPTER 8

September 2015
Where Are the Auto Finance Complaints?

On August 25, the Consumer Financial Protection Bureau released its monthly complaint portal report. Of the 26,704 complaints handled in July, approximately 8,224 of them, or 31%, were about debt collection—the most complained-about financial product or service. The runner-up was credit reporting, with about 6,696 complaints. Mortgages came in third, accounting for approximately 4,498 complaints.

For all the *sturm und drang* (or storm and stress, in English) recently coming from the Bureau regarding auto finance, you'd have expected that car dealers and finance companies would be high on the list of complaints. You'd be wrong.

I invite you to read through the Bureau's press release and the 25-page report itself. Maybe you can find some references to auto finance. I couldn't.

Admittedly, it's possible that other categories contain auto finance complaints. At least one category, installment loans, might involve some auto financing, but because of the Bureau's inexplicable refusal to use the term "loan" correctly (as the name of a product that is different from an "installment sale"), it is difficult to say for sure. In any event, the installment loan category does not expressly mention auto finance.

I suspect that some car finance companies and some dealers subject to the CFPB's jurisdiction might have had some of the general problems identified by the Bureau. That might make it instructive for those companies to look at the sorts of complaints consumers file.

Most of the credit report complaints (77%) dealt with incorrect information in the reports. Consumers frequently complain of debts they have paid or debts not yet due showing up on their reports and negatively affecting their credit scores.

2015: MANNING THE RAMPARTS

Consumers also complained about trouble accessing reports. Apparently this difficulty is a result of rigorous online identity authentication procedures. Consumers unable to access reports over the Internet have to send copies of sensitive, identifying documents by mail, which they feel is time consuming and potentially unsecure (perhaps they should complain about the post office).

The report identifies high-volume complaint companies. The three companies with the most complaints from March through May 2015 were Equifax, Experian, and Bank of America. Of the five most complained-about companies, three of them—Equifax, Experian, and Transunion—are credit reporting companies. Even the Bureau recognizes that company-level information should be considered in context of company size, and says it is seeking ways to help portal users understand the complaint data and the effect of size on the numbers. Until that little problem is solved, some companies with lots of customers but with few problems will continue to get an undeserved bad rap.

The report also contains information about complaint distribution by state and by product and looks at increases from one reporting period to the next. Other than the absence of any complaint information identified as being applicable to auto finance, the state and product breakdowns weren't particularly revealing. The period-to-period increases were large in many instances, but the complaint portal is new, and I suspect that the big jumps are more attributable to the fact that the portal is becoming better known—thereby increasing its use—rather than to any surge of bad acting on the part of creditors.

Notwithstanding the lack of complaints that deal expressly with auto finance, you should monitor the portal and watch for

285

any complaints from your customers. It only takes one to pique the interest of a CFPB enforcer, and you need to head off anything that would draw the CFPB's attention to your business.

September 2015
Data Nuggets

I always look forward to the National Independent Automobile Dealers Association's Used Car Industry Report. It's probably the best source for aggregate data on used car dealers, and it's chock full of revealing information.

Because I had been thinking about the effect that the Consumer Financial Protection Bureau is having on independent car dealers and how, as small businesses, those dealers face pretty much the same regulatory and compliance burdens as much larger businesses, a few items jumped off the pages of the report. These caught my eye.

The first question the report answers is the percentage of car dealerships that qualify for the exemption from CFPB jurisdiction in the Dodd-Frank Act. Buy-here, pay-here dealers don't qualify for the exemption because they hold their own retail installment contracts or leases (or sell them to their related finance companies). Dealers who sell their retail installment contracts or leases but who do not have vehicle servicing capabilities don't qualify for the exemption either. The report indicates that about four of 10 responding dealers had no service bays, indicating that at least 40% of dealers don't qualify for an exemption for this reason alone. Add to that number those BHPH dealers who have servicing facilities, and you end up with the total percentage of independent dealers subject to the CFPB's tender mercies. There's an outstanding question about what constitutes enough of a servicing capability to qualify for the exemption, but we'll leave that one for another day.

I have long thought of independent car dealerships as real "mom and pop" operations. I didn't know how descriptive that characterization was until I noted in the report that 96% of the respondents had only a single sales location. Those locations don't appear to be jam-packed with employees—63.1% of the respondents have one to four employees, and 17% have at least five but fewer than nine employees. Those numbers don't leave a lot of room for an on-staff compliance officer, do they? Think about the federal law requirements that small shops face, and tell me how anyone realistically believes that these dealers can comply.

If you have read any of the *New York Times* or *Los Angeles Times* articles on evil car dealers, or listened to the baying consumer advocates who show up at every CFPB field hearing, you would think that independent car dealers, and especially BHPH dealers, sell cars that are so bad they would need a lot of work to be classified as junk. It ain't so. Over 80% of the cars sold by the respondents had less than 100,000 miles showing on the odometer, while half had 80,000 miles or less. I've spent a lot of time behind the wheels of cars with over 80K on the clock, and they were pretty good cars. Dealers are paying an average of $7,150 for these vehicles, indicating that the dealers collectively think these cars have miles left on them. Dealers are a savvy lot, and they don't lay out seven large for sleds. Most of these dealers are selling cars with a substantial amount of life left in them.

Finally, the report shows that dealers are spending more on legal and regulatory compliance expenses. Those costs, as a percentage of revenue, more than doubled from 2014. Look for those costs to continue to escalate.

CHAPTER 8

As interpreted by the CFPB, the federal consumer financial protection laws and regulations have become much more robust. As an example, it is no longer sufficient for a dealer to abide by the law—the CFPB requires that dealers have a compliance management system (CMS) detailing their compliance efforts. That CMS imposes corporate oversight, auditing, and recordkeeping requirements. Complying with the CFPB's expansive reading of these laws adds to a dealership's expenses and headaches.

Mulling over these nuggets of information makes me wonder if the members of Congress who enacted the Dodd-Frank Act, creating the CFPB, had any knowledge about the industry they were regulating.

September 2015
How Good Do You Look in Orange?

I'm talking prison uniform orange, not Clemson orange. Not Orioles orange. Prison orange. Here's why I ask.

A number of federal consumer financial laws that apply to dealers and finance companies are set up to administer a triple whammy to violators. They impose civil liability on the creditor for consumers who are harmed, fines or penalties that must be paid to the regulators, and (gasp!) criminal penalties. The federal Truth in Lending Act is such a law, and there are others.

Most dealers and finance companies are generally familiar with the provisions of these laws that allow for compensation to injured consumers. When private lawyers bring lawsuits for individual consumers or for a class of "similarly situated" consumers, they seek such damages. As an example, TILA provides for so-called "statutory damages" that a plaintiff may recover, even in the absence of any actual damages, and also permits a plaintiff to recover actual damages, along with attorneys' fees and court costs.

The Dodd-Frank Act added hefty penalties that can be imposed by the Consumer Financial Protection Bureau for violations of the federal consumer financial laws. These administrative penalties don't require a court action from a consumer, but can be assessed by the CFPB through enforcement or imposed by referrals to the Department of Justice following supervisory reviews.

But criminal penalties? Who ever heard of a criminal case for a disclosure violation?

OK, I confess. I have never seen a criminal case brought against a creditor for a violation of TILA. No one I know of is doing hard time for failing to disclose an accurate annual percentage rate. No one's in the slammer because the term "Finance Charge" in a disclosure statement was not more conspicuous than other required disclosures. That being the case, why am I wasting your time?

Because, as Bob Dylan will tell you, "The times, they are a-changin'."

The CFPB is interpreting the federal financial laws in a dangerously expansive way. The legal theories the Bureau is pushing are edgy, if not downright radical. One dictionary definition of "zealot" is "a person who is fanatical and uncompromising in pursuit of . . . religious, political, or other ideals." By that definition, I believe that the Bureau has more than a few zealots on the payroll, and I think that those zealots sooner or later simply will not be able to resist reaching for what would be a very powerful weapon: referring a matter to the Justice Department for a criminal charge for a violation of a federal consumer financial law.

CHAPTER 8

When that scenario eventually unfolds, you can bet your hushpuppy recipe that the facts of the case won't be pretty. You won't hear about a "mom and pop" buy-here, pay-here dealership that tried its dead-level best to keep a chronically delinquent customer in a car but made some minor technical mistake along the way. Nope, there will be some dealer or finance company really behaving badly; a consumer who hasn't done much, if anything, to deserve mistreatment; and, probably, allegations of racial discrimination, unfair, deceptive, and abusive sales or servicing practices, abuse of servicemembers, defamation of the Girl Scouts of America (just kidding), or some combination of all of these.

Lawyers say that "bad facts make bad law." This would be an example of that adage. And if the facts are that bad, an attempt to bring a criminal charge just might work. And perhaps just the threat by the regulator to make a criminal referral will be enough to force a creditor to agree to a disadvantageous settlement.

So, if the threat of civil lawsuits (including class actions) and punitive regulatory assessments has not been enough to compel you to begin to get your compliance house in order, maybe, just maybe, the possibility of jail time will. Give it some thought—orange is just not your color.

October 2015
Consumer Credit Regulation—The Long View

People think that the wave of federal and state regulation of the credit industry is something new. It ain't so.

Recently, I gave a presentation in which I tried to convey to the audience the historical sweep of the struggle between the U.S. consumer credit industry and the country's pro-consumer protection advocates. The narrative I compiled reminded me of the Hundred Years' War.

The first thing to note about the Hundred Years' War is that it wasn't. It was a series of conflicts that spanned 116 years—from 1337 to 1453. The fight, between the rulers of England and the rulers of France and their respective allies, was about who would control France.

The "war" over the regulation of credit has not yet consumed 100 years, much less 116 years, but it's beginning to get a bit long in the tooth.

I'm sure that other credit scholars could identify earlier points at which the battle was joined, but my pick is the point after World War II, when the combination of returning soldiers, high demand for household formation (they had to put us "boomer" babies somewhere), and suddenly idled industrial war capacity led to the increased production of cars, washing machines, furniture, and those "enormous" 12-inch screen TV sets. The modern credit movement arguably can be traced to companies that rushed to make it possible for people to buy the things they needed while paying for them over time.

The regulation of credit law during that time was not exactly what you'd call robust. The Uniform Law Commission first promulgated the Uniform Commercial Code in 1952 (the effort began in 1942). The UCC supplanted the Law Merchant, which was a system of rules, customs, and usages generally recognized and adopted by traders as the law for the regulation of their commercial transactions and the resolution of their controversies. Neither the original UCC nor the Law Merchant was particularly long on consumer protection.

But someone always spoils the party, and it wasn't long before creditors, including car dealers, behaved badly. Onerous credit terms, high finance charge rates, a mishmash of ways to

CHAPTER 8

calculate and disclose interest and finance charge rates, collection and repossession abuses, and other sorts of misbehavior led to a wave of state laws regulating consumer lending and the credit sale of goods to consumers. These state laws were, for the most part, a jumble of responses to the abuses emerging in the marketplace.

The uneven response by the states to consumer protection led the Uniform Law Commission to promulgate the Uniform Consumer Credit Code in 1968. The so-called "U3C" was intended as a comprehensive regulation of consumer credit in any state that chose to enact it. Later issued in modified versions, the U3C was not exactly a flop, but it didn't take the nation by storm either. Today, it, or parts of it, can be found in the laws of a double handful of states.

The same forces that propelled the development of the U3C were at work at the federal level as well. Senator William Proxmire's introduction of the Truth in Lending Act in the late '60s was followed by a tidal wave of federal consumer credit regulation, including the Equal Credit Opportunity Act, the Fair Credit Reporting Act, and the Consumer Leasing Act, to mention a few.

After the mid-'70s, things quieted down a bit. Industry actually scored a modest victory in 1980 with federal legislation that "simplified" TILA. But the quiet was only a relative quiet—the consumer advocates pressed their agendas in other places, including before the drafting committees of the Uniform Law Commission, trying to turn the UCC into a nationwide pro-consumer body of law.

But the consumer advocates went down in flames occasionally, as well. As an example, after several years of development, the Uniform Law Commissioners' Uniform Consumer Leasing Act—a veritable Christmas tree on which the consumer advocates hung every "gotcha" anti-lessor provision they could dream up—ended up being adopted in only one state.

But, the pendulum is never still. Now we have Dodd-Frank, the Consumer Financial Protection Bureau, and Elizabeth Warren. The consumer advocates are pretty much in the driver's seat at the moment, and many industry folks spend a lot of time railing about the "over-regulation" of the credit industry.

No doubt the pendulum will eventually swing back in the other direction. After all, we're only 60 years into this particular war.

October 2015
Defeating Class Actions the Old-Fashioned Way

There was a time, several years ago, when one of the biggest risks a dealership faced in connection with its F&I activities was a class action lawsuit. Regulatory actions and attorney general actions were both pretty high on the list of potential legal perils, but class actions typically involved big numbers and posed significant danger to the continuing health of the dealership.

The class action threat was so serious that many dealers and sales finance companies started using mandatory, pre-dispute arbitration agreements in their sales and finance contracts. Properly drafted agreements can serve as an effective first line of defense against class action lawsuits. But the Consumer Financial Protection Bureau, many of us believe, is poised to declare illegal the use of such agreements. If that happens, the bad old days of class action risk will return.

Arbitration, though, is not the only defense against class actions. Over the years, defense lawyers have used a number of different arguments to defeat a plaintiff's motion to "certify" a class. One such argument is that the class action process is not a better way to proceed than requiring each member of the class to file his or her own action for relief.

Here's an example of the effective employment of this argument.

In 2010, Phillys Johnson bought a car from MKA Enterprises, Inc., d/b/a Legends Toyota. The purchase agreement failed to disclose that the car had been used as a rental car. When Johnson discovered the car had been a rental car, she filed a lawsuit against Legends, seeking to represent a class of people like her, and the trial court certified Johnson's class. Facing a certified class, Legends appealed.

The Court of Appeals of Kansas reversed the trial court's decision and denied Johnson's motion for class certification. While the trial court determined that prosecuting separate actions by individual members of the class would create the risk of inconsistent results, the appellate court disagreed. The appellate court held that because the process of buying a car is inherently fact-driven, class certification would deny each individual claimant the opportunity to seek his or her actual damages or a civil penalty—which might exceed the actual damages.

Second, the trial court determined that questions of law or fact common to class members predominated over any questions that affected only individual members, making class certification the superior manner in which to manage and prosecute the claims of the individual class members. Again, the appellate court disagreed, finding that the trial court would be required to conduct multiple "mini-trials" in order to determine each class member's injury or loss—proceedings that would be time consuming and likely inefficient.

For these reasons, the appellate court reversed the trial court's certification of class action status and remanded the case to the trial court so that Johnson could proceed on her individual claims. Suddenly, a big, dangerous hurricane became a windstorm—still possibly a problem, but not nearly as bad as it was originally.

If class actions enjoy a revival after the CFPB bans arbitration, defense lawyers will need precedents like this one to counter the threat. Maybe you should share this article with your lawyer.

Johnson v. MKA Enterprises, Inc., 2015 Kan. App. Unpub. LEXIS 578 (Kan. App. July 17, 2015).

CHAPTER 8

Chapter 9

2016: No Truce in Sight

CHAPTER 9

With no hope that the feds will back off, dealers and those entities that buy the dealers' finance contracts and lease contracts are beginning to accept the fact that they must change their ways if they are to stay in this business. Examples of that acceptance can be found in the compliance training and certification programs offered by the National Automotive Finance Association, the Association of Finance and Insurance Professionals, and by other organizations.

Companies who offer various services to dealers are positioning themselves as sources of compliant forms and procedures by embedding those forms and procedures into their offerings. Entirely new technologies designed to manage the F&I closing process to keep it legal are emerging.

While there will be winners and losers as all of this shakes out, with luck, the brighter minds in our business will be able to create a sufficient number of compliance solutions to keep the regulators at bay. Those solutions won't be cheap, though, and it's likely that a wave of consolidation will occur, creating companies large enough to foot the bill for serious compliance.

March 2016
Vital Signs

My experience with dealers is that they tend to be, shall we say, frugal when it comes to spending money on F&I-related compliance. A full-blown review of all dealership F&I policies, procedures, documents, and related matters can quickly run into real money. While many dealers have come to the conclusion that such a review makes sense in light of the heat coming from the Federal Trade Commission, the Consumer Financial Protection Bureau, state attorneys general, and plaintiffs' lawyers, many others have not seen a threat substantive enough to justify the large expense.

For these dealers who haven't seen the light, I sometimes recommend a deal jacket review. The cost of plowing through a half-dozen or so representative deal jackets is substantially less than a full compliance review. A deal jacket review can be a useful first step in identifying compliance problems and in convincing a dealer to undertake a more comprehensive effort. I tell dealers that it's a bit like a doctor checking your pulse, blood pressure, temperature, and respiration. If something's amiss with one of those vitals, that's a symptom that something else—something more serious—might be going on.

What sorts of things do we find when we do these reviews? Here are a few examples.

- *Rubbish Bin Files.* Do the deal jackets look like miniature landfills, containing all sorts of extraneous stuff that shouldn't be there? Each deal jacket should have a table of contents and a checklist, and each document listed in the table of contents should appear, in order, in the deal jacket. Nothing that doesn't belong in the deal jacket should be there, and nothing that is required should be missing. Messy files that contain everything, including the kitchen sink, suggest that the dealership isn't organized, that there is no (lawyer-approved) document retention program, and that the quality control imposed by uniformly organized deal jackets is missing.
- *Signatures Would be Nice.* Many of the documents in the deal jacket constitute agreements of some sort between the dealership and the buyer. Usually, these documents have signature lines with a space for a date so that the parties can evidence that they have agreed to the terms of the document and when. It isn't unusual, in our

experience, for these documents to lack a required signature. Even when the dealership representatives are diligent about having the buyer sign documents, dealership signatures sometimes will be omitted. Unsigned documents can have dire consequences—the court refuses to enforce an arbitration agreement because the dealer didn't sign it, so the dealer's attempt to thwart a class action lawsuit is unsuccessful. The table of contents might highlight all deal jacket documents that need signatures, another form of quality control.

- *Coloring Inside the Lines.* Dealership computer systems are supposed to be programmed to print specific data entries in specific places on the forms that are used in the sales and financing transaction. You'd be surprised how often the "strike points" for printing are off enough to give the buyer's lawyer an argument that the disclosures are incorrect. "Close" doesn't cut it.

- *Contracts So Old They Are Written on Parchment.* Buyers orders, retail installment sales contracts, and leases are not cast in stone. The companies that provide these forms to dealers frequently change the forms and alert dealers when they do. Invariably, some dealers don't get the word or choose to ignore the news in order to exhaust the supply of old forms on hand. That can lead to disclosure or substantive violations for every deal in which those forms are used. It's usually easy to determine if a particular form is a vendor's latest iteration. Checking online or making a phone call can get you the form's most recent revision date.

- *Safe Harbor? What Safe Harbor?* Some laws are complicated, and the regulators who enforce those laws are considerate enough to provide "safe harbor" versions of legal forms required by those laws. As an example, the

FTC has published a safe harbor version of the privacy notice required by the FTC's privacy regulations. If I open a deal jacket and see a privacy notice that isn't in the safe harbor format, I know the dealership's F&I forms and processes are not receiving a lawyer's attention.

- *One Form Too Many?* One arbitration agreement is enough. Some dealers use a form of retail installment sale agreement that contains an arbitration clause, a buyers order with a different arbitration clause, and one or more documents evidencing the sale of ancillary products with still different arbitration clauses. A judge looking at that sort of hodgepodge will likely throw up his hands and refuse to enforce any of the arbitration clauses, leaving the dealership without protection from class actions when it is most needed.

- *Small Tricks and Traps.* An outdoorsman tracking game can sometimes track an animal from the smallest hints—crushed grass here, a broken twig there. Likewise, a quick scan through the dealer's forms can tell you if a good lawyer has laid hands on them. Does the buyers order contain the notice required by the FTC Used Car Rule? Is the notice conspicuous? If the dealer negotiates deals in Spanish, does the notice also appear in Spanish? Is the dealer's disclaimer of implied warranties in an "as-is" sale conspicuous? Is the notice required by the FTC's Preservation of Consumer Claims and Defenses Trade Regulation Rule printed in 10-point, bold-faced type?

These are just a few examples of the sorts of clues a deal jacket review will pick up. I'm sure others could be added to this list.

Does the patient have a fever? Pulse rate high? Shallow breathing? Blood pressure off the charts? Maybe it's just a

CHAPTER 9

reaction to something the patient ate . . . or perhaps these are signs of much more serious health problems.

And if a dealer's deal jackets can't pass common-sense tests like the ones discussed above, you can be pretty sure there are deeper F&I compliance problems that need to be addressed.

March 2016
Dealer Advertising—the Lowest-Hanging Regulatory Fruit

Car dealers apparently don't know, or don't care, that their ads violate some of the most basic federal advertising laws. Consider these real-life examples.

A Honda dealer in South Carolina lines up cars in front of the dealership and hangs a sign on each car showing the monthly payment for the car, with no other text.

A Mercedes dealer, also in the Palmetto State, has a billboard that displays a flashy new Mertz and a monthly payment—no other text.

An ultra-high-line used car dealer sends out a mailer showing a lot of really nice cars, each sporting a monthly payment but with no other financing information anywhere in the mailer.

A used car dealer in Arizona displays a sign on the side of a car offered for sale that says "$6,777 CASH PRICE— HAS BEEN DISCOUNTED FOR CASH PAYING CUSTOMERS."

An Arizona dealer's website shows a car with a "Showroom Price" of $18,783 and an "Internet Special" price of $17,283, then says "The Internet Cash Special is exactly that All Cash, plus applicable Sales tax, license and Title Fees and A Dealer Documentation Fee," and "When Financing, refer to the

Regular Sales Price and interest and Applicable Fees may increase the overall cost of the vehicle."

Let's consider two basic rules imposed by the federal Truth in Lending Act. Rule 1—Showing the amount of a monthly payment in an ad triggers a requirement to disclose other financing terms. Displaying only the monthly payment, without more, is about as basic a TILA advertising violation as I can think of. Rule 2—You cannot have one cash price for cash deals and a higher price for financed deals. The higher amount for the financed deal is a finance charge, not part of the cash price. Again, it's hard to imagine a more basic TILA violation.

All of the examples I note above are ones that I have seen with my own sparkly blue eyes or ones that friends have sent me. I wish I could tell you that they are atypical and that most dealers follow the rules when they advertise. Alas, I can't. These ads are much more typical than not.

So, are these dealers being blindsided by new rules enacted by the newly active federal agencies—the Consumer Financial Protection Bureau and the Federal Trade Commission—that enforce TILA? Nope. These rules, in essentially the form in which they appear today, have been around for nearly 50 years.

What has changed is that the agencies, and particularly the FTC, have ramped up enforcement of the rules to a level we have not seen before. State AGs, following the lead of the feds, have jumped on the advertising prosecution bandwagon as well.

And why not? The cases against the dealers whose ads are described above would be open and shut. In each instance, all the evidence a prosecuting agency would need to prove a violation has been thoughtfully provided by the dealer. The ad is exhibit 1. Case closed. There are simply no easier regulatory cases the agencies can bring. This is the lowest-hanging fruit for them.

CHAPTER 9

But, dealers tell me, "I'm below the radar of the federal agencies. They aren't looking at my ads." I tell them, "Think again. FTC and CFPB staffers are on the same mailing lists that your customers are on, see the same billboards and lot displays, and just love to review dealer websites. Keep on running noncompliant ads, and you'll see how good the regulatory radar is."

May 2016
Where Do Those Pesky Laws and Regulations Come From?

In monitoring the auto finance and lease legal landscape, we see what seems like an endless parade of punitive legislation and regulation aimed at car dealers. If you've noticed the same thing, perhaps you've wondered where all of those proposed laws and regulations come from.

Do you suppose that each legislative and regulatory body has a standing committee of well-informed, fair-minded folks whose jobs are to understand the auto industry and legislate or regulate it in a sensible way that protects consumers but doesn't overburden reputable dealers with layer after layer of restrictions?

Do you also believe in the Easter Bunny?

The reality behind those laws and regulations is that many, if not most, of them are measures brought on by dealer misconduct—self-inflicted wounds. A dealer will be caught doing bad stuff by a regulator, a state attorney general, or a news reporter, and it isn't long before the populace is up in arms, waving their torches and pitchforks and screaming for some dealer's head.

Consider a recent news report. In a private lawsuit, a dealer was charged with selling a new Nissan Versa to a homeless, schizophrenic woman with an income of $733 per month in Social Security disability benefits. According to the complaint, the sales price for the Versa was $2,000 over list, and, to add insult to injury, the dealership allegedly crammed a $2,275 service contract into the deal. The dealership's conduct was characterized by the plaintiff's lawyer as "rapacious."

To create a contract like this one that could be sold to a sales finance company would require "dummying up" the credit application and the stipulations that the finance companies usually require. The complaint wasn't long on the details of this sort of creativity in the dealership's F&I office, but anyone reading the complaint would conclude that if the complaint's allegations were true, such activity had occurred.

Before I go any further, let me emphasize that this is a complaint filed in court by a *car buyer's lawyer*. The dealership has not yet answered the complaint, so we don't know what the dealer will have to say, and we are a long way from a judge or a jury determining what actually are the facts of the matter.

But in at least one sense, the facts don't matter. The complaint has been filed, the newspapers have picked it up, and the public—and legislators and regulators—have yet again been reminded that car dealers are a bunch of crooks who prey on the unwary and defenseless. And that reaction leads to the next one: "There oughta be a law!"

Never mind that the allegations in this complaint, if true, mean that the dealership and its personnel have violated a number of existing state and federal laws. The dealership's alleged conduct was an outrage, and an outrage calls for action. So, we get yet another law or regulation; another layer of redundant consumer protection.

So the next time you have to spend a dollar on compliance, you can thank the Consumer Financial Protection Bureau, your

CHAPTER 9

state and federal legislators, Senator Elizabeth Warren, and the army of consumer advocates across the country who are seemingly trying to regulate the car business out of existence. But save at least one thank you for the dealership down the street, whose cowboys in the F&I office erroneously figured they could pull a fast one on the finance company without getting caught.

June 2016
NY AG Says Arbitration Is "Efficient and Effective"

If you have even a small appreciation for irony, you'll enjoy this. The Consumer Financial Protection Bureau is in the process of banning arbitration clauses in credit transactions when the clauses prohibit class relief. As part of its justification for the proposed ban, the CFPB has proffered two "studies" it conducted that purport to show that the arbitration process is unfair to consumers.

Then along comes New York Attorney General Eric T. Schneiderman, who proceeds to drop something very unpleasant in the CFPB's punchbowl. Schneiderman just announced that New York consumers recovered more than $2.5 million in arbitrated lemon law claims in 2015, bringing the total to $12.4 million since 2011. New car lemon cases—53 of them—accounted for $2 million of the amount, while 15 used car cases totaled about a half million.

Attorney General Schneiderman said, "The Lemon Law Arbitration Program has proven to be [an] efficient and effective means for both consumers and the auto industry to resolve disputes. Under this program, hundreds of auto consumers have obtained compensation without the costs and delays of going to court." Note that this is an activist, consumer-protective state attorney general characterizing the arbitration process as "efficient" and "effective" and saying the process is cheaper and quicker than going to court. This is the same process the CFPB calls unfair.

Is arbitration unfair? Perhaps in the CFPB's ivory tower, where staff studies that rely for the most part on studies dealing with small claims, and on carefully selected "facts" that agree with the policy decision that has long since been made, that may appear to be the case. But in the real world, things are apparently a bit different.

We have argued that the underlying rationale the CFPB has voiced for banning class relief—that the prohibition of class proceedings keeps consumers with small claims from aggregating those claims and effectively strips them of any legal remedy—should not apply in auto sales, finance, and lease transactions. In this part of the consumer credit world, auto buyers' claims tend to be significant and worth pursuing, whether in court or arbitration. In addition to the awards that buyers can seek for actual damages, many of the laws and regulations that apply to car transactions provide for awards of attorneys' fees and sometimes for a doubling or tripling of actual damages.

The CFPB's underlying rationale falls apart in the car world, as Schneiderman's comments describing the real-world operation of arbitration suggest, but you can search the Bureau's studies until you are blind, and you won't find any mention of the differences between a $25,000 automotive lemon law claim or a $10,000 fraud claim on the one hand and a $1.10 cell phone roaming charge on the other hand.

But I'm howling at the moon. The CFPB has requested comments on a proposed rule that will prohibit class waivers in arbitration agreements. I suspect that rule, or something similar,

CHAPTER 9

will become final. At that point, the ongoing battle between car dealers and creditors on the one hand and class action lawyers on the other hand will have swung back in the class action lawyers' favor.

All thanks to the CFPB's "don't bother me with the facts" regulatory philosophy.

Your tax dollars at work!

June 2016
Shaken, Not Stirred?

When I contemplated the reaction of the buy-here, pay-here dealership industry to the Consumer Financial Protection Bureau's $800,000 enforcement action alleging unfair pricing and sales practices against Herbies Auto Sales, a single-lot BHPH dealership in Colorado, I was reminded of James Bond's famous request for a martini, "shaken, not stirred."

I had expected that our law firm's phones would be ringing off the hook with calls from BHPH dealers trying to avoid being the next pelt the CFPB nailed on the barn wall. We received a spate of calls from concerned dealers after the Herbies settlement agreement was announced, but it wasn't as if the floodgates opened. That's worrisome because, based on what I've seen, BHPH dealers are in great peril from the CFPB.

Why? The settlement with Herbies was noteworthy for the CFPB's reliance on decades-old federal disclosure laws and for its attack on pricing and sales practices that are common throughout the BHPH industry. It is important to note that Herbies did not admit to any of the CFPB's allegations, but the allegations are nonetheless surprising.

Note that several of the practices challenged by the CFPB are not the sorts of practices that can be identified by looking at the dealership's sales and credit documents. A retail installment contract may, for example, expressly state that a service contract is not required for credit, but if the dealer's practice is to require a service contract in connection with all sales, the language in the retail installment contract indicating that the purchase is voluntary won't make the CFPB go away.

A BHPH dealer reading the Herbies settlement would come away with concerns about not showing prices on all vehicles on the lot, limiting a buyer to a few cars based on the buyer's creditworthiness, differential pricing for cash and credit sales, requiring the purchase of service contracts, charging for GPS or starter interrupt collection devices, and "pricing to payments" without revealing the car's full price until contract signing.

So, dealers and their trade associations are "shaken" about the CFPB's allegations in Herbies, and for good reason. A number of the sales and pricing practices in Herbies are almost standard operating procedure in the BHPH business—indeed, many sales trainers actually teach dealers to do some of the things that Herbies was nailed for. And some of the practices targeted by the CFPB are common in the non-BHPH world, as well.

Being "shaken," however, doesn't solve anything. If I am a BHPH dealer, I think I'd be "stirred" to have a thorough legal review of my documents, my pricing, as well as my sales policies and procedures, using the Herbies settlement agreement as a starting point for determining how vulnerable I might be to a thumping big CFPB fine.

Or I'd be "stirred" to sell the dealership and do something less dangerous, like signing on with Her Majesty's Secret Service.

CHAPTER 9

June 2016
CFPB Targets Individual Bank Employee

A May 26 Consumer Financial Protection Bureau announcement should send chills down the spines of any dealership F&I people who are misbehaving. The announcement dealt with a CFPB enforcement action against a former Wells Fargo employee for a mortgage fee-shifting scheme the CFPB called "illegal."

The CFPB's announcement said that David Eghbali, a loan officer for the Wilshire Crescent Wells Fargo branch in Beverly Hills, California, had an arrangement with an escrow company, New Millennium Escrow, Inc., allowing him to manipulate the prices his customers would pay for escrow services. In California, an escrow company typically prepares certain documents and holds and transfers payments related to mortgage loan refinance transactions. Consumers obtaining mortgages usually do not have a preferred escrow company, often relying on their loan officers to recommend one.

The CFPB's investigation found that, based on Eghbali's directions, New Millennium reduced its fees for some customers and made up for its losses by adding fees to loans for others. This helped Eghbali generate business by allowing him to offer "no-cost" loans to price-conscious clients who might have gone to a competing bank for a cheaper loan. The CFPB found that Eghbali in return referred nearly all his clients to New Millennium.

Eghbali was paid by commission. The CFPB found that Eghbali's fee-shifting scheme ultimately increased the number of loans he was able to close and, as a result, his commissions. Eghbali also received a top-producing loan officer award from Wells Fargo each year from 2011 to 2014, resulting in a bonus for each loan he closed.

2016: NO TRUCE IN SIGHT

The CFPB filed an administrative consent order requiring Eghbali to pay an $85,000 penalty to the CFPB's Civil Penalty Fund and banning him from working in the mortgage industry for a year.

So far, CFPB enforcement actions targeting individuals have been few and far between. This action, and Director Cordray's remarks accompanying the press release about this action, stress the CFPB's willingness to take its enforcement to those in the front lines of the consumer credit business.

F&I personnel and other dealership employees dealing with car buyers in ways that are regulated by federal consumer financial protection laws would be well advised to behave themselves or face CFPB actions directed at them instead of, or in addition to, their dealerships.

CHAPTER 9

Chapter 10

2017 & Beyond: The Never-Ending Struggle

CHAPTER 10

In the introduction, I referred to "The Long Arc of Consumer Protection," the battle between consumer advocates and industry that has waged since the 1960s. That isn't quite the Hundred Years' War, which began in 1337 and ended in 1453, but it is still a healthy time span, and it shows no signs of ending any time soon.

And I don't expect it to. I also don't expect that the industry will be able to turn back the forces of consumerism in their entirety. Only a couple of times in my memory have those forces been reversed. One involved overreaching by the FTC, which in 1978 launched an ill-considered, and ultimately ill-fated campaign against children's cereal advertising, only to be taken down a notch by Congress with legislation that curbed the agency's enforcement powers. Another occurred in 1980, when Congress reacted to several years of industry pressure to remove some of the punitive "gotcha" features of TILA by enacting the Truth in Lending Simplification Act.

Even if the auto finance industry is able to make some progress in blunting some consumer initiatives, the consumer forces will not give back any significant part of what they have gained since early in this century. And they will continue to press their agenda, urging:

- a national usury rate (probably 36%);
- a "military APR"—an APR calculation that will require a creditor to include in the APR calculation the cost of voluntarily purchased ancillary products such as credit insurance, GAP, and service contracts (and they will press to have the concept applied in nonmilitary credit);
- a requirement for car dealers to post prices on vehicles offered for sale;
- a limit on the amount that a dealer marks up a used vehicle for sale (120% of book value, for example);

- rules governing the "spot delivery" process;
- that creditors determine before extending credit whether prospective obligors have the "ability to repay;"
- federal collections regulations for "first-party" creditors not presently subject to the Fair Debt Collection Practices Act;
- a prohibition on the use of starter interrupt and GPS devices in collections; and
- a ban on any sort of dealer participation in the finance charge other than a flat fee for originating a contract.

And these are just the initiatives that stand a chance at passage. I also expect to see the consumer advocates push some ideas that have been suggested by the lunatic fringe, such as a ban on self-help repossession. Those fringe arguments stand almost no chance of becoming law, but industry will have to spend time and treasure to defeat them.

So strap on that helmet and crawl back into your foxhole—here they come again!

CHAPTER 10

Appendix 1

Auto Finance Lexicon

APPENDIX 1

This book deals with the legal side of auto finance and leasing. In the chapters addressing the various subjects, we sometimes use shorthand references to legal terms. Here are some of the terms you will see from time to time and a short description of what they mean.

AG: stands for Attorney General. Every state has one, essentially the top legal officer in the state. AGs usually enforce consumer protection laws and regulations. When we are being cynical, we sometimes say the "AG" stands for "Aspiring Governor." We also sometimes say the same thing when we aren't being cynical.

CFPB: the Consumer Financial Protection Bureau. The CFPB, created by the Dodd-Frank Act, is the federal agency charged with supervising certain providers of consumer finance products and enforcing certain consumer finance laws with respect to those providers. It is also the agency charged with writing and interpreting regulations implementing the ECOA (Reg. B), the CLA (Reg. M), TILA (Reg. Z), etc., as they apply to certain car dealers. The CFPB is the new consumer-friendly "federal cop" for these car dealers.

CLA: the Consumer Leasing Act. The CLA governs disclosures in consumer lease transactions. The CLA is actually Chapter 5 of TILA (the federal Truth in Lending Act), but it is usually referred to as if it is a separate piece of legislation.

Credit Practices Rule: a Federal Trade Commission rule that regulates certain creditor practices, such as the pyramiding of late charges, garnishing wages, notifying cosigners, and the like.

Dodd-Frank Act: we use this term to refer to the Dodd-Frank Wall Street Reform and Consumer Protection Act, sponsored by Senator Chris Dodd (D-CT) and Rep. Barney Frank (D-MA) and enacted on July 21, 2010. The Dodd-Frank Act was a sweeping reform of federal laws that deal with the regulation of regulating financial institutions. One of the principal parts of the Dodd-Frank Act created the Consumer Financial Protection Bureau.

ECOA: the federal Equal Credit Opportunity Act. The ECOA prohibits credit discrimination on the basis of sex, race, marital status, etc.

F&I: finance and insurance. The "finance and insurance" department of a dealership is called the F&I department. That's where financing terms are arranged and various "add-on" products such as credit insurance and extended warranties are sold.

FCRA: the federal Fair Credit Reporting Act. The "FACT Act" is an amendment to the FCRA. The FCRA regulates those who compile and use credit reports.

FRB: the Federal Reserve Board. The FRB is a federal agency that controls monetary policy in the United States and regulates certain banking institutions. Under the Dodd-Frank Act, the FRB retains rule-writing authority for TILA (Reg. Z), the CLA (Reg. M), the ECOA (Reg. B), etc., as those laws apply to certain car dealers who are exempted by the Dodd-Frank Act from supervision and enforcement by the CFPB.

APPENDIX 1

FTC: the Federal Trade Commission. The FTC is a tough, consumer-friendly federal agency that enforces several federal laws and regulations (including the TILA, the ECOA, and Regs. Z and B) with respect to certain car dealers (new car dealers and certain used car dealers) exempt from the CFPB's enforcement authority.

Gramm-Leach-Bliley (GLB) Act: a federal law, Title 5 of which deals with the privacy of personal financial information.

Green Pea: a brand new dealership sales employee.

Holder Rule: a shorthand reference to the Federal Trade Commission's Trade Regulation Rule titled "The Preservation of Consumer Claims and Defenses." The Holder Rule permits a buyer under a retail installment sale contract to assert against the holder of the contract certain claims and defenses the buyer has against the selling dealer.

Odometer Law: a federal law designed to curb abusive practices (rollbacks, for example) dealing with vehicle odometers.

OFAC, or the Office of Foreign Asset Control: a unit of the U.S. Treasury Department that maintains the so-called "Specially Designated Nationals" or "bad guy" list. It is illegal for U.S. citizens to do business with someone whose name is on the bad guy list, and dealers who do not wish to violate the law must check the list before engaging in any business with any person.

Magnuson-Moss Warranty Act: a federal law that regulates warranties.

Reg. B: a regulation of the FRB and the CFPB implementing the ECOA.

Reg. M: a regulation of the FRB and the CFPB implementing the CLA.

Reg. P: a regulation of the FTC, the CFPB, and the federal banking agencies, which in its various forms implements the Gramm-Leach-Bliley Act's privacy provisions.

Reg. Z: a regulation of the FRB and the CFPB implementing TILA.

RISA: refers to a "retail installment sales act." Nearly every state has a RISA. Some states (about half) have a special version of a RISA for motor vehicle financing and a separate RISA for other kinds of personal property financing. RISAs typically regulate finance charge rates, late charges, grace periods, bad check charges, disclosures, and the like in auto financing agreements between dealers and customers.

RISC: a retail installment sale contract. This document is used to document a credit sale from a dealer to a buyer. Then, the dealer usually sells the RISC to a finance company or bank. Buy-here, pay-here dealers hold RISCs and collect payments from buyers, unless they have created an affiliated finance company to assign them to. If you call a RISC a "loan," Spot (the Dalmatian mascot for our legal newsletter, *Spot Delivery*®) has instructions to bite you on the ankle.

APPENDIX 1

TILA: the federal Truth in Lending Act. TILA governs disclosures in consumer credit transactions. This is the "granddaddy" of federal disclosure laws, dating from the late 1960s.

Tort: a tort is a "civil wrong." The actions that comprise a tort can also comprise a crime, but a tort is not necessarily a crime. Examples of torts are negligence, fraud, and defamation.

TRR: a Trade Regulation Rule. TRRs are issued by the FTC. The "Used Car Rule" requiring window stickers is a TRR.

UDAP: refers to unfair and deceptive acts and practices. The FTC has UDAP provisions, and the CFPB has its own UDAP provisions too. Only the FTC and the CFPB can enforce their respective versions—a consumer cannot bring a private lawsuit to enforce it. Most states have UDAP laws as well and many permit consumers to sue under them. UDAP laws are favorites of lawyers who sue dealers because they are very general in their prohibitions and usually provide for a multiple (two or three times) the consumer's actual damages, plus attorneys' fees.

USA PATRIOT Act: a federal law aimed at terrorism and specifically targeting money laundering.

Used Car Rule: the "Buyers Guide" rule issued by the FTC. It requires a Buyers Guide to be displayed on each used vehicle offered for sale and requires certain language regarding the Buyers Guide in the contract of sale.

Appendix 2
Index

APPENDIX 2

A

acquisition fees, 160, 161–163
Administrative Procedures Act (APA), 38, 151, 154
advertising/marketing
  attorneys general, 302–303
  compliance, 56, 114, 126–127, 170–172, 232
  on Craigslist, 58
  deceptive, 123, 177–179, 221–223, 230–231, 233–234, 248–250, 277
  discounts, 128
  Do Not Fax rule, 46–49
  due diligence, 283
  Federal Trade Commission rules, 44–46, 114, 115–116, 127–129, 177–179
  fonts, 222
  "free" offers in, 115–116
  FTC oversight, 44–46, 303–304
  language in, 115–116
  lead sites, 95
  liability related to, 232
  marketing companies/ad agencies, 48, 282
  Motor Vehicle Advertising Regulations, 169
  no-haggle, 223–225
  online, 57–58, 95–96, 105, 233–234, 237–238
  Operation Steer Clear, 230–232
  push, pull, drive or drag, 163–165
  requirements, 232
  in Spanish, 226
  state laws, 45–46
  upside down ads, 124–127
  violations, 45, 124–127, 302–303
  WAC (with approved credit), 116, 127–128
  warranties, 116
AFIP (Association of Finance and Insurance Professionals), 241
AFSA (American Financial Services Association), 100, 101, 120–122, 214, 276
AGs. *See* Attorneys General (AGs)
Alabama, 277
Alaska, 129, 256
Alexander, Dwain, 96–99
all-in formula, 149
American Financial Services Association (AFSA), 100, 101, 120–122, 214, 276
annual percentage rate (APR), 35, 43, 101, 149, 161, 314
Anwyl, Jeremy, 95, 100
APA (Administrative Procedures Act), 38, 151, 154
arbitration
  class action lawsuits, 35, 252–255, 293–295, 300
  Consumer Financial Protection Bureau Report, 270–273, 279–281
  Federal Arbitration Act, 9, 18, 208–209, 273, 280
  forms, 301
  Lemon Laws, 306–308
  mandatory agreements, 14, 16, 18, 35, 106, 243–244, 271–272
  restrictions on, 11, 14, 16, 20, 42
  state laws, 208–209

INDEX

Archer, Michael, 96, 97
Arizona, 129, 256, 302
Arkansas, 182–185, 226–227
ASFA (Automobile Sales Finance Act), 157
as-is sales, 184, 227, 228
Association of Finance and Insurance Professionals (AFIP), 241
Attorneys General (AGs)
   on advertising violations, 45, 302–303
   arbitration by, 253–255
   consumer complaints, 71
   debt collection, 229
   definition, 318
   enforcement powers of, 109, 150
   under FTC, 149–150
   on spot delivery regulations, 129–131, 216, 256–258, 260–264
   authority over car dealers, 37–38, 44, 55–57, 155–156
Auto Dealer Task Force, 45, 50–51, 59, 69
Automobile Sales Finance Act (ASFA), 157
AutoTrader, 104

B

Bachus, Spencer, 63
bad guy list (Specially Designated Nationals), 320
balloon payments, 24, 231
Benoit, Michael, 41, 55, 73, 265
best practices, 229–230, 252
   adoption of, 268

arbitration agreements, 255
   Bureau's decisions for, 253–254
   buy-here, pay-here dealers, 132–133
   common set of, 189
   for creditors, 271–272
   in leases/leasing, 68–69
   regulators of, 269
   repossessions, 130
   spot deliveries (yo yo deals), 66–67, 129–131, 132–133, 215, 216, 256, 258
Better Business Bureau, 99
BHPH. See buy-here, pay-here (BHPH) dealers
Bill of Rights for car buyers, 19, 42
bird dog fees (referral fees), 96–97
Blackwell, Rick, 267–269
Brauch, Bill, 73, 74
Buyers Guide, 183–184, 226–227, 322
buy-here, pay-here (BHPH) dealers
   best practices, 132–133, 256–258
   CFPB jurisdiction over, 276
   compliance issues, 239–244, 247
   debt collection, 228–230, 250, 252
   deceptive advertising, 177–179
   discriminatory behaviors of, 103
   enforcement/regulation of, 41–44, 117–118, 156–160, 276, 308–309
   in lease marketplace, 137

325

APPENDIX 2

in Oregon, 267–270
posting of prices, 119–120
subject to CFPB jurisdiction, 286
used vehicle sales, 287
buy rate, 101, 102, 192–193, 196–200

C

California, 129, 156–160, 221, 230, 256, 310
Canada, 277
CAR (Center for Automotive Research), 235–236
Car Buyers' Bill of Rights, 19, 42
case law
   Federal Trade Commission v. Ross, 232–234
   Golden v. Prosser, 250–252
   Hester v. Hubert Vester Ford, Inc., 260–264
   Johnson v. MKA Enterprises, Inc., 293–295
   See also class action lawsuits; legislation; litigation
cash pricing, 212–213, 238, 302
CCSC (Consumer Credit Safety Commission), 9–12, 14
Center for Automotive Research (CAR), 235–236
Center for Responsible Lending (CRL), 72, 73, 102, 272, 274
CFA (Consumer Fraud Act), 169, 249
CFPA (Consumer Financial Protection Agency), 20–21
CFPB. *See* Consumer Financial Protection Bureau (CFPB)

Charapp, Michael G., 74
Chiesa, Jeffrey S., 170
Choate, Chris, 101
Civil Investigation Demands (CIDs), 256–258, 265
civil liability, 288
civil wrongs (torts), 322
CLA (Consumer Leasing Act), 34, 231, 277, 283, 318
class action lawsuits
   arbitration clauses for, 18, 271, 273, 279–280, 279–281, 306–308
   avoiding, 11, 300
   defeating, 293–295
   defending, 35, 208, 209, 252
   discrimination, 42
   prohibitions on, 254
   protection from, 301
   rules for filing, 225
   threats of, 290
class action lawyers, 88, 93, 105, 244, 281, 308
CMS. *See* compliance management system (CMS)
COC (Comptroller of the Currency), 31
Cohen, Rob, 74
Colorado, 87, 129, 256, 308–309
complaints. *See* consumer complaints
compliance issues
   buy-here, pay-here, 239–244
   compliance management system (CMS), 175–177, 186–187, 204
   consumer privacy, 58, 240–241

326

INDEX

costs of, 234–236, 239, 298–302
criminal penalties, 92, 288–290
disregard for, 90–93, 260
do-it-yourself (DIY), 61
due diligence, 283
handling consumer complaints, 188–191, 243
hard costs of programs, 239
internet-related, 60, 165–167
reviews, 61, 83–85, 179, 244, 278, 283, 309
risk triage, 91, 109–110
for small dealers, 59–61
technology, 142–143
training for, 205–207, 238–239, 241
whistleblowers, 110
compliance management system (CMS)
description of, 175–177, 204
developing a, 195–196, 235
elements of effective, 188–189
reasons for/implementation of, 186–187
requirements of, 288
Comptroller of the Currency (COC), 31
Connecticut, 124, 129, 256
consumer abuse survey, 76, 78–80, 81, 99
Consumer Advisory Council, 32
consumer advocacy, 33–35, 75–77, 106–108
consumer affairs, 169, 248–250
consumer classes, 199, 288
consumer complaints
  to CFPB, 71, 146–148, 187–191, 264–266

compliance in handling, 188–191, 243
creditors/credit sales, 147, 251–252, 261, 282, 285
debt collection, 70, 123, 284
employees/staff, 190
to FTC, 69–72, 122–124, 139–140
handling, 188–191, 243
leases/leasing, 71, 140, 249
Consumer Credit Safety Commission (CCSC), 9–12, 14
consumer education, 100–101
Consumer Financial Protection Agency (CFPA), 20–21
consumer complaints to, 71, 187–191, 264–266
exemptions, 35–40, 59, 150, 154–156, 186, 218, 273–274, 276, 286–287
Consumer Financial Protection Agency Act, 19
Consumer Financial Protection Bureau (CFPB)
Company Portal, 284–286
compliance management systems (CMS), 175–177, 186–187, 204, 288
consumer complaints, 71, 146–148, 187–191
consumer finance, 148–149
creation of, 3, 6
credit card transactions, 117
criticism of, 62–64, 194–196
on deceptive practices, 42–43, 125
definition, 318

327

APPENDIX 2

exemptions, 3, 35–40, 59, 154–156, 218, 273–274, 286–287
fair lending, 191–194, 196–200
finance charges, 119–120
funding issues, 63–64, 146
jurisdiction, 41–44, 55–57, 58–59, 61, 153
nonpublic investigation, 49
Office of Servicemember Affairs, 38–39
oversight by, 62–63
staffing/budget, 145–146
Supervision, Enforcement and Fair Lending Division, 145
targeting individuals, 310–311
undercover agents, 167–169
Consumer Fraud Act (CFA), 169, 249
Consumer Leasing Act (CLA), 34, 283, 318, 319
Regulation M, 31, 45, 171, 231, 277
consumer privacy
compliance issues, 58, 240–241
data collection, 77
debt collection, 141–142
disposal policies, 172–175
disregard for, 56–57
Federal Trade Commission rules, 141–143, 172–175
Gramm-Leach-Bliley Act, 11, 20, 34, 142, 173, 240, 267
safe harbor language, 300–301
technology, 141–143

Consumer Products Safety Commission (CPSC), 18
consumer protection. *See* Dodd Frank Wall Street Reform and Consumer Protection Act (Dodd Frank Act)
Consumer Protection Act (Tennessee), 282
consumer rights, 42, 157, 246
Consumer Sentinel, 148
contracts
interest-bearing (simple interest) contracts, 24, 132
pre-computed contracts, 24, 132
sale of, 286
sales contract forms, 300–301
service contracts, 94, 116, 220, 305, 309
See also retail installment sale contracts (RISCs)
Cook, Robert, 5, 135
cooling-off period, 17, 19, 42
Cordray, Richard, 87, 117–118, 153, 253, 255, 311
Covington, Patty, 160
CPSC (Consumer Products Safety Commission), 18
Craigslist advertising, 58
credit card transactions, 117, 136–137, 177
creditors/credit sales
advertising violations, 124–127
bad behavior of, 291
battle between car dealers and, 308
BHPH dealers, 137, 228, 250, 308–309
bills related to, 11, 14

INDEX

burdens on, 22
California, 157
claims/complaints against, 147, 251–252, 261, 282, 285
class action disputes, 279
credit practices rule, 318
dealer as, 275
debt collection rules for, 229, 315
disclosure regulations for, 9, 134, 136
discriminatory practices of, 34
duties of, 16, 177
federal enforcement of, 8, 31–32
insurance coverage required by, 146
liabilities of, 198, 288
limitations on, 20
loan transactions versus, 87–90, 191–192, 245–248, 272–273, 275–276
mandatory arbitration agreements, 18, 35, 271–272
military APR requirements, 314
nonviolations, 176, 186
obligations of, 6
outreach by the Bureau to, 145
rating schemes for, 24
recharacterization attacks on, 88–90
requirements and prohibitions, 32, 172
secured, 158
self-help repossession by, 78, 99
settlement agreements, 290
TILA and, 31, 135, 289
usury rates of, 15, 162

violations by, 202
See also Consumer Financial Protection Bureau (CFPB); Fair Debt Collection Practices Act (FDCPA)
credit practices rule, 318
criminal penalties for noncompliance, 92, 288–290
CRL (Center for Responsible Lending), 72, 73, 102, 272, 274

D

data-gathering compliance, 60–61, 77, 121, 148, 150, 152
Davis, Delvin, 73
dealer markups, 42–43, 101–103, 192–193, 214, 219, 314
dealer participation, 42, 75–77, 193, 213, 274, 315
dealers
 buy-here-pay-here (*See* buy-here, pay-here (BHPH) dealers)
 franchised, 3, 41, 132, 150, 187, 235
 independent, 41, 218, 247, 286–287
 National Association of Dealer Counsel (NADC), 61
 National Automobile Dealers Association (NADA), 120–122, 155, 214, 235, 241, 274, 276
 National Independent Automobile Dealers Association (NIADA), 99, 286

329

APPENDIX 2

deal jackets, 298–302
debt collection
    buy-here, pay-here dealers, 228–230, 250, 252
    consumer complaints, 70, 123, 284
    consumer privacy and, 141–142
    Fair Debt Collection Practices Act, 20, 228–230, 250–252, 315
    lawsuits against, 141–142
    rules for, 229–230, 315
    settlements with businesses in, 142
    unfair or deceptive acts or practices in, 248
deceptive practices
    advertising/marketing, 123, 177–179, 221–223, 230–231, 233–234, 248–250, 277
    CCSC on, 10
    complaints alleging, 189
    finance and insurance (F&I) office, 304–306
    under FTC Act, 38, 210, 234
    on internet, 104–105, 110–111
    laws prohibiting, 45
    payment packing, 42
    prevention of, 8
    prohibitions on, 277–278
    spot delivery, 64, 129
    Tennessee case, 281
    upside down ads, 124–127
    See also Consumer Financial Protection Bureau (CFPB); unfair or deceptive acts or practices (UDAP)
Delahunt/Durbin bill, 9–10

Delaware, 129, 256
disclosures
    Automobile Sales Finance Act, 157
    criminal penalties for violations, 288–290
    Federal Trade Commission rules, 210–211
    finance charges, 161–162, 212–213
    financing, 101–102, 119–120, 215, 275–276
    forms, 300
    history in auto finance of, 33–35
    insurance, 147
    mortgage industry, 22–24, 32, 86
    multiple discounts, 210–211
    requirements, 31, 33–34, 161–162, 247
    in retail installment contracts, 246–248
    role in consumer protection, 134–136
    with approved credit, 127–128
    See also Truth in Lending Act (TILA)
discrimination
    buy rate, 102, 198–200
    by creditors, 34
    disparate impact, 102–103, 193, 195, 199
    fair lending, 191–194
    racial, 42, 199
    reverse redlining, 103
    See also Equal Credit Opportunity Act (ECOA)

disparate impact discrimination, 102–103, 193, 195, 199
Disposal Rule, 172–175
District of Columbia, 129, 229, 256
Division of Consumer Affairs, 248–250
Division of Financial Practices. *See* Consumer Financial Protection Bureau (CFPB)
DIY (do-it-yourself) compliance, 61. *See also* self-help repossession
Dodd, Christopher, 22, 135
Dodd Frank Wall Street Reform and Consumer Protection Act (Dodd Frank Act)
  advertising, 44–46
  arbitration, 268, 280
  Attorneys General (AGs), 109
  auto dealer exemption, 3, 35–40, 154–156, 278
  auto financing, 119, 149
  Consumer Financial Protection Bureau and, 62–63, 146
  creation, 3–4, 253
  debt collection, 228–230
  description, 319
  disclosures, 86
  enforcement of, 61, 93, 277–278, 289
  exemptions, 3, 22, 35–40, 154–156, 178, 278, 286–287, 319
  force-placed insurance, 147
  in history of consumer protection, 290–293
  mandates under, 146
  nonbanks, 145
  state laws, 152
do-it-yourself (DIY) compliance, 61. *See also* self-help repossession
Dolan, Reilly, 73
Domonoske, Thomas, 95, 98
do-not-call/do-not-fax/do-not-email rules, 159
due diligence, 201–202, 283
Durbin, Richard, 9–10
Durkin, Thomas, 102

E

ECOA. *See* Equal Credit Opportunity Act (ECOA)
Edmunds, Inc., 100
education/training. *See* training/education
Eghbali, David, 310
employees/staff
  CFPB supervision of, 176
  complaints about, 190
  compliance by, 287
  compliance officers, 283
  dealer profits per, 236
  green peas, 320
  having staff lawyers, 91
  lawsuits related to, 261–263, 310–311
  law violations by, 168
  legal requirements for, 287
  loyalty/lack of loyalty of, 47–48
  protections and prohibitions created by, 67

331

APPENDIX 2

time spent by and on, 236–244
turnover rates, 126
See also training/education
Equal Credit Opportunity Act
  (ECOA), 20, 101, 246
  CFPB oversight of, 318
  creation of, 34, 292
  description, 319
  Regulation B, 67, 159,
    191–194, 240, 267
  violations/claims based on,
    105, 202
  See also discrimination
equity, negative, 10, 16, 99,
  124–126, 127–129, 164–165
ethical issues, 64, 67–69, 97, 98,
  240
exemptions
  advertising-related, 44
  CFPB, 35–40, 59, 150,
    154–156, 186, 218,
    273–274, 276, 286–287
  Dodd Frank Act, 3, 22,
    35–40, 154–156, 178, 278,
    286–287, 319
  FDCPA, 229, 252
  qualifying for, 287
  special interest groups, 21
  under TILA, 16

F

FAA (Federal Arbitration Act), 9,
  18, 208–209, 273, 280
Fair and Accurate Credit
  Transactions Act (FACTA), 28
Fair Credit Reporting Act
  (FCRA), 11, 20, 28, 319

Fair Debt Collection Practices Act
  (FDCPA), 20, 228–230,
  250–252, 315
FAIR (fee and interest rate)
  formula, 43
fair lending practices, 102,
  191–194
FDIC (Federal Deposit Insurance
  Corporation), 31
the Fed (Federal Reserve System),
  31–32, 146
Federal Arbitration Act (FAA), 9,
  18, 208–209, 273, 280
Federal Communications
  Commission (FCC), 46–49
Federal Deposit Insurance
  Corporation (FDIC), 31
federal laws/rules
  consumer privacy, 141–143,
    172–175
  credit sales, 8, 31–32
  disclosures, 210–211
  Federal Trade Commission's,
    44–46, 114, 115–116,
    127–129, 177–179
  financing, 35–37
  underwriting practices, 10,
    11, 23
  usury, 15–17, 17–18
Federal Register, 60, 75, 215
Federal Reserve Board (FRB)
  Consumer Advisory Council,
    32
  criticism of, 30–32
  dealer markup, 101–102
  description, 319
  disclosures, 215
  fee-harvester rules, 136–138

332

INDEX

"Keys to Vehicle Leasing," 242
mortgage crisis, 23–24
Office of Servicemember Affairs, 38–39
Risk-Based Pricing Rule, 27–28
rule-writing authority, 150
Federal Reserve System (the Fed), 31–32, 146
Federal Trade Commission (FTC)
   advertising, 44–46, 114, 115–116, 127–129, 177–179
   Attorneys General, 149–150
   authority over car dealers, 37–38, 44, 55–57, 155–156
   Auto Dealer Task Force, 45, 50–51, 59, 69
   Buyers Guide rule, 322
   Civil Investigation Demands (CIDs), 256–258, 265
   compliance with, 49, 51, 61, 283
   consumer complaints to, 69–72, 122–124, 139–140
   consumer privacy, 141–143, 172–175
   Consumer Sentinel, 148
   cooling-off period, 19
   credit practices rule, 318
   description, 320
   disclosures, 210–211
   Disposal Rule, 172–175
   Division of Financial Practices (*See* Consumer Financial Protection Bureau (CFPB))
   enforcement by, 93, 172–175, 302–304
   FTC Act (Federal Trade Commission Act), 142, 149, 173, 178, 210, 221, 231, 233, 277
   Holder Rule, 49–51, 301
   individual liability, 232–234
   negative equity advertising, 164–165
   Office of Servicemember Affairs, 38–39
   Operation Ruse Control, 277–278, 281
   Operation Steer Clear, 221–223, 230–232, 237, 248, 276–278, 281
   public roundtables, 54, 72–77, 80–82, 93–103, 105–108, 138, 156
   Risk-Based Pricing Rule, 26–27, 27–28
   Safeguarding Rule, 83–85
   safe harbor language, 300–301
   settlement orders, 124
   undercover agents, 167–169
   "Understanding Vehicle Financing," 241, 276
   unfair or deceptive acts or practices (UDAP) authority, 38, 142, 147, 149, 182, 283
   upside down ads, 124–127
   Used Car Rule, 182–185, 207–208, 226–228, 301
Federal Trade Commission v. Ross, 232–234
fee-harvester rules, 136–138
finance and insurance (F&I)
   closing process, 298
   deceptive practices, 304–306

333

APPENDIX 2

description, 4, 319
document fees, 11
illicit practices, 56–57
power booking, 56
regulation of, 19
remittance transfers, 20
training, 241
finance charges, 15, 56, 66, 119–120, 161–162, 212–213, 214, 273
financing
  acquisition fees, 160, 161–163
  all-in formula, 149
  APR, 14, 17, 35, 43
  balloon payments, 23, 24, 231
  buy rate, 101, 102, 192–193, 196–200
  data collection, 152
  dealer markup, 214
  dealer participation, 35, 56, 192–194
  debt-to-income ratios, 32
  disclosures, 101–102, 119–120
  due diligence, 201
  federal oversight for, 35–37
  history, 33
  interest-bearing (simple interest) contracts, 24, 132
  licensing, 152
  liquidity, 200–202
  loan-to-value (LTV), 24, 32
  no-doc loans, 32
  payday lending, 43
  payment packing, 35, 42, 56, 220
  pre-computed contracts, 24, 132
  prepaid finance charges, 162

pre-payment penalties, 23, 24, 215
pricing, 214
promissory notes, 132
ratings system, 23–24
trade-in allowances, 164–165
See also loans/lending practices; pricing; sales
force-placed insurance, 147
Fortney, Anne, 41
franchised dealerships, 235
Frank, Barney, 19, 22, 135
fraud/fraudulent practices
  class actions for, 273
  Consumer Fraud Act (NJ), 169, 249
  Hester v. Hubert Vester Ford, Inc., 260–264
  laws prohibiting, 158
  study on, 81
  types of, 277
  See also spot deliveries (yo yo deals); unfair or deceptive acts or practices (UDAP)
FRB. *See* Federal Reserve Board (FRB)
"free" offers in advertising, 115–116
FTC Act (Federal Trade Commission Act), 142, 149, 173, 178, 210, 221, 231, 233, 277. *See also* Federal Trade Commission (FTC)

G

General Motors Acceptance Corporation (GMAC), 42
Georgia, 129, 221, 230, 256
Golden v. Prosser, 250–252
government. *See* federal laws/rules; state laws
GPS (Global Positioning System), 77, 137, 139, 315
Gramm-Leach-Bliley Act (GLBA), 11, 20, 34, 142, 173, 240, 267, 320
Grzeskiewicz, Greg, 74, 75
Guaranteed Auto Protection (GAP), 14, 96, 220, 225, 242

H

Hackett, Rick, 143–154
Hall, Steve, 95, 96
Harvey, Stephen, 102–103
Hawaii, 129, 256
Henrick, Randy, 73
Hester v. Hubert Vester Ford, Inc., 260–264
Hoffman, John J., 248
Holder Rule (Preservation of Consumer Claims and Defenses Trade Regulation Rule), 49–51, 301, 320
Hornblass, JJ, 72
Hudson, Thomas B., 72

I

Idaho, 129, 256
Illinois, 73, 74–75, 129, 173–174, 221, 230, 256
indirect lenders, 192

individual liability, 232–234
information-gathering compliance, 60–61, 77, 121, 148, 150, 152
interest-bearing (simple interest) contracts, 24, 132
internet
  advertising on, 126–127, 170, 210, 211–213, 233–234
  compliance information on, 60–61
  deceptive practices, 104–105, 110–111
  legal research using, 165–167
  liability for online actions, 233
  special sales prices for, 237–239, 302–304
  use by consumers, 95–96
Iowa, 73, 129, 256
Irvine, Susie, 100, 101

J

Johnson v. MKA Enterprises, Inc., 293–295

K

Kansas, 294
Keest, Kathleen, 5, 135
Kessler, Glenn, 274–276
"Keys to Vehicle Leasing" (FRB), 242
Kiser, Keith, 75
Kitzmiller, J. Peter, 75
Koblenz, Andrew D., 73, 75, 101–102, 155–156
Kueckelhan, Deanya, 183
Kukla, Chris, 72, 101–102

L

language issues
  for retail installment sale contracts, 115–116, 154
  safe harbor language, 300–301
  Spanish language, 142, 183–184, 226, 241–242, 301
Law Merchant, 291
laws
  class action lawsuits, 35, 252–255, 293–295, 300
  deceptive practices prohibition, 45
  federal (*See* federal laws/rules)
  Lemon Laws, 169, 306–308
  odometer law, 320
  state (*See* state laws)
  usury, 152, 162
  violations by employees, 168
  See also case law; legislation
lawsuits. *See* case law
lead sites, 95
leases/leasing
  advertising rules, 221
  approaches to compliance in, 260
  best practices in, 68
  BHPH as part of, 137
  CFPB agenda for, 155, 218
  complaints about, 71, 140, 249
  contract forms, 300
  dealers licensed only for, 40
  employee training for, 242
  by franchised dealers, 187
  lease forms, 86
  lease-to-own deals, 43
  monitoring of, 304
  paying up front, 221–222, 231
  retail leases, 36–37
  sale of contracts, 286, 298
  small claims lawsuits, 307
  state laws, 234
Lee, Steve, 249
Leedom, Christopher M., 74
legislation
  Administrative Procedures Act (APA), 38, 151, 154
  Automobile Sales Finance Act (ASFA), 157
  Car Buyers' Bill of Rights, 19
  Consumer Financial Protection Agency Act, 19
  Consumer Fraud Act (CFA), 169, 249
  Consumer Leasing Act (CLA), 31, 34, 45, 171, 231, 277, 283, 318, 319
  Consumer Protection Act, 282
  Dodd Frank Act (*See* Dodd Frank Wall Street Reform and Consumer Protection Act (Dodd Frank Act))
  Equal Credit Opportunity Act (*See* Equal Credit Opportunity Act (ECOA))
  Fair and Accurate Credit Transactions Act (FARCTA), 28
  Fair Credit Reporting Act (FCRA), 11, 20, 28, 319
  Fair Debt Collection Practices Act (FDCPA), 20, 228–230, 250–252, 315

INDEX

Federal Arbitration Act
 (FAA), 9, 18, 208–209,
 273, 280
Federal Trade Commission
 Act (FTC Act), 142, 149,
 178, 210
Federal Trade Commission
 (FTCA) Act, 38, 210, 234
Gramm-Leach-Bliley Act
 (GLBA), 11, 20, 34, 142,
 173, 240, 267, 320
Magnuson-Moss Warranty
 Act, 267, 320
Motor Vehicle Retail
 Installment Sales Act, 268
New Jersey Consumer Fraud
 Act, 169, 249
odometer law, 320
Oregon Motor Vehicle Retail
 Installment Sales Act, 268
Servicemembers Civil Relief
 Act, 267
Tennessee Consumer
 Protection Act, 282
Truth in Lending (*See* Truth
 in Lending Act (TILA))
Truth in Lending Act (*See*
 Truth in Lending Act
 (TILA))
Uniform Commercial Code
 (UCC), 158, 291
Uniform Consumer Credit
 Code (U3C), 292
Uniform Consumer Leasing
 Act (UCLA), 292–293
USA PATRIOT Act, 322
See also case law
Leibowitz, Jon, 55

Lemon Laws, 169, 306–308
lending. *See* loans/lending
 practices
liability
 advertising-related, 232
 civil, 288
 for credit discrimination, 198
 fair lending issues, 102
 individual, 232–234
 negation of, 252
 for online actions, 233
Liblang, Dani, 74
Lieu, Ted, 156, 160
liquidity, 19, 200, 275
litigation, 102–103, 170, 193,
 195, 199, 277, 307. *See also*
 case law; class action lawsuits
loans/lending practices
 Center for Responsible
  Lending (CRL), 72, 73,
  102, 272, 274
 credit sales versus, 87–90,
  191–192, 245–248,
  272–273, 275–276
 fair lending, 191–194, 196–200
 indirect lenders, 192
 liability issues, 102
 loan-to-value (LTV) financing,
  24, 32
 loan transactions versus credit
  sales, 87–90, 191–192,
  245–248, 272–273,
  275–276
 no-doc loans, 32
 payday loans, 43
 predatory lending, 82

337

retail installment sales contracts (RISCs) versus, 245–248, 272–273
See also financing; Truth in Lending Act (TILA)
loan-to-value (LTV) financing, 24, 32
Long, Denny, 48–49
Los Angeles Times, 287
LTV (loan-to-value) financing, 24, 32
Lund, Will, 73
Lyngklip, Ian, 74

M

Madigan, Lisa, 211, 223
Magnuson-Moss Warranty Act, 267, 320
Maine, 129, 256
mandatory arbitration agreements, 14, 16, 18, 35, 106, 243–244, 271–272
marketing. *See* advertising/marketing
Markey, Edward J., 213–216
markup (pricing), 42–43, 101–103, 192–193, 214, 219, 314
Maryland, 129, 210, 256
Massachusetts, 129, 213, 221, 230, 256
McLelland, Pam, 99–100
Mercer, Shawn, 96, 97, 98
Michigan, 221, 230, 235
military/servicemembers
  abuse of, 282
  agencies serving, 148

APR requirements, 314
financial literacy, 99–101
military APR, 314
Office of Servicemember Affairs, 38–39
paying allotments for financing, 168
predatory lending, 82
procedures and processes for, 94–100
protection for, 229
referral fees (bird dog fees), 96–97
regulatory reinforcement authority for, 140, 153
Servicemembers Civil Relief Act, 267
Minnesota, 129, 256
Mississippi, 129, 256
Missouri, 129, 256
Monello, S. Allen, 74
Moore, Jr., Thomas A., 73
Mortgage Acts and Practices Advertising Rule, 178
mortgage crisis, 23–24
  disclosures, 32
  effect on auto finance industry, 6, 8–9, 135
  Federal Reserve Board, 30–32
  legislative response, 19, 22–23
Mosher, Alan, 100–101
Motor Vehicle Advertising Regulations, 169
mutual rescission, 65–66, 131, 257

INDEX

N

National Automobile Dealers Association (NADA), 235, 274
National Automotive Finance Association (NAF Association), 143
National Consumer Law Center (NCLC), 76, 77–80, 78–80, 81, 99, 213
National Credit Union Administration (NCUA), 31
National Highway Traffic Safety Administration (NHTSA), 23
negative equity, 10, 16, 99, 124–126, 127–129, 164–165
negative equity advertising, 164–165
Nevada, 129, 256
New Hampshire, 129, 256
New Jersey, 129, 169, 248–250, 249, 256
New Mexico, 129, 256
New York, 129, 256, 306–308
New York Times, 287
NHTSA (National Highway Traffic Safety Administration), 23
Nissan Motors Acceptance Corporation (NMAC), 42
no-doc loans, 32
no haggle advertising/pricing, 223–225
nonbanks, 117–118, 145–156, 152–153
North Carolina, 124, 221, 230, 262–263

O

Obama, Barack, 3, 16, 41, 63, 87, 156
Obamacare, 8
odometer law, 320
Office of Foreign Asset Control (OFAC), 57, 320
Office of Servicemember Affairs, 38–39
Ohio, 48, 87, 129, 210, 235, 256
O'Laughlin, Terry, 96–97, 98
Operation Ruse Control, 277–278, 281
Operation Steer Clear, 221–223, 230–232, 237, 248–250, 276–277, 276–278, 281
Oregon, 129, 237–239, 256, 268

P

payday loans, 43
payment packing, 42, 56
Pearce, Charles, 73
Pearlstein, Steven, 30–31
Pennsylvania, 129, 249, 256
Perry, Chip, 104
Petraeus, Holly, 95, 118
power booking, 56
pre-computed contracts, 24, 132
predatory lending, 82
pre-payment penalties, 24
Preservation of Consumer Claims and Defenses Trade Regulation Rule (Holder Rule), 49–51, 301, 320
price tags, 219, 314
pricing
  cash, 212–213, 238, 302

339

APPENDIX 2

dealer markup, 42–43, 101–103, 192–193, 214, 219, 314
no-haggle, 223–225
posting of prices, 119–120
price tags, 219, 314
reference pricing, 238
See also financing; sales
privacy. *See* consumer privacy
prohibitions
  on class action lawsuits, 254
  creditors/credit sales, 32, 172
  on deceptive practices, 277–278
  by employees, 67
  fraudulent practices, 158
  repossession, 268, 269
  unfair or deceptive acts or practices, 45
promissory notes, 132
protected class consumers, 199
Proxmire, William, 33, 135, 292
Public Citizen (consumer advocacy group), 255
public roundtables, 54, 72–77, 80–82, 93–103, 105–108, 138, 156
push, pull, drive or drag advertising, 163–165

R

racial discrimination, 199
Ramirez, Edith, 213
RBP (Risk-Based Pricing Rule), 26–27, 38–39, 56–57, 60, 143, 228
real estate financing, 36
recharacterization attacks, 88–90

Red Flags Rule, 57, 85, 142–143, 228
reference pricing, 238
referral fees (bird dog fees), 96–97
Regulation B, 67, 159, 191–194, 192, 321
Regulation M, 31, 45, 171, 231, 277, 321
Regulation P, 321
regulations. *See* rules/regulations
Regulation Z, 31, 45, 119, 135, 159, 171, 231, 277, 321
rent-to-own deals, 40, 43
Repo Madness, 43, 78, 99
repossession
  abuses of, 292
  best practices, 130
  by dealer, 65
  illegal, 132
  prohibitions on, 268, 269
  regulations for, 133, 152
  remedies for, 192
  results of, 92
  self-help (*See* self-help repossession)
  selling repossessed cars, 158
  threatening rules, 257, 261–263
  violence occurring with, 99
  voluntary, 94
rescission (unwind) agreements, 65, 66, 67, 130, 131, 157, 257, 258, 263
retail installment contracts (RICs), 245–246
retail installment sale acts (RISAs), 65–66, 321

INDEX

retail installment sale contracts (RISCs), 8–9, 245–248, 272–273
  acquisition fees, 160–163
  buy-here, pay-here, 132–133, 228–230, 308–309
  consumer disclosure, 101–102
  discriminatory behaviors, 196–200
  due diligence, 200
  enforcement authority for, 41, 150, 155, 187, 213–216, 218, 286
  Holder Rule and, 50–51
  language of, 115–116, 154
  loan versus, 245–248, 272–273
  negative equity, 127
  spot deliveries, 64, 66–67, 260–264
reverse redlining, 103
Reynolds, Carole, 74
Rhode Island, 129, 256
Rich, Jessica, 226
RICs. *See* retail installment sale acts (RISAs)
RICs (retail installment contracts), 245–246
rights, consumer, 42, 157, 246
RISAs (retail installment sale acts), 65–66, 321
RISCs. *See* retail installment sale contracts (RISCs)
Risk-Based Pricing Rule (RBP), 26–27, 27–28, 38–39, 56–57, 60, 143, 228
risk triage, 91, 109–110
Romney, Mitt, 156
Ross, Kathy, 233–234

roundtables, public, 54, 72–77, 80–82, 93–103, 105–108, 138, 156
rules/regulations
  buy-here, pay-here (BHPH), 41–44, 156–160
  credit practices rule, 318
  Disposal Rule, 172–175
  do-not-call/do-not-fax/do-not-email rules, 159
  fee-harvester rules, 136–138
  Holder Rule, 49–51, 301
  leases/leasing, 45, 304–306
  Lemon Laws, 169, 306–308
  Mortgage Acts and Practices Advertising Rule, 178
  National Consumer Law Center (NCLC), 76, 77–80, 78–80, 81, 99, 213
  odometer law, 320
  Preservation of Consumer Claims and Defenses Trade Regulation Rule, 49–51, 301
  Red Flags Rule, 57, 85, 142–143, 228
  Regulation B, 67, 159, 191–194, 192, 321
  Regulation M, 31, 45, 171, 231, 277, 321
  Regulation P, 321
  Regulation Z, 31, 45, 119, 135, 159, 171, 231, 277, 321
  Risk-Based Pricing Rule, 26–27, 38–39, 56–57, 60, 143, 228
  Safeguarding Rule, 83–85, 142
  spot delivery, 129–131, 216, 256–258, 260–264

341

APPENDIX 2

Trade Regulation Rule, 322
Truth in Lending (*See* Truth in Lending Act (TILA))
Uniform Law Commission, 291
USA PATRIOT Act, 322
Used Car Lemon Law, 169
Used Car Rule, 321
writing regulations, 67–69
See also case law; legislation; litigation
rule-writing authority, 150

S

Safeguarding Rule, 83–85, 142
safe harbor language, 300–301
sales
   as-is, 301
   contract forms, 300–301
   cooling-off period, 19, 42
   deal jackets, 299
   GAP (Guaranteed Auto Protection), 14, 96, 220, 225, 242
   online, 95–96, 104–105
   rent-to-own, 40, 43
   service contracts, 94, 116, 220, 305, 309
   title pawn, 43
   transparency, 242
   unsigned documents, 299–300
   violations, 309
   See also financing; pricing
Schneiderman, Eric T., 306–308
self-help repossession
   do-it-yourself (DIY) compliance, 61
   limitations on, 43, 257

Repo Madness report, 43, 78, 99
spot deliveries, 65, 260–264
use of starter interrupt devices, 99, 315
service contracts, 94, 116, 220, 305, 309
servicemembers. *See* military/servicemembers
Servicemembers Civil Relief Act, 267
settlement orders, 124
Seward, Jon, 102–103
Shahan, Rosemary, 75
Sheptak, Peter J., 73
simple interest (interest-bearing) contracts, 24, 132
small claims lawsuits, 277, 307
small dealers, 59–61
South Carolina, 208–209, 212–213, 302
South Dakota, 102, 105, 124
Spanish language issues, 142, 183–184, 226, 241–242, 301
Specially Designated Nationals (bad guy list), 320
spot deliveries (yo yo deals), 215–216
   abuses, 64–65
   best practices, 66–67, 215
   compliance review, 258, 263–264
   consumer advocates' concerns with, 97–99
   discriminatory behaviors, 196–200
   mutual rescission, 66, 131, 257
   regulations for, 129–131

state AGs, 256–257
unwinding, 67, 130–131, 257–258, 263
staff. *See* employees/staff
starter interrupt devices, 77, 99, 137, 309, 315
State Division of Consumer Affairs (NJ), 169
state laws
   advertising, 45–46
   arbitration, 208–209
   Dodd Frank Wall Street Reform and Consumer Protection Act (Dodd Frank Act), 152
   leases/leasing, 234
   spot deliveries (yo yo deals), 256–257
   unfair or deceptive acts or practices (UDAP), 224
   usury, 152, 162
   See also specific state

T

Tatman, David, 267–269
Taylor, Joseph A., 73
Tennessee, 42, 129, 205, 256, 281–283, 282
Texas, 221, 230
threatening rules (repossession), 257, 261–263
Thurston, Robin, 75
TILA. *See* Truth in Lending Act (TILA)
title pawns, 43
torts, 322
Tracey, Jack, 143

Trade Regulation Rule (TRR), 322
training/education
   advertising as specialty, 171
   advertising requirements, 232
   compliance issues, 205–207, 238–239, 241, 283, 298
   compliance officers, 235
   consumer education, 100–101
   dealers, 133, 205
   effective methods for, 100
   employees, 148
   finance and insurance (F&I) staff, 241
   lack of, 141
   leasing rules, 242
   legal aspects of advertising, 45
   legal training for staff, 166–168
   mandatory, 205–206, 243
   policies for, 193
   re-training, 176, 258
   sales trainers, 309
   sources for, 207
   teaching bad practices, 168
TRR (Trade Regulation Rule), 322
Truth in Lending Act (TILA), 16, 20, 23, 31–32, 86, 154, 159, 319
   auto financing, 16
   CFPB oversight of, 318
   Consumer Leasing Act under, 318
   creation, 292
   criminal penalties, 92, 288–290
   description, 322
   disclosure requirements, 31, 33–34, 161–162, 247
   finance charges, 15, 161

343

Regulation Z, 31, 45, 119, 135, 159, 171, 231, 277
  violations, 212–213, 277
20-week Rule, 96

U

U3C (Uniform Consumer Credit Code), 292
UCC. *See* Uniform Commercial Code (UCC)
UCLA (Uniform Consumer Leasing Act), 292–293
UDAP. *See* unfair or deceptive acts or practices (UDAP)
undercover agents, 167–169
"Understanding Vehicle Financing" (FTC), 241, 276
underwriting practices
  disparities in your, 193
  in exit strategies, 202
  federal, 10, 11, 23
  increasing burdens of, 16
  as part of financial markets collapse, 135
  reviews of your, 244
  standards imposed for, 15, 32
unfair, deceptive, or abusive acts or practices (UDAAP), 6, 10, 42–43, 68, 322. *See also* deceptive practices; unfair or deceptive acts or practices (UDAP)
unfair or deceptive acts or practices (UDAP)
  in advertising, 164
  California, 158–159
  challenges to, 6
  claims of, 105, 179
  debt collection, 248
  defined, 42–43
  definition of "abusive," 149
  determination of, 119–120
  employee engagement in, 191
  FTC rules, 38, 142, 147, 149, 182, 283
  individual liability, 232–234
  laws prohibiting, 45
  litigation under, 261–262
  Oregon's, 268
  payment packing, 42
  plaintiffs, 224–225
  self-help repossession, 260–264
  spot deliveries (yo-yo deals), 64–67
  state law variations of, 224
  violations of, 185, 215, 248
  See also deceptive practices; Truth in Lending Act (TILA)
Uniform Commercial Code (UCC), 158, 291
Uniform Law Commission, 291
unwind (rescission) agreements, 65, 66, 67, 130, 131, 157, 257, 258, 263
up front payments, 231
upside down ads, 124–127
USA PATRIOT Act, 322
Used Car Lemon Law, 169
Used Car Rule, 182–185, 207–208, 226–228, 301, 322
used vehicle market
  Buyers Guide, 183–184, 227
  dealer licensing, 156
  Lemon Laws in, 169, 306–308

National Independent Automobile Dealer's Association Used Car Industry Report, 286–288
Used Car Rule, 182–185, 207–208, 226–228, 301
usury
    bills aimed at, 14
    criminal, 162
    federal cap on, 17–18
    federal rate, 15–17
    national rate, 314
    state laws and statutes on, 152, 162
Utah, 129, 141, 256

V

Van Alst, John, 73, 99, 100
Vermont, 129, 256
violations
    advertising, 45, 124–127, 302–303
    by creditors, 186, 202
    criminal penalties for, 288–290
    by employees/staff, 168
    of Equal Credit Opportunity Act, 105, 202
    Oregon advertising, 237–239
    sales, 309
    of Truth in Lending Act, 212–213, 277
    of unfair or deceptive acts or practices (UDAP), 185, 215, 248
Vladeck, David, 125
Voegler, Jerry, 103

W

WAC (with approved credit), 116, 127–128
warranties
    advertised, 116
    disclaimers, 208
    extended, 116
    implied, 184, 208, 301
    in Spanish, 301
    Used Car Rule, 184–185
    validity overseas, 94
Warren, Elizabeth, 6, 8, 63–64, 220, 273–276, 306
Washington, 129, 256
Washington Post, 30, 203, 274
Washington Times, 167
Wayne Mazda/Wayne Auto Mall Hyundai, 248
websites. *See* internet
Westcott, David W., 73
West Virginia, 124, 129, 256
Whann, Keith, 74, 75, 99
whistleblowers, 110
White, Kate, 73
Winston, Joel, 72, 75, 144, 224
with approved credit (WAC), 116, 127–128
Worthman, Katie, 74

Y

yo-yo deals. *See* spot deliveries (yo yo deals)

Z

Zak, Greg, 100